AWS Certified DevOps Engineer – Professional

Exam # DOP-C01

Practice Questions

www.ipspecialist.net

Document Control

Proposal Name	:	AWS – DevOps Engineer - Professional – Practice Questions
Document Version	:	1.0
Document Release Date	:	10-Feb-2019
Reference	:	DOP-C01

Feedback:

If you have any comments regarding the quality of this book, or otherwise alter it to better suit your needs, you can contact us through email at info@ipspecialist.net

Please make sure to include the book title and ISBN in your message

About IPSpecialist

IPSPECIALIST LTD. IS COMMITTED TO EXCELLENCE AND DEDICATED TO YOUR SUCCESS.

Our philosophy is to treat our customers like family. We want you to succeed, and we are willing to do anything possible to help you make it happen. We have the proof to back up our claims. We strive to accelerate billions of careers with great courses, accessibility, and affordability. We believe that continuous learning and knowledge evolution are most important things to keep re-skilling and up-skilling the world.

Planning and creating a specific goal is where IPSpecialist helps. We can create a career track that suits your visions as well as develop the competencies you need to become a professional Network Engineer. We can also assist you with the execution and evaluation of proficiency level based on the career track you choose, as they are customized to fit your specific goals.

We help you STAND OUT from the crowd through our detailed IP training content packages.

Course Features:

❖ Self-Paced learning
  • Learn at your own pace and in your own time
❖ Covers Complete Exam Blueprint
  • Prep-up for the exam with confidence
❖ Case Study Based Learning
  • Relate the content with real life scenarios
❖ Subscriptions that suits you
  • Get more pay less with IPS Subscriptions
❖ Career Advisory Services
  • Let industry experts plan your career journey
❖ Virtual Labs to test your skills
  • With IPS vRacks, you can testify your exam preparations
❖ Practice Questions
  • Practice Questions to measure your preparation standards
❖ On Request Digital Certification
  • On request digital certification from IPSpecialist LTD

About the Authors:

This book has been compiled with the help of multiple professional engineers. These engineers specialize in different fields e.g Networking, Security, Cloud, Big Data, IoT etc. Each engineer develops content in its specialized field that is compiled to form a comprehensive certification guide.

About the Technical Reviewers:

Nouman Ahmed Khan

AWS-Architect, CCDE, CCIEX5 (R&S, SP, Security, DC, Wireless), CISSP, CISA, CISM is a Solution Architect working with a major telecommunication provider in Qatar. He works with enterprises, mega-projects, and service providers to help them select the best-fit technology solutions. He also works closely as a consultant to understand customer business processes and helps select an appropriate technology strategy to support business goals. He has more than 14 years of experience working in Pakistan/Middle-East & UK. He holds a Bachelor of Engineering Degree from NED University, Pakistan, and M.Sc. in Computer Networks from the UK.

Abubakar Saeed

Abubakar Saeed has more than twenty-five years of experience, Managing, Consulting, Designing, and implementing large-scale technology projects, extensive experience heading ISP operations, solutions integration, heading Product Development, Presales, and Solution Design. Emphasizing on adhering to Project timelines and delivering as per customer expectations, he always leads the project in the right direction with his innovative ideas and excellent management.

Syed Hanif Wasti

Syed Hanif Wasti is a Computer science graduate working professionally as a Technical Content Developer. He is a part of a team of professionals operating in the E-learning and digital education sector. He holds a bachelor's degree in Computer Sciences from PAF-KIET, Pakistan. He has completed training of MCP and CCNA. He has both technical knowledge and industry sounding information, which he uses efficiently in his career. He was working as a Database and Network administrator while having experience of software development.

Areeba Tanveer

Areeba Tanveer is working professionally as a Technical Content Developer. She holds Bachelor's of Engineering degree in Telecommunication Engineering from NED University of Engineering and Technology. She also worked as a project Engineer in Pakistan Telecommunication Company Limited (PTCL). She has both technical knowledge and industry sounding information, which she uses effectively in her career.

Uzair Ahmed

Uzair Ahmed is a professional technical content writer holding bachelor's degree in Computer Science from PAF-KIET university. He has sound knowledge and industry experience in SIEM implementation, .NET development, machine learning, Artificial intelligence, Python programming and other programming and development platforms like React.JS Angular JS Laravel.

Afia Afaq

Afia Afaq works as a Technical Content Developer. She holds a Bachelor of Engineering Degree in Telecommunications Engineering from NED University of Engineering and Technology. She also has worked as an intern in Pakistan Telecommunication Company Limited (PTCL) as well as in Pakistan Meteorological Department (PMD). Afia Afaq uses her technical knowledge and industry sounding information efficiently in her career.

Hira Arif

Hira Arif is an Electrical Engineer Graduate from NED University of Engineering and Technology, working professionally as a Technical Content Writer. Prior to that, she worked as Trainee Engineer at Sunshine Corporation. She utilizes her knowledge and technical skills profoundly when required.

Free Resources:

With each workbook you buy from Amazon, IPSpecialist offers free resources to our valuable customers.

Once you buy this book you will have to contact us at support@ipspecialist.net or tweet @ipspecialistnet to get this limited time offer without any extra charges.

Free Resources Include:

Exam Practice Questions in Quiz Simulation: IP Specialists' Practice Questions have been developed keeping in mind the certification exam perspective. The collection of these questions from our technology workbooks is prepared to keep the exam blueprint in mind covering not only important but necessary topics as well. It is an ideal document to practice and revise your certification.

Career Report: This report is a step by step guide for a novice who wants to develop his/her career in the field of computer networks. It answers the following queries:

- Current scenarios and future prospects.
- Is this industry moving towards saturation or are new opportunities knocking at the door?
- What will the monetary benefits be?
- Why to get certified?
- How to plan and when will I complete the certifications if I start today?
- Is there any career track that I can follow to accomplish specialization level?

Furthermore, this guide provides a comprehensive career path towards being a specialist in the field of networking and also highlights the tracks needed to obtain certification.

Our Products

Technology Workbooks

IPSpecialist Technology workbooks are the ideal guides to developing the hands-on skills necessary to pass the exam. Our workbook covers official exam blueprint and explains the technology with real life case study based labs. The content covered in each workbook consists of individually focused technology topics presented in an easy-to-follow, goal-oriented, step-by-step approach. Every scenario features detailed breakdowns and thorough verifications to help you completely understand the task and associated technology.

We extensively used mind maps in our workbooks to visually explain the technology. Our workbooks have become a widely used tool to learn and remember the information effectively.

vRacks

Our highly scalable and innovative virtualized lab platforms let you practice the IP Specialist Technology Workbook at your own time and your own place as per your convenience.

Quick Reference Sheets

Our quick reference sheets are a concise bundling of condensed notes of the complete exam blueprint. It's an ideal handy document to help you remember the most important technology concepts related to certification exam.

Practice Questions

IP Specialists' Practice Questions are dedicately designed for certification exam perspective. The collection of these questions from our technology workbooks are prepared to keep the exam blueprint in mind covering not only important but necessary topics as well. It's an ideal document to practice and revise your certification.

AWS Certifications

AWS Certifications are industry-recognized credentials that validate your technical cloud skills and expertise while assisting in your career growth. These are one of the most valuable IT certifications right now since AWS has established an overwhelming lead in the public cloud market. Even with the presence of several tough competitors such as Microsoft AZure, Google Cloud Engine, and Rackspace, AWS is by far the dominant public cloud platform today, with an astounding collection of proprietary services that continues to grow.

The two key reasons as to why AWS certifications are prevailing in the current cloud-oriented job market:

- There's a dire need for skilled cloud engineers, developers, and architects – and the current shortage of experts is expected to continue into the foreseeable future.
- AWS certifications stand out for their thoroughness, rigor, consistency, and appropriateness for critical cloud engineering positions.

Value of AWS Certifications

AWS places equal emphasis on sound conceptual knowledge of its entire platform, as well as on hands-on experience with the AWS infrastructure and its many unique and complex components and services.

For Individuals

- Demonstrate your expertise to design, deploy, and operate highly available, cost-effective, and secure applications on AWS.
- Gain recognition and visibility for your proven skills and proficiency with AWS.
- Earn tangible benefits such as access to the AWS Certified LinkedIn Community, invite to AWS Certification Appreciation Receptions and Lounges, AWS Certification Practice Exam Voucher, Digital Badge for certification validation, AWS Certified Logo usage, access to AWS Certified Store.
- Foster credibility with your employer and peers.

For Employers

- Identify skilled professionals to lead IT initiatives with AWS technologies.
- Reduce risks and costs to implement your workloads and projects on the AWS platform.
- Increase customer satisfaction.

Types of Certification

Role-Based Certifications:

- **Foundational** - Validates overall understanding of the AWS Cloud. Prerequisite to achieving Specialty certification or an optional start towards Associate certification.
- **Associate** - Technical role-based certifications. No prerequisite.
- **Professional** - Highest level technical role-based certification. Relevant Associate certification required.

Specialty Certifications:

- Validate advanced skills in specific technical areas.
- Require one active role-based certification.

About AWS – Certified DevOps Engineer - Professional Exam

Exam Questions	Multiple choice and multiple answer
Number of Questions	---
Time to Complete	170 minutes
Available Languages	English and Japanese
Practice Exam Fee	40 USD
Exam Fee	300 USD

The AWS Certified DevOps Engineer – Professional exam validates advanced technical skills and experience in designing distributed applications and systems on the AWS platform. Example concepts you should understand for this exam include:

- ➤ Designing and deploying dynamically scalable, highly available, fault-tolerant, and reliable applications on AWS
- ➤ Selecting appropriate AWS services to design and deploy an application based on given requirements
- ➤ Migrating complex, multi-tier applications on AWS
- ➤ Designing and deploying enterprise-wide scalable operations on AWS
- ➤ Implementing cost-control strategies

Recommended AWS Knowledge

- One or more years of hands-on experience developing and maintaining an AWS based application

- In-depth knowledge of at least one high-level programming language

- Understanding of core AWS services, uses, and basic AWS architecture best practices

- Proficiency in developing, deploying, and debugging cloud-based applications using AWS

- Ability to use the AWS service APIs, AWS CLI, and SDKs to write applications

- Ability to identify key features of AWS services

- Understanding of the AWS shared responsibility model

- Understanding of application lifecycle management

- Ability to use a CI/CD pipeline to deploy applications on AWS

- Ability to use or interact with AWS services

- Ability to apply a basic understanding of cloud-native applications to write codes

- Ability to write codes using AWS security best practices (e.g. using IAM roles instead of using secret and access keys in the code)

- Ability to author, maintain, and debug code modules on AWS

- Proficiency writing code for server-less applications

- Understanding of the use of containers in the development process

	Domain	%
Domain 1	Continuous Delivery & Process Automation	55%
Domain 2	Monitoring, Metrics, and Logging	20%
Domain 3	Security, Governance, and Validation	10%
Domain 4	High Availability and Elasticity	15%
Total		100%

Practice Questions

1. To change the instance type of the production instance which is running as the part of an auto-scaling group. There are currently four instances running in a group, and the whole architecture is deployed by using CloudFormation template, and you have to ensure that there are always two instances running during the updating session without creating any interruption. Which is the most favorable option below for the scenario?
   a. AutoScalingRollingUpdate
   b. AutoScalingScheduledAction
   c. AutoScalingReplacingUpdate
   d. AutoScalingIntegrationUpdate

2. There is a large multi-tiered Windows-based web application situated behind a load balancer and running on an EC2 instance. The problem occurs of slow customer page load time, and the manager asks you to sort out this problem and ensure that customer load time is not affected by too many requests per second. Which one of the following techniques solves this problem?
   a. Re-deploy your infrastructure using AWS CloudFormation template. Configure Elastic load balancing health check to initiate a new AWS CloudFormation stack when health checks return failed.
   b. Re-deploy your infrastructure using an AWS CloudFormation template. Spin up a second AWS CloudFormation stack. Configure Elastic load balancing spillover functionality to spill over any slow connections to the second AWS CloudFormation stack.
   c. Re-deploy your infrastructure using AWS CloudFormation, Elastic BeanStalk, and auto-scaling. Set up your auto-scaling group policies to scaled-based on the number of requests per second as well as the current customer load time.
   d. Re-deploy your application using an auto-scaling template. Configure the auto-scaling template to spin up a new Elastic BeanStalk application when the customer load time surpasses your threshold.

3. Amazon SQS queue is processing messages of an auto-scaling group instance. This processing involves calling third-party web services. The third-party complaints of failed and repeated calls it is receiving from you. During the inspection, it is seen that

instances are terminated when the group scales-in. What could be the possible solution to reduce the number of incomplete process attempts?

    a. Creating a new auto-scaling group with minimum and maximum of 2 and instances running web proxy software. Configure the VPC route table to route HTTP traffic to these web proxies.

    b. Modify the application running on the instances to enable termination protection while it processes a task and disable it when the processing is complete.

    c. Increase the minimum and maximum size for the auto-scaling group. And change the scaling policies, so they scale less dynamically.

    d. Modify the application running on the instances to put itself into an auto-scaling standby state while it processes a task and return itself to Inservice when the processing is complete.

4. There is a company that has different applications built on different programming languages. How can the application be built as quickly as possible in this case?

    a. Develop each app in one Docker container and deploy using Elastic BeanStalk.

    b. Create a Lambda function deployment package consisting of code and any dependencies.

    c. Develop each app in a separate Docker container and deploy using Elastic BeanStalk.

    d. Deploy each app in a separate Docker container and deploy using CloudFormation.

5. To do live debugging of a highly secure environment, the development team wants account- level access to the production instance. What should be done?

    a. Place the credentials provided by EC2 into S3 bucket with encryption enabled. Assign AWS IAM users to each developer so they can download the credential files.

    b. Place an internally created private key into a secure S3 bucket with server-side encryption using customer keys and configuration management, create a service account on all the instances using this private key, and assign IAM users to each developer so they can download the file.

    c. Place each developer own public key into a private S3 bucket, use instance profiles and configuration management to create a user account for each

developer on all instances, and place the user's public keys into the appropriate account.

    d. Place the credentials provided by Amazon EC2 onto an MFA encrypted USB drive, and physically share it with each developer, so that the private key never leaves the office.

6. For the deployment of the application, you have used CloudFormation instead of OpsWorks and the Elastic BeanStalk. But this resource system is not supported by CloudFormation. What would you do now?

    a. Specify more mappings and separate your template into multiple templates by using nested stacks.

    b. Creates a custom resource type using a template developer, custom resource template, and CloudFormation.

    c. Specify the custom resource by separating your template into multiple templates by using nested stacks.

    d. Use a configuration management tool such as chef, puppet, and Ansible.

7. To store credentials on Amazon EC2 instances for connecting to an Amazon RDS MYSQL database instance. How can these credentials be securely stored?

    a. Give the Amazon EC2 instance an IAM role that allowed read access to a private Amazon S3 bucket. Store a file with database credentials in the Amazon S3 bucket. Have your configuration management system pull the file from the bucket when it is needed

    b. Launch an Amazon EC2 instance and use the configuration management system to bootstrap the instance with the Amazon RDS DB credentials. Create an AMI from this instance.

    c. Store the Amazon RDS DB credentials in Amazon EC2 user data. Import the credential into the instance on boot.

    d. Assign an IAM role to your Amazon EC2 instance, and use this IAM role to access the Amazon RDS DB from your Amazon EC2 instances.

8. Which is the first transition state an instance enter after leaving the steady state due to health check failure or decreased load?

    a. Terminating

    b. Detaching

    c. Terminating: Wait

    d. Entering Standby

9. There is an application which is currently running on EC2 instance behind a load balancer, and now the management decides to deploy the application on blue/ green deployment strategy. How can you deploy the application?

    a. Setup Amazon Route53 health checks to fail over from any Amazon EC2 instance that is currently being deployed to.

    b. Using AWS CloudFormation, create a test stack for validating the code, and then deploy the code to each production Amazon EC2 instance.

    c. Create a new load balancer with new Amazon EC2 instances, carry out the deployment, and then switch DNS over to the new load balancer using Amazon Route53 after testing.

    d. Launch more Amazon EC2 instance to ensure high availability, deregister each Amazon EC2 instance from the load balancer, upgrade it, and test it and then register it again with the load balancer.

10. The management is concerned with the extreme increasing cost as management has reported the increase in monthly bills. After reviewing the billing report, it is noticed that there is an increase in data transfer cost. Now how can you provide management with better insight into data transfer use?

    a. Update your Amazon CloudWatch metrics to use 5- second granularity, which will give better-detailed metrics that can be combined with your billing data to pinpoint anomalies.

    b. Use Amazon CloudWatch logs to run a map- reduce on your logs to determine high usage and data transfer.

    c. Deliver custom metrics to Amazon CloudWatch per application that breaks down application data transfer into multiple, more specific data point.

    d. Using Amazon CloudWatch metrics, pull your Elastic load balancing outbound data transfer metrics monthly, and include them with your billing report to show which application is causing higher bandwidth usage.

11. To maintain version control and achieve automation for the application in your organization, you are requested to use CloudFormation. To keep everything agile and maintain while reducing the cost how you can use CloudFormation?

a. Create separate templates based on functionality, create nested stacks with CloudFormation.
b. Use CloudFormation custom resources to handle dependencies between stacks.
c. Create multiple templates in one CloudFormation stack.
d. Combine all resources into one template for version control and automation.

12. To change the current alarm threshold defined in the CloudWatch alarm in a CloudFormation template defined in AWS. How can you achieve this?
a. Currently, there is no option to change what is already defined in the CloudFormation template.
b. Update the template and then update the stack with the new template. Automatically all resources will be changed in the stack.
c. Update the template and then update the stack with the new template. Only those resources that need to be changed will remain as they are.
d. Delete the current CloudFormation template. Create a new one which will update the current resources.

13. When an EC2 instance is running in an auto-scaling group, the application rapidly scales up or down in response to load. However, after the load peaks, the problem starts in the configuration management system where previously terminated EC2 instance is still active. What is the reliable and efficient way o handle the EC2 resources within the configuration management system? (Choose 2)
a. Write a script that is run by a daily cron job on an Amazon EC2 instance, and that executes API describe calls of the EC2 auto-scaling group and removes terminated instances from the configuration management system.
b. Configure an Amazon SQS queue for auto-scaling actions that has a script that listens for new messages and removes terminated instances from the configuration management system.
c. Use your existing configuration management system to control the launching and bootstrapping of instances to reduce the number of moving parts in the automation.
d. Write a small script that will run during Amazon EC2 instance shutdown to de-register the resource from the configuration management system.

14. In this scenario, there is an EC2 instance running on the auto-scaling group. In this, the instances are bootstrapped dynamically and take 15 minutes to complete

bootstrapping. Auto-scaling reports that instances are being in services as before the completion of bootstrapping and application alarms for new instances also generated before the completion of bootstrapping which creates confusion. The cause is that the application monitoring tool is pooling the auto-scaling service API for instances that are in service and creating an alarm for previously unknown instances. Which one of the following ensures that new instances are not added in application monitoring tool before the bootstrapping?

    a. Create an auto-scaling group life cycle hook to hold the instance in the pending:wait state until your bootstrapping is complete. Once bootstrapping is complete, notify auto-scaling to complete the life cycle hook and move the instance into pending:proceed state.

    b. Use the default Amazon CloudWatch application metrics to monitor your application's health. Configure an Amazon SNS topic to send these CloudWatch alarms to the correct recipients.

    c. Tag all instances on launch to identify that they are in a pending state. Change your application monitoring tool to look for this tag before adding new instances, and then use the Amazon API to set the instance state to 'pending' until bootstrapping is complete.

    d. Increase the desired number of instances in your auto-scaling group configuration to reduce the time it takes to bootstrap future instances.

15. You are using Docker to get high consistency between staging and application for the application in EC2 instance, but you are asked for de-risk deployment at the company. How do you further de-risk the rest of the execution environment?

    a. Develop models of your entire cloud system in CloudFormation. Use this model in staging and production to achieve greater parity.

    b. Use AWS Config to force the staging and production stacks to have configuration parity. Any differences will be detected for you, so you are aware of risks.

    c. Use AMI's to ensure the whole machine, including the kernel of the virtual machines, is consistent, since Docker uses Linux container (LXC) technology, and we need to make sure the container environment is consistent.

    d. Use AWS ECS and Dockers clustering. This will make sure that the AMI's and machine sizes are the same across both the environments.

16. You are using chef in your datacenter. Which service is designed to let the customer leverage existing chef recipes in AWS?
    a. AWS Elastic BeanStalk
    b. AWS OpsWorks
    c. AWS CloudFormation
    d. Amazon Simple Workflow Service

17. There is a recently deployed application on EC2 instances behind ELB and customers start complaining about errors received from the application. You have to diagnose the error, but the problem is that the ELB access logs are empty. What would be the reason?
    a. You do not have the appropriate permissions to access the logs.
    b. You do not have your CloudWatch metrics correctly configured
    c. ELB access logs are only available for the maximum of one week.
    d. Access logging is an optional feature of ELB that is disabled by default.

18. Currently, an infrastructure is running on EC2 instance behind an auto-scaling group. The application logs are written on ephemeral storage. The company experienced a major bug which triggered the auto-scaling group up and down before successfully retrieve the logs of the server. What technique is suitable to retrieve logs after the instance's shutdown?
    a. Configure the ephemeral policies on your auto-scaling group to back up on terminate.
    b. Configure your auto-scaling policies to create a snapshot of all ephemeral storage on terminate.
    c. Install the CloudWatch logs agent on your AMI, and configure CloudWatch logs agent to stream your logs.
    d. Install the CloudWatch monitoring agent on your AMI, and set up new SNS alert for CloudWatch metrics that trigger the CloudWatch monitoring agent to backup all logs on the ephemeral drive.

19. While testing Amazon RDS MySQL database, CPU utilization hit 100% and make the system non-responsive. The application is read-heavy. What are the methods which can scale the data tiers in order the meet the application needs? (Choose 3)
    a. Add Amazon RDS DB read replicas, and have your application direct read queries to them.

b. Add your Amazon RDS DB instance to an auto-scaling group and configure your CloudWatch metrics based on CPU utilization.

c. Use an Amazon SQS queue to throttle data going to the Amazon RDS DB instance.

d. Use ElastiCache in front of your Amazon RDS DB to cache common queries.

e. Shard your data set among multiple Amazon RDS DB instances.

f. Enable multi-AZ for your Amazon RDS DB instance.

20. In case of the continuous deployment process, the application using new AMI's undergoes an I/O performance test before deploying to production. The application utilizes one EBS PIOPS volume per instance and requires consistent I/O performance. Which of the following yield the correct result in a repeatable manner for I/O performance test?

a. Ensure that the I/O block sizes for the test are randomly selected.

b. Ensure that the Amazon EBS volumes have been pre-warmed by reading all the blocks before the test.

c. Ensure that snapshots of the Amazon EBS volumes are created as a backup.

d. Ensure that the Amazon EBS volume is encrypted.

21. There is a large number of web servers in an auto-scaling group behind the load balancer. Hourly, you need to filter and process the data and put it back in the durable data store to run reports. The Auto-scaling group continuously launches or terminates the web servers according to the scaling policies assigned to them, but you do not want to lose any access log during this launching and termination. What are the two approaches to meet the demand? (Choose 2)

a. Install an Amazon CloudWatch log agent on every web server during the bootstrap process. Create a CloudWatch log group and define metric filters to create custom metrics that track unique visitors from the streaming web server logs. Create a scheduled task on an Amazon EC2 instance that runs every hour to generate a new report based on the CloudWatch custom metrics.

b. On the web servers, create a scheduled task that executes a script to rotate and transmit the logs to Amazon Glacier. Ensure that the operating system shutdown procedure triggers a logs transmission when the Amazon EC2 instance is stopped/ terminated. Use Amazon data pipeline to process the data in Amazon Glacier and run reports every hour.

c. On the web servers, create a scheduled task that executes a script to rotate and transmit the logs to an Amazon S3 bucket. Ensure that the operating system shutdown procedure triggers a logs transmission when the Amazon EC2 instance is stopped/ terminated. Use AWS data pipeline to move log data from the Amazon S3 bucket to Amazon redshift in order to process and run reports every hour.

d. Install an AWS data pipeline logs agent on every web server during the bootstrap process. Create a log group object in AWS data pipeline, and define metric filters to move processed log data directly from the web servers to Amazon RedShift and run reports every hour.

22. To implement blue/green deployment for several multi-tier web application having infrastructure EC2 front end server, Amazon ElastiCache clusters, Amazon SQS queues, and Amazon relational database instance. Which service combination gives the ability to control traffic between the different deployed version of the application?

a. Create one AWS Elastic BeanStalk application and all AWS resources (using configuration files inside the application source bundle) for each web application. New versions would be deployed using Elastic BeanStalk environments and using the swap URLs feature.

b. Using AWS CloudFormation templates creates one Elastic BeanStalk application and all AWS resources (in the same template) for each web application. A new version would be deployed using AWS CloudFormation templates to create new Elastic BeanStalk environments, and traffic would be balanced between them using weighted round robin (WRR) records in Amazon Route53.

c. Using AWS CloudFormation templates creates one Elastic BeanStalk application and all AWS resources (in the same template) for each web application. New versions would be deployed updating a parameter on the CloudFormation template and passing it to the cfn-hup helper daemon, and traffic would be balanced between them using weighted round robin (WRR) records in Amazon Route53.

d. Create one Elastic BeanStalk application and all AWS resources (using configuration files inside the application source bundle) for each web application. New versions would be deployed updating the Elastic BeanStalk application version for the current Elastic BeanStalk environment.

23. To create Route53 records automatically in CloudFormation during all launches of a template when not running in production. How can this be implemented?
    a. Use a parameter of the environment, and add a condition on the Route53 resource in the template to create the record only when the environment is not production.
    b. Create two templates, one with the Route53 record value and one with the null value for the record. Use the one without it when deploying to production.
    c. Use a parameter for the environment, and add a condition on the Route53 resource in the template to create the record with the null string when the environment is production.
    d. Create two templates, one with the Route53 record and one without it. Use the one without it when deploying to production.

24. You are using IAM roles to access AWS API's, and an application is running on an EC2 instance. How can you configure your application running on that instance to retrieve the API keys for use with the AWS SDK's?
    a. When assigning an EC2 IAM role to your instance in the console, in the "chosen SDK" drop-down list, select the SDK that you are using, and the instance will configure the correct SDK on launch with the API keys.
    b. Within your application code, make a get request to the IAM service API to retrieve credential for your user.
    c. When using AWS SDK's and Amazon EC2 roles, you do not have to explicitly retrieve API keys, because the SDK handle retrieving them from the Amazon EC2 metadata service.
    d. Within your application code, configure the AWS SDK to get the API's keys from environment variables, because assigning an Amazon EC2 role stores keys in environment variables on launch.

25. To protect information that your application is stored on an EBS volume attached to the EC2 instance. How can you make this sensitive information secure?
    a. Unmount the EBS volume, take a snapshot and encrypt a snapshot. Re-mount the Amazon EBS volume.
    b. It is not possible to encrypt an EBS volume, you use a lifecycle policy to transfer data to S3 for encryption.

c. Copy the unencrypted snapshot and check the box to encrypt the new snapshot. Volumes restored from this encrypted snapshot will also be encrypted.

d. Create and mount a new encrypted Amazon EBS volume. Move the data to the new volume. Delete the old Amazon EBS volume.

26. In a project, you are working on a single AWS CloudFormation template to deploy AWS infrastructure which supports multi-tier web application. You have to maintain the AWS CloudFormation resource in such a way that the departments such as networking and security can review the architecture before it goes to production. How can you accommodate each department and maintain the resource?

a. Organize the AWS CloudFormation template so that related resources are next to each other in the template, such as VPC subnets and routing rules for networking and security groups and IAM information for security.

b. Separate the AWS CloudFormation template into a nested structure that has individual templates for the resources that are to be governed by different departments, and use the outputs from the networking and security stacks for the application template that you control.

c. Organize the AWS CloudFormation templates, so that related resources are next to each other in the template for each department's use, leverage your existing continuous integration tool to constantly deploy changes from all parties to the production environment, and then run tests for validation.

d. Use a custom application and the AWS SDK to replicate the resources defined in the current AWS CloudFormation template, and use the existing code review system to allow other departments to approve changes before altering the application for future deployments.

27. What services can Elastic BeanStalk perform for you, when your application takes a long time to run?

a. Manages an Amazon SQS queue and running a daemon process on each instance.

b. Manages an Amazon SNS topic and running a daemon process on each instance.

c. Manages Lambda function and running a daemon process on each instance.

d. Manages the ELB and running a daemon process on each instance.

28. For the primary monitoring of a web application, CloudWatch is used. After recent deployment of software, 500 internal server occurs on the web application. You need to create a CloudWatch alarm which notifies on-call engineer when these errors occur. How can you accomplish this using AWS services? (Choose 3)

    a. Deploy your web application as an AWS Elastic BeanStalk application. Use the default Elastic BeanStalk CloudWatch metrics to capture 500 internal servers. Set a CloudWatch alarm on that metric.

    b. Install a CloudWatch logs agent on your server to stream web application logs to CloudWatch.

    c. Use Amazon Simple Email Service to notify an on-call engineer when a CloudWatch alarm is triggered.

    d. Create a CloudWatch logs group and create metric filters that capture 500 internal server errors. Set a CloudWatch alarm on that metric.

    e. Use Amazon simple notification service to notify an on-call engineer when a CloudWatch alarm is triggered.

29. A company develops a variety of web applications using different platform and programming languages with different application dependencies. Each application must be developed and deployed quickly and must be highly available all the time in order to satisfy the business. What methods are used for this purpose?

    a. Develop the application in Docker containers, and then deploy them to Elastic BeanStalk environments with auto-scaling and elastic load balancing.

    b. Use the AWS CloudFormation docker import service to build and deploy the applications with high availability and multiple availability zones.

    c. Develop each application code in DynamoDB, and then use hooks to deploy it to Elastic Beanstalk environments with auto-scaling and elastic load balancing.

    d. Store each application code in a Git repository, develop custom package repository managers for each application dependencies, and deploy to AWS OpsWorks in multi availability zones.

30. You have deployed Elastic BeanStalk in a new application without losing the current state of the environment in a document. You want to make sure that you can restore the current state later or possibly can create a new environment. You have to make a restoring point. What should be your strategy?

    a. Use CloudFormation templates

    b. Configuration Management template

c. Saved Configuration

d. Saved Templates

31. To design a system, which needs at least 8 m4.large instances to operate service traffic. When a system with high availability in the us-east-1 region which has 6 availability zone is designing, your company needs to ne able to handle the full death of the availability zone. How can you distribute the servers to minimize the cost, while assuming all EC2 nodes are linked with ELB. VPC account can utilize us-east-1's availability zone a through f, inclusively.

   a. 3 servers in each of availability zones a through d, inclusive.

   b. 8 servers in each of availability zones a and b.

   c. 2 servers in each of availability zones a through e, inclusive.

   d. 4 servers in each of availability zones a through c, inclusive.

32. In AWS CloudFormation, this is not an intrinsic function?

   a. Fn::Equal

   b. Fn::If

   c. Fn::Not

   d. Fn::Parse

33. EC2 instances are running behind an ELB in AWS setup. And you have to monitor the incoming connections of ELB. Which is the best option for this purpose?

   a. Use AWS CloudTrail with the load balancer.

   b. Enable access logs on the load balancer.

   c. Use a CloudWatch logs agent.

   d. Create a custom metric CloudWatch filter on your load balancer.

34. You have to set up some applications in AWS. A web tier hosted on EC2 instances, Session data to be written on DynamoDB, Logfiles to be written to Microsoft SQL server. How can you allow an application to write data to DynamoDB table?

   a. Add an IAM user to a running EC2 instance.

   b. Add an IAM user that allows write access to the DynamoDB table.

   c. Create an IAM role that allows read access to the DynamoDB table.

   d. Create an IAM role that allows write access to the DynamoDB table.

35. An E-Commerce store is managed by using Elastic BeanStalk, and the store is the open-source e-commerce platform and deployed across multiple instances in an auto-scaling group. Development team creates a new extension for the store which is PHP source code as well as SQL upgrade script which is used to make necessary updates in the database schema. Some of the extensions deployment fails while SQL upgrade system due to some errors. This is because SQL script is being executed on Amazon EC2 instances. You have to make sure that the SQL script only executed once per deployment regardless of instances running at that time. How can you achieve this?
    a. Use a "Container Command" within an Elastic BeanStalk configuration file to execute the script, ensuring that the "leader only" flag is set to true.
    b. Make use of the Amazon EC2 metadata service to query whether the instance is marked as the leader in the auto-scaling group. Only execute the script if "true" is returned.
    c. Use a "Solo Command" within an Elastic BeanStalk configuration file to execute the script. The Elastic BeanStalk service will ensure that the command is only executed once.
    d. Update the Amazon RDS security group to only allow write access from a single instance in the auto-scaling group; that way, only one instance will successfully execute the script on the database.

36. In an auto-scaling group health check, one of the instances returns to the status of impaired to auto-scaling. What will auto-scale do?
    a. Terminate the instance and launch the new instance.
    b. Send an SNS notification.
    c. Perform a health check until cool down before declaring that the instance is failed.
    d. Wait for the instance to become healthy before sending traffic.

37. There is a set of EC2 instances hosted on AWS. You create a role named DemoRole and assigned that role to a policy, but you are unable to use that role with any instance. What is the reason?
    a. You need to create an instance profile and associate it with that specific role.
    b. You are not able to associate an IAM role with an instance.

c. You won't be able to use that role with an instance unless you also create a user and associate it with that specific role.
d. You won't be able to use that role with an instance unless you also create a user group and associate it with that specific role.

38. To monitor specific applications and send real-time alerts to DevOps Engineer which service is the best to fulfill this requirement?
    a. Amazon CloudWatch
    b. Amazon Simple Notification Service
    c. Amazon Simple Queue Service
    d. Amazon Simple Email Service

39. You want to migrate your applications to the cloud, and you want to migrate gradually so that application is tested with a small percentage of the user. It will be increased over time. What is the required implementation?
    a. Use DirectConnect to route traffic to the on-premise location. In DirectConnect, configure the amount of traffic to be routed to the on-premise location.
    b. Implement a Route53 failover routing policy that sends traffic back to the on-premises application if the AWS application fails.
    c. Configure an Elastic Load Balancer to distribute the traffic between the on-premises application and AWS application.
    d. Implement a Route53 weighted routing policy that distributes the traffic between your on-premises application and the AWS application depending on weight.

40. For video game scores, you are creating a new API. In this case, reads are 100 times better than writes, and the 1% of scores are read 100 times more faster than the rest of the scores. Using DynamoDB what is the best suitable design for this system?
    a. DynamoDB table with 100x higher read than write throughput, with cloud front caching.
    b. DynamoDB with roughly equal read and write throughput, with cloud front caching.
    c. DynamoDB table with 100x higher read than write throughput, with ElastiCache caching.

d. DynamoDB table with roughly equal read and write throughput, with ElastiCache caching.

41. There is an application which consists of EC2 instance in an auto-scaling group. During a particular time frame, users complaining about the poor response time of application due to the increase in traffic. You have to deploy new EC2 instance for an auto-scaling group when utilization of CPU is greater than 60% for 2 consecutive periods of 5 minutes. What is the way to solve this problem?

   a. Decrease the consecutive number of collection periods.
   b. Increase the minimum number of instances in the auto-scaling group.
   c. Decrease the collection period to ten minutes.
   d. Decrease the threshold CPU utilization percentage at which to deploy a new instance.

42. Multiple applications are running on AWS. The company wants you to develop a tool that immediately calls the team when the alarm is triggered. You also have to make sure that alarm for on-call team generated must handle to notify correct team at the correct time. How can this be implemented?

   a. Create an Amazon SNS topic and an Amazon SQS queue. Configure the Amazon SQS queue as a subscriber to the Amazon SNS topic. Configure CloudWatch alarms to notify this topic when an alarm is triggered. Create an Amazon EC2 auto-scaling group with both minimum and desired instances configured to 0. Worker node in this group spawns when messages are added to the queue. Workers then use Amazon Simple Email Service to send messages to your on-call teams.
   b. Create an Amazon SNS topic and configure your on-call team email addresses as a subscriber. Use the AWS SDK tools to integrate your application with Amazon SNS and send messages to this new topic. Notifications will be sent to on-call users when a CloudWatch alarm is triggered.
   c. Create an Amazon SNS topic and configure your on-call email addresses as subscribers. Create a secondary Amazon SNS topic for alarms and configure your CloudWatch alarms to notify this topic when triggered. Create an HTTP subscriber to this topic that notifies your application via HTTP post when an alarm is triggered. Use the AWS SDK tools to integrate your application with Amazon SNS and messages to the first topic so that on-call engineers receive alerts.

d. Create an Amazon SNS topic for each on-call group, and configure each of these with the team member emails as a subscriber. Create another Amazon SNS topic and configure your CloudWatch alarms to notify this topic when triggered. Create an HTTP subscriber to this topic that notifies your application via HTTP post when an alarm is triggered. Use the AWS SDK tools to integrate your application with Amazon SNS and send messages to the correct team topic when on shift.

43. You are a DevOps engineer in a company, and you are requested to create a rolling deployment solution with minimal downtime and cost-effective. How can you achieve this? (Choose 2)

    a. Re-deploy your application using a CloudFormation template to deploy Elastic BeanStalk.
    b. Re-deploy with a CloudFormation template, define update policies on auto-scaling groups in your CloudFormation template.
    c. Use update policy attribute to specify how CloudFormation handles updates to auto-scaling group resource.
    d. After each stack is deployed, tear down the old stack.

44. Which of the configuration files can be used to deploy Docker containers as an Elastic BeanStalk application as you want to deploy multi docker environment to AWS?

    a. Dockerrun.aws.json
    b. .ebextensions
    c. Dockerrun.json
    d. Dockerfile

45. Elastic Load Balancing HTTP health check is enabled. In AWS management console all the instance pass through health checks but customer reports that your site is not responding. What will be the reason?

    a. The HTTP health checking system is misreporting due to latency in inter-instance metadata synchronization.
    b. The health check in place is not sufficiently evaluating the application function.
    c. The application is returning a positive health check too quickly for the AWS management console to respond.

d. Latency in DNS resolution is interfering with Amazon EC2 metadata retrieval.

46. Elastic BeanStalk is using to manage the plications. There is an SQL script that only needs to be executed at once per deployment no matter how many instances are running. How can you achieve this?
   a. Use a "Container Command" within an Elastic BeanStalk configuration file to execute the script, ensuring that the "leader only" flag is set to false.
   b. Use Elastic Beanstalk version and a configuration file to execute the script, ensuring that the "leader only" flag is set to true.
   c. Use a "Container Command" within an Elastic BeanStalk configuration file to execute the script, ensuring that the "leader only" flag is set to true.
   d. Use a "Leader Command" within an Elastic BeanStalk configuration file to execute the script, ensuring that the "container only" flag is set to true.

47. The company developed a web application and hosted it in Amazon S3 bucket configured for static website hosting. The application using AWS SDK for JavaScript in the browser to access the data stored in the DynamoDB table. How can you secure API keys which access data from DynamoDB table?
   a. Create an Amazon S3 role in IAM with access to the specific DynamoDB tables, and assign it to the buckets hosting your website.
   b. Configure S3 bucket tags with your AWS access keys for your bucket hosting your website so that the application can query them for access.
   c. Configure a web identity federation role within IAM to enable access to the correct DynamoDB resources and retrieve temporary credentials.
   d. Store AWS keys in global variables within your application and configure the application to use these credentials when making requests.

48. You are hired as the new head of operation of SaaS company, and your CTO has asked you to make debugging. The CTO complains that there is no idea what is going on in the complex, service-oriented architecture because it is very difficult to find the errors in the logs and other services too as a developer just log in to disk. How can you satisfy the CTO?
   a. Copy all log files into AWS S3 using a cron job on each instance. Use an S3 notification configuration on the put bucket event and publish an event to

AWS Lambda. Use the Lambda to analyze logs as soon as they come in and flag issues.

b. Begin using CloudWatch logs on every service. Stream all log groups into S3 objects. Use AWS EMR cluster jobs to perform adhoc map reduce analysis and write new queries when needed.

c. Copy all log files into AWS S3 using a cron job on each instance. Use an S3 notification configuration on the put bucket event and publish an event to AWS Kinesis. Use apache sparks on AWS EMR to perform at-scale stream processing queries on the log chunks and flag issues.

d. Begin using CloudWatch logs on every service. Stream all log groups into an AWS elastic search service domain running kibana 4 and perform log analysis on a search cluster.

49. You have a setup in AWS that contains an elastic load balancer, an auto-scaling group which launches EC2 instances and AMI's with your code pre-installed. You want a cost-effective solution and deploy the updates up to a certain number of users and able to revert quickly. What is the best approach?

a. Create a second ELB, and a new auto-scaling group assigned a new launch configuration. Create a new AMI with an updated app. Use Route53 weighted round robin records to adjust the proportion of traffic hitting the two ELBs.

b. Create new AMI's with a new app. Then use the new EC2 instances in half proportion to the older instances.

c. Redeploy with AWS Elastic Beanstalk and Elastic BeanStalk versions. Use Route53 weighted round robin records to adjust the proportion of traffic hitting the two ELB's.

d. Create a full second stack of instances, cut the DNS over to the new stack of instances, and change the DNS back if a rollback is needed.

50. While analyzing the metrics, you got to know that the company website is experiencing response time higher than the anticipated during peak hours. You rely on auto-scaling to make sure you are scaling your time during peak windows. How can you enhance your auto-scaling policy to decrease the response time which is high?

a. Push custom metrics to CloudWatch to monitor your CPU and network bandwidth from your servers, which will allow your auto-scaling policy yo have better fine-grain insight.

b. Increase your auto-scaling group's number of max servers.

    c. Create a script that runs and monitors your servers; when it detects an anomaly in load, it posts to an Amazon SNS topic that triggers elastic load balancing to add more servers to the load balancer.

    d. Push custom metrics to CloudWatch for your application that include more detailed information about your web application, such as how many requests it is handling and how many are waiting to be processed.

51. A mobile application includes photo sharing service, expecting thousands of users at the time of launch. You have Amazon S3 bucket for the storage of the images you also make sure how to authenticate and authorize your users at the time of access to the image. You also have to manage the storage. What are the approaches to obtain the solution? (Choose 2)

    a. Create an Amazon S3 bucket per user, and use your application to generate the S3 URL for the appropriate content.

    b. Use AWS IAM user accounts as your application level user database, and offload the burden of authentication from your application code.

    c. Authenticate your users at the application level, and use AWS security token service (STS) to grant token-based authorization to S3-object.

    d. Authenticate your users at the application level, and send an SMS token message to the user. Create an Amazon S3 bucket with the same name as the SMS message token, and move the user's objects to that bucket.

    e. Use a key-based naming scheme comprised from the user ID's for all user objects in a single Amazon S3 bucket.

52. Current log analysis of an application took 4 hours to generate the report for the top 10 web application user. You have to make sure that system is capable of reporting with in real time, ensure that the report will be up to date and able to handle the increase in the number of requests of the web application. Choose the cost-effective option that can fulfill the requirements?

    a. Publish your data to CloudWatch logs, and configure your application to auto-scale to handle the load on demand.

    b. Publish your log data to an Amazon S3 bucket. Use AWS CloudFormation to create an auto-scaling group to scale your post-processing application which is configured to pull down your log files stored on Amazon S3.

    c. Post your log data to an Amazon Kinesis Data Stream, and subscribe your log processing application, so that is configured to process your logging data.

d.   Create a multi-AZ Amazon RDS MySQL cluster, post the logging data to MySQL, and run a map reduce job to retrieve the required information on user accounts.

53. You agreed that using blue/green deployment structure benefits the team, after the scrum with your development team. How can you deliver this requirement?

a.   Re-deploy your application on AWS Elastic BeanStalk, and take advantage of Elastic BeanStalk deployment types.

b.   Using an AWS CloudFormation template, re-deploy your application behind a load balancer, launch a new AWS CloudFormation stack during each deployment, update your load balancer to send half your traffic to the new stack while you test, after verification update the load balancer to send 100% of the traffic to the new stack, and then terminate the old stack.

c.   Create a new auto-scaling group with the new launch configuration and desired capacity same as that of the initial auto-scaling group and associate it with the same load balancer. Once the new auto-scaling group instances got registered with ELB modify the desired capacity of the initial auto-scaling group to zero and gradually delete the old auto-scaling group.

d.   Using an AWS OpsWorks stack, re-deploy your application behind an elastic load balancing load balancer and take advantage of OpsWorks stack versioning, during deployment create a new version of your application, tell OpsWorks to launch the new configuration behind your load balancer, and when the new version is launched, terminate the old OpsWorks stack.

54. A start-up launches a new photo-sharing application for mobile devices. Within a few months, the application users increase which decreases the application performance due to the increase in loads. The application has a two-tier architecture which is composed of an auto-scaling PHP application tier and a MySQL RDS instance initially deployed with CloudFormation. The auto-scaling group has a minimum value of 4 and the maximum value of 8, but the desired capacity is eight because of the CPU utilization increases. You decide to move from the general purpose M3 instances to the compute optimized C3 instances. How you bring this change without interrupting the users?

a.   Sign into the AWS management console, copy the old launch configuration, and create a new launch configuration that specifies the C3 instances. Update

the auto-scaling group with a new launch configuration. Auto-scaling will then update the instance type of all running instances.

b. Sign in to the AWS management console, and update the existing launch configuration with the new C3 instance type. Add an update policy attribute to your auto-scaling group that specifies auto-scaling rolling update.

c. Update the launch configuration specified in the AWS CloudFormation template with the new C3 instance type. Run a stack update with the new template. Auto-scaling will then update the instances with the new instance type.

d. Update the launch configuration specified in the AWS CloudFormation template with the new C3 instance type. Also, add an update policy attribute to your auto-scaling group that specifies auto-scaling rolling update. Runa stack update with the new template.

55. There is an application hosted on AWS, and the application was created using CloudFormation template and auto-scaling. Now the number of application users increases which decreases the performance of the application. According to analysis, the change in the instance type to C3 would resolve the issue. Which is the best option which is capable of resolving the issue while minimizing the downtime of the end user?

a. Copy the old launch configuration, and create a new launch configuration with the C3 instances. Update the auto-scaling group with the new launch configuration. Auto-scaling will then update the instance type of all running instances.

b. Update the launch configuration in the AWS CloudFormation template with the new C3 instance type. Add an update policy attribute to the auto-scaling group that specifies an auto-scaling rolling update. Run a stack update with the updated template.

c. Update the existing launch configuration with the new C3 instance type. Add an update policy attribute to your auto-scaling group that specifies an auto-scaling rolling update in order to avoid downtime.

d. Update the AWS CloudFormation template that contains the launch configuration with the new C3 instance type. Run a stack update with the updated template, and auto-scaling will then update the instances one at a time with the new instance type.

56. An application is hosted on AWS, and you have to make sure that the DevOps is notified when the certain thresholds are reached. (Choose 3)
    a. Use CloudWatch logs agent to send log data from the app to CloudWatch logs from Amazon EC2 instances.
    b. Pipe data from EC2 to the application logs using AWS data pipeline and CloudWatch.
    c. Once a CloudWatch alarm is triggered, use SNS to notify the senior DevOps engineer.
    d. Set the threshold your application can tolerate in a CloudWatch logs group and link a CloudWatch alarm on that threshold.

57. A specific process running an application which is critical to application functionality and health check is added to the auto-scaling group. The instances are showing healthy, but the application is not working properly. What is the problem with the health checks?
    a. You do not have the time range in the health check properly configured.
    b. It is not possible for a health check to monitor a process that involves application.
    c. The health check is not configured properly.
    d. The health check is not checking the application process.

58. There is a stateless web server tier application running on Amazon EC2 instances behind the load balancer, and using Amazon RDS with read replicas. To implement seal-healing and cost-effective architecture which is the most suitable method. (Choose 2)
    a. Set up a third-party monitoring solution on a cluster of Amazon EC2 instances in order to emit custom CloudWatch metrics to trigger the termination of unhealthy Amazon EC2 instances.
    b. Set up scripts on each Amazon EC2 instance to frequently send ICMP pings to the load balancer in order to determine which instance is unhealthy and replace it.
    c. Set up an auto-scaling group for the web server tier along with an auto-scaling policy that uses the Amazon RDS DB CPU utilization CloudWatch metric to scale the instances.

d. Set up an auto-scaling group for the web server tier along with an auto-scaling policy that uses the Amazon EC2 CPU utilization CloudWatch metric to scale the instances.

e. Use a larger Amazon EC2 instance type for the web server tier and a larger DB instance type for the data storage layer to ensure that they don't become unhealthy.

f. Set up an auto-scaling group for the database tier along with an auto-scaling policy that uses the Amazon RDS read replica log CloudWatch metric to scale out the Amazon RDS read replicas.

g. Use an Amazon RDS multi-AZ deployment.

59. You have two availability zones in an EC2 instance. One AZ has four instances while the other has three instances and none of the instance is protected by scale-in. By default, auto-scaling termination policy what will happen?

 a. Auto-Scaling selects an instance to terminate randomly.

 b. Auto-Scaling will terminate un-protected instances in the availability zone with the oldest launch configuration.

 c. Auto-Scaling terminates which unprotected instances are closest to the next billing hour.

 d. Auto-Scaling will select the AZ with 4 EC2 instances and terminate an instance.

60. Management observed the increase in billing cost after reviewing the last quarter monthly bills from Amazon. On researching for the increase in cost, you found that one of the new services is doing a lot of GET bucket API calls to S3 to build a metadata cache of all objects in the application bucket. You need to provide a solution to come up with the problem which reduces the amount of these GET bucket API calls. What would be your strategy?

 a. Update your Amazon S3 bucket's lifecycle to automatically push a list of objects to a new bucket, and use this list to view objects associated with the applications bucket.

 b. Create a new DynamoDB table. Use the new DynamoDB table to store all metadata about all objects uploaded to Amazon S3. Anytime a new object is uploaded, update the application's internal Amazon S3 object metadata cache from DynamoDB.

 c. Using Amazon SNS, create a notification on any Amazon S3 objects that automatically updates a new DynamoDB table to store all metadata about the

new object. Subscribe the application to the Amazon SNS topic to update its internal Amazon S3 object metadata cache from the DynamoDB table.

d. Upload all files to an ElastiCache file cache server. Update your application to now read all files metadata from the ElastiCache file cache server, and configure the ElastiCache policies to push all files to Amazon S3 for long-term storage.

61. For deploying a scalable distributed system using AWS OpsWorks. And it is required to scale on demand. When it is distributed, each node must contain a configuration file that includes the hostname of the other instances inside the layer. How can you configure AWS OpsWorks to manage this configuration dynamically?

a. Create a chef recipe to update this configuration file, configure your AWS OpsWorks stack to use custom cookbooks, and assign this recipe to the configure life cycle event of the specific layer.

b. Update this configuration file by writing a script to poll the AWS OpsWorks service API service for new instances. Configure your base AMI to execute this script on operating system start-up.

c. Create a chef recipe to update this configuration file, create your AWS OpsWorks stack to use custom cookbooks, and assign this recipe to execute when instances are launched.

d. Configure your AWS OpsWorks layer to use the AWS provided a recipe for distributed host configuration, and configure the instance hostname and file path parameters in your recipe's settings.

62. In an insurance company, you are responsible for the day-to-day operation of your companies' online quotes system which is used to provides insurance quotes to the member of the public. To understand better the customer's behavior, your company wants to use the application logs generated by the system. You have tasked with the designing a log management system with the following requirements. Even during unplanned instance failure, all log entries must be retained by the system. The customer insight teams must require immediate access to the logs from the past seven days, and lastly, the fraud investigation teams require access to all the historical logs, but it will wait up to 24 hours before the logs are available. How would you achieve these requirements? (Choose 3)

a. Configure your application to write logs to the instances ephemeral disk, because this storage is free and has good write performance. Create a script that moves the logs from the instance to Amazon S3 once an hour.

b. Write a script that is configured to be executed when the instance is stopped or terminated and that will upload any remaining logs on the instance to Amazon S3.

c. Create an Amazon S3 lifecycle configuration to move log files from Amazon S3 to Amazon Glacier after seven days.

d. Configure your application to write logs to the instance's default Amazon EBS boot volume, because this storage already exists. Create a script that moves the logs from the instance to Amazon S3 once an hour.

e. Configure your application to write logs to a separate Amazon EBS volume with the "delete or termination" field set to false. Create a script that moves the logs from the instance to Amazon S3 once an hour.

f. Create a housekeeping script that runs on T2 micro instance managed by an auto-scaling group for high availability. The script uses the AWS API to identify any unattached Amazon EBS volumes containing log files. Your housekeeping script will mount the Amazon EBS volume, upload all logs to Amazon S3, and then delete the volume.

63. Web Identity Federation is defined as:
    a. Use of an identity provider like Google or Facebook to become an AWS IAM user.
    b. Use of an identity provider like Google or Facebook to exchange for temporary AWS security credentials.
    c. Use of AWS IAM user tokens to log in as a Google or Facebook user.
    d. Use STS service to create a user on AWS which will allow them to log in from Facebook or Google app.

64. The company releases some new features with high frequency and demanding high availability of the application In application A/B testing; it is to ensure that each EC2 instance of the application must be analyzed in real time to make sure that application is working flawlessly after the deployment. If the behavior of the log is anomalous, then the instances are changes to a more stable one. What would be your strategy?
    a. Ship the logs to Amazon S3 for durability and use Amazon EMR to analyze the logs in a batch manner each hour.

b. Ship the logs to Amazon CloudWatch logs and use Amazon EMR to analyze the logs in a batch manner each hour.

c. Ship the logs to an Amazon Kinesis Stream and have the consumers analyze the logs in a live manner.

d. Ship the logs to a large Amazon EC2 instance and analyze the logs in a live manner.

65. An application is deployed which uses auto-scaling for launching the new instances. To change the instance type of the new instances which of the action items is deployed?

a. Use Elastic BeanStalk to deploy the new application with new instance type.

b. Use CloudFormation to deploy the new application with new instance type.

c. Create a new launch configuration with the new instance type.

d. Create new EC2 instances with the new instance type and attach it to the auto-scaling group.

66. There is a code repository that is stored in Amazon S3. In a recent audit of security control, some question arises about maintaining the integrity of the data stored in Amazon S3, and another concern was securely deploying code from S3 to running application on EC2 in a virtual private cloud. How you reduce these concerns? (Choose 2)

a. Add an Amazon S3 bucket policy with a condition statement to allow access only from Amazon EC2 instances with RFC 1918 IP addresses and enable bucket versioning.

b. Add an Amazon S3 bucket policy with a condition statement that requires multi-factor authentication in order to delete objects and enable bucket versioning.

c. Use a configuration management service to deploy AWS identity and access management user credentials to the Amazon EC2 instances. Use these credentials to securely access the Amazon S3 bucket when deploying code.

d. Create an Amazon identity access and management role with authorization to access the Amazon S3 bucket, and launch all of your application's Amazon EC2 instances with this role.

e. Use AWS data pipeline to lifecycle the data in your Amazon S3 bucket to Amazon Glacier on a weekly basis.

    f. Use AWS pipeline with multi-factor authentication to securely deploy code from the Amazon S3 bucket to your Amazon EC2 instances.

67. While administering a continuous integration application which polls version control for changes and then launches new Amazon EC2 instances for a full suite of the built test, how can you make ensure the lowest cost while all the test runs in the parallel?

    a. Perform syntax checking on the continuous integration system before launching a new Amazon EC2 instance for build test, unit, and integration tests.

    b. Perform syntax and build test on the continuous integration system before launching the new Amazon EC2 instance units and integration tests.

    c. Perform all test on continuous integration system, using AWS OpsWorks for units, integration, and build tests.

    d. Perform syntax checking on the continuous integration system before launching a new AWS data pipeline for coordinating the output of unit, integration, and build tests.

68. There is a complex system which involves networking, IAM policies, and multiple, three-tier applications. And there are still requirements left for the new system, so you have no idea what more components are added in the final design. You want to start using CloudFormation to automate or version control the infrastructure using AWS resources. How can you use CloudFormation to provide a new environment to your customer in a more reliable and cost-effective manner?

    a. Manually create one template to encompass all the resources that you need for the system, so you only have a single template to version-control.

    b. Create multiple separate templates for each logical part of the system, create a nested stack in AWS CloudFormation, and maintain several templates to version-control.

    c. Create multiple separate templates for each logical part of the system, and provide output from one to the next using an Amazon EC2 instance running the SDK for finer granularity of control.

    d. Manually construct the networking layer using Amazon VPC because this does not change often and then use AWS CloudFormation to define all other ephemeral resources.

69. There is an application that is developed in Node.js and code is hosted in a Git repository. To deploy this application on AWS which of the options can achieve this requirement? (Choose 2)

    a. Create an Elastic BeanStalk application. Create a Docker file to install Node.js. Get the code from Git. Use the command "aws git.push" to deploy the application.

    b. Create an AWS CloudFormation template which creates an instance with the AWS::EC2::Container resource type. With user data, install Git to download the Node.js application and then set it up.

    c. Create a docker file to install Node.js and gets the code from git. Use the docker files to perform the deployment on a new AWS Elastic BeanStalk application.

    d. Create an AWS CloudFormation template which creates an instance with the AWS::EC2::Instance resource type and an AMI with docker pre-installed. With user data, install Git to download the Node.js application and then set it up.

70. You are assigned a task for improving the current deployment process by making it easier and reduce the time it takes. You have been tasked with creating a Continuous Integration pipeline that can create AMI's. Which of the following get it done? It is assuming that the development team will be deploying builds five times a week.

    a. Use a dedicated EC2 instance with an EBS volume. Download and configure the code and then create an AMI out of that.

    b. Use OpsWorks to launch an EBS-backed instance, then use a recipe to bootstrap the instance, and then have the CI system use the CreateImage API call to make an API from it.

    c. Upload the code and dependencies to Amazon S3, launch an instance, download the package from Amazon S3, then create the AMI with the CreateSnapshot API call.

    d. Have the CI system launch a new instance, then bootstrap the code and dependencies on that instance, and create an AMI using the CreateImage API call.

71. A development team is continuously spending a lot of time in rolling back the updates for an application. They work for change, and if the changes fail, they spend 5-6 hours for rolling back the update. What strategy can reduce the rolling time?

    a. Use Elastic BeanStalk and re-deploy using application versions.

b. Use S3 to store each version and then re-deploy with the Elastic BeanStalk.

c. Use CloudFormation and update the stack with the previous template.

d. Use OpsWorks and re-deploy using rollback features.

72. You want to deploy an application on Node.js, and you have no experience with AWS. Which is the easier method for you to deploy?

   a. AWS Elastic BeanStalk

   b. AWS CloudFormation

   c. AWS EC2

   d. AWS OpsWorks

73. Which auto-scaling process would be helpful before sending the traffic when testing a new instance, while still keeping them in the auto-scaling group?

   a. Suspend the process AZ rebalance.

   b. Suspend the process health check.

   c. Suspend the process replace unhealthy.

   d. Suspend the process AddToLoadBalancer.

74. The operation and Development wants a place where it can show both the operation system and application logs. How can you activate this service using AWS? (Choose 2)

   a. Using AWS CloudFormation, create a CloudWatch Log, log group and send the operating system and application logs of interest using the CloudWatch logs agent.

   b. Using AWS CloudWatch and configuration management, set up remote logging to send events through UDP packets to CloudTrail.

   c. Using configuration management, set up remote logging to send events to Amazon Kinesis and insert these into Amazon cloud search or Amazon RedShift, depending on the available analytic tool.

   d. Using AWS CloudFormation, merge the application logs with the operating system logs, and use IAM roles to allow both teams to have access to view console output from Amazon EC2.

75. There is an auto-scaling group associated with a load balancer. You want to suspend auto-scaling AddToLoadBalancer for some time. What is the effect of this on launched instances during the suspension period?

a. The instances will be registered with ELB once the process has resumed.
b. Auto-scaling will not launch the instances during this period because of the suspension.
c. The instances will not be registered with ELB. You must manually register when the process is resumed.
d. It is not possible to suspend the AddToLoadBalancer process.

76. You are utilizing CloudFormation to launch an EC2 instance and configure the application just after the application is launched. You required the stack creation of ELB and auto-scaling to wait until the instance is launched and configured properly. How you achieve this?

a. It is not possible for the stack creation to wait until one service is created and launched.
b. Use the Wait Condition resource to hold the creation of the other dependent resources.
c. Use a Creation Policy to wait for the creation of the other dependent resources.
d. Use the Hold Condition resource to hold the creation of the other dependent resources.

77. The application uses CloudFormation to orchestrate your application's resources. In the testing phase before the application went live, The RDS instance type changes and causes the instance to be re-created, which lost the test data. How can you prevent from this in future?

a. Within the AWS CloudFormation parameter with which users can select the Amazon RDS instance type, set Allowed Values to only contain the current instance type.
b. Use an AWS CloudFormation stack policy to deny updates to the instance. Only allow Update Stack permission to IAM principles that are denied SetStackPolicy.
c. In the AWS CloudFormation Template, set the AWS::RDS::DB instances class property to be read-only.
d. Subscribe to the AWS CloudFormation notification "BeforeResourceUpdate," and call CancelStackUpdate if the resources identified is the Amazon RDS instance.
e. Update the stack using Change Sets.

78. You have an auto-scaling group with the elastic load balancer. And you need to phase out all the instances and replace them with new instance type. This can be achieved by which ways? (Choose 2)
    a. Use Newest Instance to phase out all instances that use the previous configuration.
    b. Attach an additional ELB to your auto-scaling configuration and phase in newer instances while removing older instances.
    c. Use Oldest Launch Configuration to phase out all instances that use the previous configuration.
    d. Attach an additional auto-scaling configuration behind the ELB and phase in newer instances while removing older instances.

79. Which is true for AWS Elastic Beanstalk model?
    a. Applications have many deployments, deployments have many environments.
    b. Environments have many applications, applications have many deployments.
    c. Applications have many environments, environments have many deployments.
    d. Deployments have many environments, environments have many applications.

80. You have to retain log files of an application for ten years, and you need to retrieve regularly the recent logs for troubleshooting. Logging system gives the large volume of logs and must be cost effective. What technique should you use to achieve this?
    a. Store your log in Amazon CloudWatch Logs.
    b. Store your logs in Amazon Glacier.
    c. Store your logs in Amazon S3, and use lifecycle policies to archive to Amazon Glacier.
    d. Store your logs on Amazon EBS, and use Amazon EBS snapshots to archive them.

81. There is a requirement of hosting a cluster of NoSQL databases. It is expected that there will be a lot of I/O on these databases. Which of the EBS Volume type is best for high-performance NoSQL cluster deployment?
    a. io1
    b. gp1
    c. standard
    d. gp2

82. If you are configuring AWS Elastic BeanStalk worker tier for easy debugging if there are a problem finishing queue job, what you configure?
    a. Configure Rolling Deployments
    b. Configure Enhanced Health Reporting
    c. Configure Blue-Green Deployments
    d. Configure a Dead Letter Queue.

83. There is an Asynchronous application using auto-scaling and Amazon SQS. The auto-scaling scales concerning the depth of the queue. This results in the completion velocity go down, and auto-scaling group size has maxed out, but there is no increase in inbound velocity. What is the reason?
    a. Some of the new jobs coming in are malformed and processable.
    b. The routing table changed, and none of the workers can process events anymore.
    c. Someone changed the IAM role policy on the instances in the worker group and broke permissions to access the queue.
    d. The scaling metric is not functioning correctly.

84. You run 2000-engine organization and about to begin using AWS for the first time at a large scale. You wish to integrate your identity management system which is running on Microsoft active directory because the organization is power-user of Active Directory. How can you easily manage AWS directories?
    a. Use AWS Directory Service Simple AD
    b. Use AWS Directory Service AD Connector.
    c. Use a sync domain running on AWS Directory Service.
    d. Use an AWS Directory Sync Domain running on AWS Lambda.

85. There is a large number of web servers in an auto-scaling group behind a load balancer. On an hourly basis, you need to filter and process the logs to collect data for unique visitors and then put the data back in a durable store to run the report. Web Servers are constantly launching and terminating according to the defined policy, and you don't want to lose any of the log data during this launching and termination. Which approaches can meet the demand? (Choose 2)

a. Install an Amazon CloudWatch Logs agent on every web server during the bootstrap process. Create a CloudWatch Log Group and define a metric filter to create custom metrics that track unique visitors for the streaming web server logs. Create a scheduled task on an Amazon EC2 instance that runs every hour to generate a new report based on the CloudWatch custom metrics.

b. On the web server, create a scheduled task that executes a script that rotates and transmit the logs to Amazon Glacier. Ensure that the operating system shut down procedure triggers a log transmission when the EC2 instance is stopped/terminated. Use Amazon data pipeline to process the data in Amazon Glacier and run reports every hour.

c. On the web servers, create a scheduled task that executes a script to rotate and transmit the logs to an Amazon S3 bucket. Ensure that the operating system shut down procedure triggers a log transmission when the EC2 instance is stopped/terminated. Use AWS data pipeline to move log data from the Amazon S3 bucket to Amazon Redshift in order to process and run reports every hour.

d. Install an AWS Data pipeline logs agent on every web server during the bootstrap process. Create a log group object in AWS Data pipeline, and define metric filters to move processed log data directly from the web servers to Amazon Redshift and run reports every hour.

86. You have performed a deployment using Elastic BeanStalk with All at Once method, but the application is unavailable. What could be the reason?
    a. You need to configure ELB along with Elastic BeanStalk.
    b. You need to configure Route53 along with Elastic BeanStalk.
    c. There will always be a few seconds of downtime before the application is available.
    d. The cooldown period is not properly configured for Elastic BeanStalk.

87. AWS CodeCommit supports which credential types ? (Choose 3)
    a. Git Credentials
    b. SSH Keys
    c. Username/Password
    d. AWS Access Keys

88. Which of the following services are used to provision EC2 cluster containing the following components in an automated way:

- An application load balancer for distributing the traffic among different task instances running on EC2 instance.
- Single task instance on each EC2 running as part of the auto-scaling group.
- Ability to support different types of deployment strategies.

    a. SAM
    b. OpsWorks
    c. Elastic BeanStalk
    d. CodeCommit

89. You planned to use Amazon RDS facility for fault tolerance for the application. How Amazon RDS Multi-Availability Zone model works:

    a. A second, standby database is deployed and maintained in a different availability zone from the master, using synchronous replication.
    b. A second, standby database is deployed and maintained in a different availability zone from the master, using asynchronous replication.
    c. A second, standby database is deployed and maintained in a different region from the master, using asynchronous replication.
    d. A second, standby database is deployed and maintained in a different region from the master, using synchronous replication.

90. You are running accounting software on the AWS cloud. This software needs to be online every day, and week and the static requirement for computing resources. Also, other batch jobs are needed to be run without interruption. How can you minimize the cost?

    a. Purchase Standard Reserve Instances to run the accounting software. Use scheduled reserved instances to run the batch jobs.
    b. Purchase Standard Reserve Instances to run the accounting software. Use spot instances to run the batch jobs
    c. Purchase a light utilization reserved instance to run the accounting software. Turn it off after hours. Run the batch jobs with the same instance class, so the reserved instance credits are also applied to the batch jobs.

d. Purchase a full utilization reserved instance to run the accounting software. Turn it off after hours. Run the batch jobs with the same instance class, so the reserved instance credits are also applied to the batch jobs.

91. Your CTO is worried about the security of AWS account, and you have to prevent hackers from completely hijacking your account. What do you do?
    a. Use a short but complex password on the root account and any administrators.
    b. Use AWS IAM Geo-Lock and disallow anyone from logging in except for in your city.
    c. Use MFA on all users and accounts, especially on the root account.
    d. Don't write down or remember the root account password after creating the AWS account.

92. During total regional AWS failure, you need API backup by DynamoDB to stay online. You can only tolerate a few minutes of failure or slowness, but the system should recover those minutes with normal operation. How can you achieve this?
    a. Set-up DynamoDB cross-region replication in a master-standby configuration, with a single standby in another region. Create an auto-scaling group behind an ELB in each of the two regions for your application layer in which DynamoDB is running in. Add a Route53 latency DNS record with DNS failover, using the ELBs in the two regions as the resource records.
    b. Set-up a DynamoDB global table. Create an auto-scaling group behind an ELB in each of the two regions for your application layer in which the DynamoDB is running in. Add a Route53 latency DNS record with DNS failover, using the ELBs in the two regions as the resource records.
    c. Set-up a DynamoDB multi-region table. Create a cross region ELB pointing to a cross-region auto-scaling group, and direct a Route53 latency DNS record with DNS failover to the cross-region ELB.
    d. Set-up DynamoDB cross-region replication in a master-standby configuration, with a single standby in another region. Create a cross-region ELB pointing to a cross-region auto-scaling group, and direct a Route53 latency DNS record with DNS failover to the cross-region ELB.

93. To deploy multiple stacks of AWS in a repeatable manner in multiple environments, you selected CloudFormation. Now you found that there is a resource type that you

need to create and model, but it is unsupported by CloudFormation. What is the strategy to overcome this challenge?

    a. Use a CloudFormation custom resource template by selecting an API call to proxy for create, update and delete actions. CloudFormation will use the AWS SDK, CLI, or API method of your choosing as the state transition function for the resource type you are modeling.

    b. Submit a ticket to the AWS Forums. AWS extend CloudFormation resource types by releasing tooling to the AWS labs organization on GitHub. Their response time is usually one day, and they complete requests within a week or two.

    c. Instead of depending on CloudFormation, use Chef, puppet or ansible to author heat templates, which are declarative stack resource definitions that operate over the open stack hypervisor and cloud environment.

    d. Create a CloudFormation custom resource type by implementing create, update and delete functionality, either by subscribing a custom resource provider to an SNS topic or by implementing the logic in AWS Lambda.

94. The development team is using an access key to develop an application that can access S3 or DynamoDB. A new security policy declared that the credentials should not be older than two months and must be rotated. How can you achieve this?

    a. Use the application to rotate the keys in every 2 months via the SDK

    b. Use a script which will query the data the keys are created. If older than 2 months, delete them and create new keys.

    c. Delete the user associated with the keys after every 2 months. Then recreate the user again.

    d. Delete the IAM role associated with the keys after every 2 months. Then recreate the IAM role again.

95. An auto-Scaling group is configured to launch EC2 instances for the application, but you observed that auto-scaling group is not launching the instances in the right proportion. Instances are launches too fast. How you resolve this issue? (Choose 2)

    a. Adjust the cool down period set for the auto-scaling group.

    b. Set a custom metric which monitors a key application functionality for the scale-in and scale-out process.

    c. Adjust the CPU threshold set for the auto-scaling scale-in and scale-out process.

d. Adjust the memory threshold set for the auto-scaling scale-in and scale-out process.

96. In the deployment application revision using CodeDeploy, write the correct sequence of initial steps.
    - Specify the development configuration.
    - Upload Version
    - Create an application
    - Specify deployment group

    a. 3,2,1 and 4
    b. 3,1,2 and 4
    c. 3,4,1 and 2.
    d. 3,4,2 and 1.

97. In software stack in AWS you are building out a layer, that needs to be able to scale out as fast as possible to react to an increase in demand. The code is running on EC2 instance on an auto-scaling group behind a load balancer. Which application deployment method is used?
    a. SSH into new instances that come online, and deploy new code onto the system by pulling it from an S3 bucket, which is populated by code that you refresh from source control on new pushes.
    b. Bake an AMI when deploying new versions of code, and use that AMI for the auto-scaling launch configuration.
    c. Create a Docker file when preparing to deploy a new version to production and publish it to S3. Use User data in the auto-scaling launch configuration to pull down the docker file from S3 and run it when new instances launch.
    d. Create a new Auto-scaling launch configuration with user data scripts configured to pull the latest code at all times.

98. An application consists of 10% write and 90% read. You are currently servicing all the records through Route53 alias record directed toward an AWS ELB, EC2 auto-scaling group. The system becomes expensive due to large traffic spikes during certain news events, during which people request to read similar data all at the same time. What is the simplest possible way to reduce cost and scale with spikes like this?

a. Create an S3 bucket and asynchronously replicate common requests responses into S3 objects. When a request comes in for a pre-computed response, redirect to AWS S3.

b. Create another ELB and auto-scaling group layer mounted on top of another system, adding a tier to the system. Serve most read requests out of the top layer.

c. Create a cloud front distribution and direct Route53 to the distribution. Use the ELB as an origin and specify cache behaviors to proxy cache requests which can be served late.

d. Create a Memcached cluster in AWS ElastiCache. Create cache logic to serve requests which can be served late from the in-memory cache for increased performance.

99. There are some applications and services running at any time and company wants to understand from where the cost is coming from in company's production AWS account. How best you can give the business a good understanding of which application cost the most per month to operate, without expending much initial development time?

a. Create an automation script which periodically creates AWS support tickets requesting detailed intra-month information about your bill.

b. Use custom CloudWatch metrics in your system, and put a metric data point whenever cost is incurred.

c. Use AWS cost allocation tagging for all resources which support it. Use the cost explorer to analyze costs throughout the month.

d. Use the AWS price API and constantly running resource inventory scripts to calculate total price based on multiplication of consumed resources over time.

100. A team wants to begin practicing the continuous delivery using CloudFormation, to enable the automated build and deployment of the whole, versioned stacks, and stack layers and you only have a 3-tier mission critical system. Which one is not the correct option for CloudFormation in a continuous delivery environment?

a. Use the AWS CloudFormation validate template call before publishing changes to AWS.

b. Model your stack in one template, so you can leverage CloudFormation's state management and dependency resolution to propagate all changes.

c. Use CloudFormation to create a brand new infrastructure for all stateless resources on each push, and run integration tests on that set of infrastructure.

d. Parametrize the template and use mappings to ensure your template works in multiple regions.

101. To view both the operating system and application logs, operation team and development team want a single place. How can you implement this using AWS resources? (Choose 2)

a. Using AWS CloudFormation, create a CloudWatch logs, log group and send the operating system and application logs of interest using the CloudWatch logs agent

b. Using AWS CloudFormation and configuration management, set up remote logging to send events via UDP packets to CloudTrial

c. Using configuration management, set up remote logging to send events to Amazon Kinesis and insert these into Amazon Cloud Search or Amazon Redshift, depending on available analytic tools

d. Using AWS CloudFormation, merge the application logs with the operating system logs, and use IAM roles to allow both teams to have access to view console output from Amazon EC2

102. Which features of Elastic BeanStalk Service allow you to perform Blue/Green deployment?

a. Rebuild Environment

b. Swap Environment.

c. Swap URL's

d. Environment Configuration

103. Which deployment types are available in CodeDeploy Service? (Choose 2)

a. In-place Deployment.

b. Rolling Deployment.

c. Immutable Deployment.

d. Blue/Green Deployment.

104. In a very large organization that have multiple applications, which are different and constructed on different programming languages. How can you deploy applications as fast as possible?
    a. Develop each app in one docker container and deploy using Elastic BeanStalk.
    b. Create a Lambda function deployment package consisting of code and any dependencies.
    c. Develop each app in a separate docker container and deploy using Elastic BeanStalk.
    d. Develop each app in a separate docker container and deploy using CloudFormation.

105. You have to monitor API calls against your AWS account by different entities and users, to have the history of those calls. The history of those calls is needed in excess for future review. Which services used in this case?
    a. AWS Config; AWS Inspector
    b. AWS Cloud Trial; AWS Config
    c. AWS CloudTrial; CloudWatch Events
    d. AWS Config; AWS Lambda

106. Swap URL feature in Elastic BeanStalk most directly aids in what?
    a. Immutable Rolling Deployments.
    b. Mutable Rolling Deployments.
    c. Canary Deployments.
    d. Blue/Green Deployments.

107. Highest possible network performance is required for cluster computing application. You already selected homogenous instance type supporting 10Gb enhanced networking, make sure that the workload is network bound and put the instances in the placement group. What would be the last optimization that you can make?
    a. Use 9001 MTU instead of 1500 for jumbo frames, to raise packet body to packet overhead ratios.
    b. Segregate the instances into different peered VPC's while keeping them all in a placement group, so each one has its own internet gateway.

c. Bake an AMI for the instances and relaunch, so the instances are fresh in the placement group and do not have noisy neighbors.

d. Turn off SYN/ACK on your TCP stack or begin using UDP for higher throughput.

108. Create an audit log to customer banking data with all the changes, and DynamoDB is used to store all customer banking data. You are not allowed to lose information due to server failure. What I the correct way to accomplish this?

a. Use a DynamoDB stream specification and stream all changes to AWS Lambda. Log the changes to AWS CloudWatch logs, removing sensitive information before logging.

b. Before writing to DynamoDB, do a pre-write acknowledgment to disk on the application server, removing sensitive information before logging. Periodically rotate these log files into S3.

c. Use a DynamoDB stream specification and periodically flush to an EC2 instance store, removing sensitive information before putting the objects. Periodically flush these batches to S3.

d. Before writing to DynamoDB, do q pre-write acknowledgment to disk on the application server, removing sensitive information before logging. Periodically pipe these files into CloudWatch Logs.

109. There is an API which requires to stay online during AWS regional failure. You do not have a database. The API does not store any state, it only aggregates data from other users. What is the best way to complete this goal?

a. Use a cloud front distribution to serve up your API. Even if the region your API is in goes down, the edge location cloud front uses will be fine.

b. Use an ELB and a cross-zone ELB deployment to create redundancy across data centers. Even if a region fails, the other AZ will stay online.

c. Create a Route53 weighted round robin record, and if one region goes down, have that region redirect to the other region.

d. Create a Route53 latency-based routing record with failover and point it to two identical deployments of your stateless API in two different regions. Make sure both regions use auto-scaling group behind ELBs.

110. There is an application hosted on AWS, on EC2 instance behind a load balancer. You add new features on an application which causes the sites to slow down, and now you are receiving complains. How you recover this issue?
    a. Use CloudTrail to log all the API calls, and then traverse the log files to locate the issue.
    b. Use CloudWatch, monitor the CPU utilization to see the times when the CPU peaked.
    c. Review the Elastic Load Balancer logs.
    d. Create some custom CloudWatch metrics which are pertinent to the key features of your application.

111. Which one of the following deployment mechanisms provides the fastest roll back after failure?
    a. Rolling-Immutable
    b. Canary
    c. Rolling-Mutable
    d. Blue/Green

112. To investigate one instance which is the part of your auto-scaling group, how you do this?
    a. Suspend the AZ re-balance process so that auto-scaling will not terminate the instance.
    b. Put the instance in a standby state.
    c. Put the instance in an Inservice state.
    d. Suspend the AddToLoadBalancer process.

113. To perform ad-hoc analysis on log data, which includes searching quickly for specific error codes and reference number. Which should be evaluated first?
    a. AWS Elasticsearch Service
    b. AWS Redshift
    c. AWS EMR
    d. AWS DynamoDB

114. To perform ad-hoc business analytics queries on well-structured data. The data come in constantly at a high velocity. Your business intelligence team understand SQL. Which service should you look first?
    a. Kinesis Firehose + RDS
    b. Kinesis Firehose + Redshift
    c. EMR using Hive
    d. EMR running Apache Spark

115. There is a serious outage at AWS. The EC2 is not affected, but the EC2 instance deployment script stopped working with the outage in the region. What can be the reason?
    a. The AWS console is down, so your CLI commands do not work.
    b. S3 is unavailable, so you can't create EBS volumes from the snapshot you use to deploy new volume.
    c. AWS turns off the deploy code API call when there are major outages, to protect from system floods.
    d. None of the other answers make sense. If EC2 is not affected, it must be some other issues.

116. To build a ruby on rail application, for internet, non-production use that utilizes the MySQL database. You need a less AWS experienced developers to deploy code with a single command line push and make it simple. Which is the best tool for this setup?
    a. AWS CloudFormation
    b. AWS OpsWorks
    c. AWS ELB + EC2 with CLI push
    d. AWS Elastic BeanStalk

117. There is an application deployed that uses auto-scaling to launch new instances. But now you need to change the instance type. Which item is used to achieve the following action?
    a. Use Elastic BeanStalk to deploy the new application with the new instance type.
    b. Use CloudFormation to deploy the new application with the new instance type.
    c. Create a new launch configuration with the new instance type.

d. Create a new EC2 instance with the new instance type and attach it to the auto-scaling group.

118. Which services used in conjunction with CloudWatch Logs? (Choose 3)
    a. Amazon Kinesis
    b. Amazon S3
    c. Amazon SQS
    d. Amazon Lambda

119. Which service is used to deploy application code content which is stored in the Amazon S3 bucket, bit bucket repositories and Git hub repositories?
    a. CodeCommit
    b. CodeDeploy
    c. S3 Lifecycles
    d. Route53

120. To implement DevOps in your company, which services should be used?
    a. AWS Elastic BeanStalk
    b. AWS OpsWorks
    c. AWS CloudFormation
    d. All of the above

121. There is a system which automatically provisions EIPs to EC2 instances on boot in VPC. The system provisions the whole VPC and stack at once, and you have two of them per VPC. You attempt to create a development environment failed on your new AWS account, after successfully creating a staging and production environment in the same region. What happens now?
    a. You didn't choose the development version of the AMI you are using.
    b. You didn't set the development flag to true when deploying EC2 instances.
    c. You hit the soft limit of 5 EIPs per region and requested a 6th.
    d. You hit the soft limit of 2 VPCs per region and requested a third.

122. For the system's general availability and uptime, you need to create a simple, holistic check. And the system presents itself as the HTTP speaking API. How to achieve this with a tool on AWS?
    a. Route53 Health Checks
    b. CloudWatch Health Checks
    c. AWS ELB Health Checks
    d. EC2 Health Checks

123. To fix your auto-scaling group which scales too quickly, too much and scaled when the traffic is decreasing what you should do?
    a. Set a longer cooldown period on the group, so the system stops overshooting the target capacity. The issue is that the scaling system doesn't allow enough time for new instances to begin servicing requests before measuring aggregate load again.
    b. Calculate the bottleneck or constraint on the computer layer, then select that as the new metric, and set the metric thresholds to the bounding values that begin to affect response latency.
    c. Raise the CloudWatch alarm thresholds associated with your auto-scaling group, so the scaling takes more of an increase in demand before beginning.
    d. Use larger instances instead of lots of smaller ones, so the group stops scaling out so much and wasting resources at the OS level since the OS uses a higher proportion of resources on smaller instances.

124. To get CloudFormation stack status updates to show up in a continues delivery system as close to real time as possible. What should you do?
    a. Use a long-poll on the resources object in your CloudFormation stack and display those state changes in the UI for the system.
    b. Use a long-poll on the List stacks API call for your CloudFormation stack and display those state changes in the UI for the system.
    c. Subscribe your continuous delivery system to an SNS topic that you also tell your CloudFormation stack to publish events into.
    d. Subscribe your continuous delivery system to an SQS queue that you also tell your CloudFormation stack to publish events into.

125. You meet your operation team to discuss the last month data. During the meeting, you realized that three weeks ago, your monitoring system which pings over HTTP from outside the AWS recorded a large spike in latency on your 3 tier web service API. DynamoDB is used for database layer, EBS, ELB, EC2 for the business logic tiers and SQS, EC2, and ELB for the presentation layer. Which technique will not figure out what happens?
    a. Check your CloudTrail log history around the spikes time for any API calls that caused slowness.
    b. Review CloudWatch metrics for one-minute interval graphs to determine which component(s) slowed the system down.
    c. Review your ELB access logs in S3 to see if any ELBs in your system saw the latency.
    d. Analyze your logs to detect bursts in traffic at that time.

126. There is an application deployed using EBS. You have to deploy a new application and ensure that the EBS has detached from the current instance and then re-attach to the new instance. But the new instances are not receiving any kind of traffic. What is the case?
    a. The instances are of the wrong AMI, hence they are not being detected by the ELB.
    b. It takes time for the ELB to register the instances, hence there is a small time frame before your instances can start receiving traffic.
    c. You need to create a new Elastic BeanStalk application because you cannot detach and then reattach instances to an ELB within an Elastic BeanStalk application.
    d. The instances needed to be reattached before the new application version was deployed.

127. A vendor requires that to have access to S3 bucket in your account. The vendor already has an AWS account. How can you provide access to the bucket?
    a. Create a new IAM user and grant the relevant access to the vendor on that bucket.
    b. Create a new IAM group and grant the relevant access to the vendor on that bucket.
    c. Create a cross-account role for the vendor account and grant that role access to the S3 bucket.

d. Create an S3 bucket policy that allows the vendor to read from the bucket from their AWS account.

128. You have an Ops stack status in AWS and want to install updates in the Linux instances in the stack. How you perform those updates? (Choose 2)
    a. Create and start new instances to replace your current online instances. Then delete the current instances.
    b. Use auto-scaling to launch new instances and then delete the older instances.
    c. On Linux-based instances in Chef 11.10 or older stacks, run the Update Dependencies stack command.
    d. Delete the stack and create a new stack with the instances and their relevant updates.

129. There is a CloudFormation stack is deployed which is used to spin up resources in your account. Which represents a failure in CloudFormation?
    a. UPDATE-COMPLETE-CLEANUP-IN-PROGRESS
    b. DELETE-COMPLETE
    c. ROLLBACK-IN-PROGRESS
    d. UPDATE-IN-PROGRESS

130. For building a high score game table in DynamoDB, which will store each user's highest score for each game within many games. And each of which has similar usage and the same number of players. What will be the DynamoDB structure?
    a. Highest score as the hash/ only key.
    b. Game ID as the hash key, Highest score as the range key.
    c. Game ID as the hash / only key.
    d. Game ID as the range/the only key.

131. For monitoring of stack, which tool does not directly support the AWS OpsWorks?
    a. AWS Config
    b. Amazon CloudWatch Metrics
    c. Amazon CloudTrail
    d. Amazon CloudWatch Logs

132.   You are building an application that posts cat pictures online, and images are stored in AWS S3 bucket. You want to run the system cheaply and simply. Which one of the following allows to implement a photo sharing application with authentication and authorization?

   a. Build the application out using AWS Cognito and web identity federation to allow users to log in using Facebook or Google accounts. Once they are logged in, the secret token passed to that user is used to directly access resources on AWS, like AWS S3.

   b. Use JWT or SAML compliant system to build authorization policies. Users log in with a user name and password and are given a token they can use indefinitely to make calls against the photo infrastructure.

   c. Use AWS API gateway with a constantly rotating API key to allow access from the client-side. Construct a custom build of the SDK and include S3 access in it.

   d. Create an AWS Auth service domain and grant public sign up and access to the domain. During set-up add at least one major social media site as a trusted identity provider for users.

133.A CI is needed to build the AMI's with the pre-installed on images on every new code push, and you need to do this at a lower cost. How can you do this?

   a. Bid on spot instances just above the asking price as soon as new commits come in, perform all instances configuration and setup, then create an AMI based on the spot instance.

   b. Have the CI launch a new on-demand EC2 instance when new commits come in, perform all instance configuration and setup, then create an AMI based on the on-demand instance.

   c. Purchase a Light Utilization Reserved Instance to save money on the continuous integration machine. Use these credits whenever you create AMIs on instances.

   d. When the CI instance receives commits, attach a new EBS volume to the CI machine. Perform all set up on this EBS volume, so you don't need a new EC2 instance to create the AMI.

134.   An EC2 instance has failed a health check. Now, what will the ELB do?

   a. The ELB will terminate the instance.

   b. The ELB stops sending traffic to the instance that failed its health check.

   c. The ELB does nothing.

    d. The ELB will replace the instance.

135. Which is required for building a multi-container docker platform by using Elastic BeanStalk?
    a. Docker File to create custom images during deployment.
    b. Prebuilt images stored in public or private online image repository.
    c. Kurbernetes to manage the Docker containers.
    d. RedHat Opensift to manage the Docker containers.

136. To maintain the version control and achieve automation for the application in your organization, you are requested to use CloudFormation. How can you best maintain multiple environments while keeping the cost down by using CloudFormation?
    a. Create separate templates based on functionality, create nested stacks with CloudFormation.
    b. Use CloudFormation custom resources to handle dependencies between stacks.
    c. Create multiple templates in one CloudFormation stack.
    d. Combine all resources into one template for version control and automation.

137. Service is designed that aggregates the clickstream data in batch and deliver reports to the subscriber through the emails. The data is extremely spikey, high-scaled, geographically distributed and unpredictable. How you design this system?
    a. Use a large shift cluster to perform the analysis, and a fleet of Lambdas to perform record inserts into the Redshift tables. Lambda will scale rapidly enough for the traffic spikes.
    b. Use a Cloud Front distribution with access log delivery to S3. Clicks should be recorded as query string GETs to the distribution. Reports are built and sent by periodically running EMR jobs over the access logs in S3.
    c. Use API Gateway invoking Lambdas which Put records into Kinesis, and EMR running spark performing Get record on Kinesis to scale with spikes. Spark on EMR outputs the analysis to S3, which are sent out via email.
    d. Use AWS Elasticsearch service and EC2 auto-scaling groups. The auto-scaling groups scale based on click throughput and stream into the Elasticsearch domain, which is also scalable. Use Kibana to generate reports periodically.

138.   You are operating 10% writes, and 90% reads based on your logging data, and you have to scale RDS deployment. How can you best scale this in an easier way?

    a. Create a second master RDS instance and peer the RDS groups.

    b. Cache all the database responses on the read side with Cloud Front.

    c. Create Read Replicas for RDS since the load is mostly read.

    d. Create a multi-AZ RDS installs and route read traffic to standby.

139.   You want to automate the 3 layers of large cloud deployment, and want to make it capable of tracking all the changes over time in deployment and carefully control any alteration. Which is the best way to achieve these requirements?

    a. Use OpsWorks stacks with 3 layers to model the layering in your stack.

    b. Use CloudFormation Nested Stack templates, with three child stacks to represent the three logical layers of your cloud.

    c. Use AWS config to declare a configuration set that AWS should roll out to your cloud.

    d. Use Elastic BeanStalk Linked Applications, passing the important DNS entries between layers using the metadata interface.

140.   How can you achieve gigabit network throughput on EC2, when you already selected cluster-compute, 10 GB instances with enhanced networking, network-bounded workload? But you do not see 10-gigabit speeds.

    a. Enable biplex networking on your servers, so packets are non-blocking in both directions, and there's no switching over-head.

    b. Ensure the instances are in different VPCs so you don't saturate the internet gateway on anyone VPC.

    c. Select PIOPS for your drives and mount several, so you can provision sufficient disk throughput.

    d. Use a placement group for your instances so the instances are physically near each other in the same availability zone.

141. Your CTO thinks that your AWS account was hacked. What is the only way to know if there were unauthorized access or not and what they did? They are assuming that you have a very sophisticated AWS engineer and can help you out to cover the whole track.

    a. Use CloudTrail Log File Integrity Validation.

b. Use AWS config SNS Subscriptions and process events in real time.

c. Use CloudTrail backed up to AWS S3 and Glacier.

d. Use AWS Config Timeline forensics.

142.   When is the application created through Console or EB CLI, which of the following is the default deployment mechanism used by Elastic BeanStalk?

a. All at Once

b. Rolling Deployments

c. Rolling with an additional batch

d. Immutable

143.   To store a large volume of data, that is accessible for a short period and archived indefinitely after that. What is the possible cost-effective solution?

a. Keep all your data in S3 since this is durable storage.

b. Store your data in Amazon S3, and use lifecycle policies to archive to Amazon Glacier.

c. Store your data in an EBS volume, and use lifecycle policies to archive to Amazon Glacier.

d. Store your data in Amazon S3, and use lifecycle policies to archive to S3-infrequently-access.

144.   An application is loaded on OpsWorks Stack. Which of the following events are triggered by OpsWorks?

a. Deploy

b. Setup

c. Configure

d. Shutdown

145.   In AWS auto-scaling, what is the first transition state an existing instance enters after leaving the Standby state?

a. Detaching

b. Terminating: Wait

c. Pending

d. Entering Standby

146. The company is hosting resources using AWS. They want to record all API calls and transitions help in understanding what resources are present in the account. And want the facility to allow auditing credentials and logins. Which services can fulfill the requirements?

    a. AWS Config, CloudTrail, IAM Credential Reports.
    b. CloudTrail, IAM Credential Reports, AWS Config
    c. CloudTrail, AWS Config, IAM Credential Reports.
    d. AWS Config, IAM Credential Reports, CloudTrail

147. You are running a very large data processing jib one time per day, and the source data exist on S3, and the output processing should also be written on S3 when finished. What approach should you use to version control this processing job and all set up, tear down logic for the system?

    a. Model an AWS EMR job in AWS Elastic BeanStalk application.
    b. Model an AWS EMR job in AWS CloudFormation.
    c. Model an AWS EMR job in AWS OpsWorks.
    d. Model an AWS EMR job in AWS CLI Composer.

148. Your CTO wants you to know that what your AWS accounts users are doing to change the resources at all times. She wants a report describing of who is doing what overtime and reported to her once per week. What you do now?

    a. Create a global AWS CloudTrail Trail. Configure a script to aggregate the log data delivered to S3 once per week and deliver this to the CTO.
    b. Use CloudWatch events rules with an SNS topic subscribed to all AWS API calls. Subscribe the CTO to an email type delivery on this SNS topic.
    c. Use AWS IAM Credential reports to deliver a CSV of all uses of IAM user tokens over time to the CTO.
    d. Use AWS Config with an SNS subscription on a Lambda, and insert these changes over time into a DynamoDB table. Generate reports based on the contents of this table.

149. You want to provide vendor access to your AWS account. They need to be capable of reading protected messages in private S3 bucket and they also use AWS. How can you accomplish this?

a. Create an IAM user with API access keys. Grant the user permissions to access the bucket. Give the vendor the AWS access key ID and AWS secret access key for the user.

b. Create an EC2 instance profile on your account. Grant the associated IAM role full access to the bucket. Start an EC2 instance with this profile and give SSH access to the instance to the vendor.

c. Create a cross-account IAM role with permission to access the bucket, and grant permission to use the role to the vendor AWS account.

d. Generate a signed S3 PUT URL and a signed S3 PUT URL, both with wildcard values and 2 years duration. Pass the URLs to the vendor.

150.   What are the three configurations presented to you while configuring the Elastic BeanStalk environment?

a. Choosing the type of environment- Web or worker environment.

b. Choosing the platform type- Node.js, IIS, etc.

c. Choosing the type of notification- SNS or SQS

d. Choosing whether you want a highly available environment or not.

151. Currently, an application is running with an auto-scaling group with an elastic load balancer configured in Amazon web services. The customers complain about slow response time after the deployment. How to diagnose the issue?

a. Use CloudWatch to monitor the Healthy Host Count Metric

b. Use CloudWatch to monitor the ELB latency.

c. Use CloudWatch to monitor the CPU Utilization.

d. Use CloudWatch to monitor the Memory Utilization.

152.   Which one of the following Cache engine OpsWorks has built-in support for?

a. Redis

b. Memcache

c. Both Redis and Memcache

d. There is no built-in support as of yet for any cache engine.

153.   How can you pass queue messages that are 1 GB each?

a. Use Kinesis as a buffer stream for message bodies. Store the checkpoint ID for the placement in the Kinesis Stream in SQS.

b. Use the Amazon SQS Extended Client Library for Java and Amazon S3 as a storage mechanism for message bodies.

c. Use SQS's support for message portioning and multi-part uploads on Amazon S3.

d. Use AWS EFS as a shared pool storage medium. Store file system pointers to the files on disk in the SQS message bodies.

154. You are creating an application that can store extremely sensitive financial information. And all the stored information must be encrypted at rest and in transit. Which of the following violate this policy?

a. ELB SSL Termination.

b. ELB using Proxy Protocol v1.

c. Cloud Front viewer Protocol Policy set to HTTPS redirection.

d. Telling S3 to use AES256 on the server side.

155. You plan to use the encrypted snapshots in the AWS infrastructure design. Which statement is true in regards to EBS encryption?

a. Snapshotting an encrypted volume makes an encrypted snapshot; restoring an encrypted snapshot creates an encrypted volume when specified/requested.

b. Snapshotting an encrypted volume makes an encrypted snapshot when specified/requested; restoring an encrypted snapshot creates an encrypted volume when specified/requested.

c. Snapshotting an encrypted volume makes an encrypted snapshot; restoring an encrypted snapshot always creates an encrypted volume.

d. Snapshotting an encrypted volume makes an encrypted snapshot when specified/requested; restoring an encrypted snapshot always creates an encrypted volume.

156. A new application version is deployed for production. The deployment is high risk, and you have to make sure that the deployment is working properly by rolling out the new versions to the user over many hours and you must be able to control the proportion of users seeing the new application version down to the percentage point. You are using ELB and EC2 with the auto-scaling group and custom AMI's with your pre-installed code assigned to the launch configuration. There are no database level changes, and the deployment must be cheap therefore you are not allowed to increase

the number of instances, but you must be able to check back the code quickly if something goes wrong. How you meet these requirements?

a. Create a second ELB, Auto-Scaling Launch Configuration, Auto-Scaling Group using the Launch Configuration. Create AMIs with all codes pre-installed. Assign the new AMI with Auto-scaling Launch Configuration. Use Route53 Weighted Round Robin Records to adjust the proportion of traffic hitting two ELBs.

b. Use the Blue/Green deployment method to enable the fastest possible roll back if needed. Create a full second stack of instances and cut the DNS over to the new stack of instances, and change the DNS back if a rollback is needed.

c. Create AMI's with all code pre-installed. Assign the new AMI to the Auto-Scaling Launch Configuration, to replace the old one. Gradually terminate instances running the old code (launched with the old Launch Configuration) and allows the new AMIs to boot to adjust the traffic balance to the new code. On rollback, reverse the process by doing the same thing, but changing the AMI on the launch config back to the original code.

d. Migrate to use AWS Elastic BeanStalk. Use the established and well-tested rolling deployment setting AWS provides on the new application environment, publishing a zip bundle of the new code and adjusting the wait period to spread the deployment over time. Re-deploy the old code bundle to roll back if needed.

157. A serverless architecture included the AWS API Gateway, AWS Lambda, and AWS DynamoDB and experienced a large increase in traffic to a sustained 3000 requests per second, which increases the failure rate. The request on operation lasts for 500 milliseconds on average. The DynamoDB table did not exceed 50% throughput provision, and primary keys are assigned correctly. What can ne the reason for failure?

a. Your API gateway deployment is throttling your request.

b. Your AWS API Gateway deployment is bottlenecking on request (de)serialization.

c. You did not request a limit increase on concurrent Lambda function executions.

d. You used consistent read requests on DynamoDB and are experiencing semaphore lock.

158. Currently, you have EC2 instances hosting an application and instances are the part of the auto-scaling group. You want to change the instance type. How can you manage the deployment cost-effectively?
   a. Terminate the existing Auto-Scaling group. Create a new Launch Configuration with the new instance type. Attach that to the new Auto-Scaling Group.
   b. Use the Auto-Scaling Rolling Update Policy on CloudFormation template auto-scaling group.
   c. Use the Rolling Update feature which is available for EC2 instances.
   d. Manually terminate the instances, launch new instances with the new instance type and attach them to the auto-scaling group.

159. You received a failure notification after launching a CloudFormation template. What is the default behavior in such case of CloudFormation?
   a. It will rollback all the resources that were created up to the failure point.
   b. It will keep all the resources that were created up to the failure point.
   c. It will prompt the user on whether to keep or terminate the already created resources.
   d. It will continue with the creation of the next resource in the stack.

160. You are DevOps engineer and are requested to create a rolling deployment solution which is lesser in cost and have minimal downtime? (Choose 2)
   a. Re-deploy your application using a CloudFormation template to deploy Elastic BeanStalk.
   b. Re-deploy with a CloudFormation template, define update policies on Auto-Scaling groups in your CloudFormation template.
   c. Use Update Policy attribute with Auto-Scaling Rolling update policy on CloudFormation to deploy new code.
   d. After each stack is deployed, tear down the old stack.

161. A company has video games, and for that, they are creating new API. The number of reads is 100 times more than writes. The top 1% of scores are 100 times more frequently than the rest of the scores. How you as developer professional engineer design the use of DynamoDB?
   a. DynamoDB table with roughly equal read and write throughput, with CloudFront caching.

b. DynamoDB table with roughly equal read and write throughput, with ElastiCache caching.

c. DynamoDB table with 100x higher read than write throughput, with CloudFront caching.

d. DynamoDB table with 100x higher read than write throughput, with ElastiCache caching.

162. An organization has its application on AWS EC2 instance, and they give secure access to AWS Service API's by defining IAM roles. Now they want to fetch the API keys for using with AWS SDK then how you as developer professional engineer configure the application on the instance?

   a. When using AWS SDKs and Amazon EC2 roles, you do not have to explicitly retrieve API keys, because the SDK handles retrieving them from the Amazon EC2 MetaData service.

   b. When assigning an EC2 IAM role to your instance in the console, in the "Chosen SDK" drop-down list, select the SDK that you are using, and the instance will configure the correct SDK on launch with the API keys.

   c. Within your application code, configure the AWS SDK to get the API keys from environment variables, because assigning an Amazon EC2 role stores keys in environment variables on launch.

   d. Within your application code, make a GET request to the IAM Service API to retrieve credentials for your user.

163. If a company has an application on AWS and they want that if application hits the defined threshold, then they will get a notification about that hitting. How they achieve this? (Choose 2)

   a. Once a CloudWatch alarm is triggered, use SNS to notify the Senior DevOps Engineer.

   b. Use CloudTrail Logs agent to send log data from the app to CloudTrail Logs from Amazon EC2 instances

   c. Set the threshold your application can tolerate in a CloudWatch metric and link a CloudWatch alarm on that threshold.

   d. Pipe data from EC2 to the application logs using AWS Data Pipeline and CloudWatch

164. A company has an application in which the changes occur, but if the changes fail, then they rollback the updates, but it took 5-6 hrs for rolling back. Then how you as DevOps engineer provide a solution to reduce the rolling back duration?
    a. Use OpsWorks and re-deploy using rollback feature.
    b. Use S3 to store each version and then re-deploy with Elastic BeanStalk
    c. Use Elastic BeanStalk and re-deploy using Application Versions
    d. Use CloudFormation and update the stack with the previous template

165. Consider a company has its multiple branches in multiple regions and they deployed their application via Elastic BeanStalk in a new environment. Now they need to save the environment current state so that they can use that environment state in a new environment or restoring the same environment with that state. How you can achieve this?
    a. Saved Templates
    b. Saved Configurations
    c. Configuration Management Templates
    d. Use CloudFormation templates

166. A company saves its code for web application in the Git Repository, and now they need to deploy this application in AWS which is Node.js. How they do this? (Choose 2)
    a. Create an AWS CloudFormation template which creates an instance with the AWS::EC2::Instance resource type and an AMI with Docker pre-installed. With UserData, install Git to download the Node.js application and then set it up.
    b. Create a Docker file to install Node.js and gets the code from Git. Use the Dockerfile to perform the deployment on a new AWS Elastic BeanStalk application.
    c. Create an AWS CloudFormation template which creates an instance with the AWS::EC2::Container resources type. With UserData, install Git to download the Node.js application and then set it up.
    d. Create an Elastic BeanStalk application. Create a Docker file to install Node.js. Get the code from Git. Use the command "aws git.push" to deploy the application

167. A company has its code store in S3, and they need to maintain the integrity of S3 bucket data and want to securely deploy code from S3 to EC2 in VPC on which application is running. How they achieve this? (Choose 2)
    a. Use AWS Data Pipeline with multi-factor authentication to securely deploy code from the Amazon S3 bucket to your Amazon EC2 instances.
    b. Use a configuration management service to deploy AWS Identity and Access Management user credentials to the Amazon EC2 instances. Use these credentials to securely access the Amazon S3 bucket when deploying code.
    c. Add an Amazon S3 bucket policy with a condition statement that requires multi-factor authentication in order to delete objects and enable bucket versioning.
    d. Create an Amazon Identity and Access Management role with authorization to access the Amazon S3 bucket, and launch all of your application's Amazon EC2 instances with this role.

168. You want to use Blue/Green Deployment for an application running on EC2 instances that are behind ELB. How you can implement deployment?
    a. Launch more Amazon EC2 instances to ensure high availability, de-register each Amazon EC2 instance from the load balancer, upgrade it, and test it, and then register it again with the load balancer.
    b. Set up Amazon Route53 health checks to fail over from any Amazon EC2 instance that is currently being deployed to.
    c. Using AWS CloudFormation, create a test stack for validating the code, and then deploy the code to each production Amazon EC2 instance.
    d. Create a new load balancer with new Amazon EC2 instances, carry out the deployment, and then switch DNS over to the new load balancer using Amazon Route53 after testing.

169. A company wants storage of log files for the long term, and they also want retrieval of most recent logs. The storage must be cost-effective and large in size as the volume of logs is large. How you as DevOps engineer provide a solution for storage?
    a. Store your logs on Amazon EBS, and use Amazon EBS snapshots to archive them.
    b. Store your logs in Amazon S3, and use lifecycle policies to archive to Amazon Glacier.
    c. Store your log in Amazon CloudWatch Logs.

d. Store your logs in Amazon Glacier.

170. An organization has an application, and now they release a new feature of that application which is a highly available application. For testing the new feature, they use A/B testing. The logs from each updated instances need to analyze real-time to observe the working and if they found any issue then version of application changes to stable one. How they perform analyzing of the logs in the highly available way?

    a. Ship the logs to a large Amazon EC2 instance and analyze the logs in a live manner.

    b. Ship the logs to Amazon CloudWatch Logs and use Amazon EMR to analyze the logs in a batch manner each hour.

    c. Ship the logs to Amazon S3 for durability and use Amazon EMR to analyze the logs in a batch manner each hour.

    d. Ship the logs to an Amazon Kinesis Stream and have the consumers analyze the logs in a live manner.

171. A company needs to migrate its application from on-premises to the cloud, but gradually migration is needed as they can't bear any downtime. First, they need to shift a small amount of user toward AWS and then increases with time. How they achieve this?

    a. Implement a Route53 weighted routing policy that distributes the traffic between your on-premises application and the AWS application depending on weight.

    b. Configure an Elastic Load Balancer to distribute the traffic between the on-premises application and the AWS application.

    c. Use DirectConnect to route traffic to the on-premise location. In DirectConnect, configure the amount of traffic to be routed to the on-premise location.

    d. Implement a Route53 failover routing policy that sends traffic back to the on-premises application if the AWS application fails.

172. An educational institution uses AWS to host their application. They use CloudFormation templates and auto-scaling. Now they observe that the number of students using application is increasing and they face performance issue. If they change the EC2 instance type, they will improve the performance. How they change the instance type?

a. Update the AWS CloudFormation template that contains the launch configuration with the new C3 instance type. Run a stack update with the updated template, and Auto Scaling will then update the instances one at a time with the new instance type.

b. Update the existing launch configuration with the new C3 instance type. Add an UpdatePolicy attribute to your Auto Scaling group that specifies an AutoScaling rolling update in order to avoid downtime.

c. Update the launch configuration in the AWS CloudFormation template with the new C3 instance type. Add an UpdatePolicy attribute to the Auto Scaling group that specifies an AutoScalingRollingUpdate. Run a stack update with the updated template.

d. Copy the old launch configuration, and create a new launch configuration with the C3 instances. Update the Auto Scaling group with the new launch configuration. Auto Scaling will then update the instance type of all running instances.

173. A company wants to make easier deployment and reduce the time taken by the deployment for improvement of deployment as they deploy five times a week maximum. They hired DevOps engineer to create CI pipeline that can build AMI's. How he does this?

a. Have the CI system launch a new instance, then bootstrap the code and dependencies on that instance, and create an AMI using the CreateImage API call.

b. Use OpsWorks to launch an EBS-backed instance, then use a recipe to bootstrap the instance, and then have the CI system use the CreateImage API call to make an AMI from it.

c. Use a dedicated EC2 instance with an EBS Volume. Download and configure the code and then create an AMI out of that.

d. Upload the code and dependencies to Amazon S3, launch an instance, download the package from Amazon S3, then create the AMI with the CreateSnapshot API call

174. John has CloudFormation template in AWS. Now he wants to change the alarm threshold define in template under CloudWatch Alarm. How he achieves this?

a. Delete the current CloudFormation template. Create a new one who will update the current resources.

b. Update the template and then update the stack with the new template. Only those resources that need to be changed will be changed. All other resources which do not need to be changed will remain as they are.

c. Update the template and then update the stack with the new template. Automatically all resources will be changed in the stack.

d. Currently, there is no option to change what is already defined in Cloudformation templates.

175. An organization has an application that uses stateless web tier on EC2 instances that are behind the ELB and use RDS read replicas. From the following options which option is best to implement self-healing and cost-effective architecture?

a. Use a larger Amazon EC2 instance type for the web server tier and a larger DB instance type for the data storage layer to ensure that they don't become unhealthy.

b. Use an Amazon RDS Multi-AZ deployment.

c. Set up a third-party monitoring solution on a cluster of Amazon EC2 instances in order to emit custom CloudWatch metrics to trigger the termination of unhealthy Amazon EC2 instances.

d. Set up an Auto Scaling group for the web server tier along with an Auto Scaling policy that uses the Amazon EC2 CPU utilization CloudWatch metric to scale the instances.

176. An organization uses CodeBuild to build Docker image and register it to ECR. After that CodePipeline uses CodeDeploy to deploy the recent Docker image on EC2 by using ECS. For CodeBuild 3 logic steps are define in buildspec.yaml file.

- Pre-build stage
- Build a stage
- Post-build stage

In the build stage, they need to build recent Docker image. Then what he should need to be done with the pre-build stage and post-build stage?

a. Pre-build stage: Set the repository URI and an image tag if needed. Post-build stage: Push the image to your ECR repository such as "docker push $REPOSITORY_URI:latest."

b. Pre-build stage: Login into ECR using "aws ecr get-login" and set the repository URI. Post-build stage: Push the image to your ECR repository such as "aws ecr push $REPOSITORY_URI:latest."

c. Pre-build stage: Login into ECR using "aws ecr get-login" and set the repository URI. Post-build stage: Push the image to your ECR repository such as "docker push $REPOSITORY_URI:latest."

d. Pre-build stage: Nothing needs to be done as what you need to do is just push the image to ECR, which will be done in Post-build stage. Post-build stage: Push the image to your ECR repository such as "docker push $REPOSITORY_URI:latest."

177. An online company has its application on which multiple web and non-web services are running for its operations. The application makes use of EC2 instance belong to a different type like Windows, Linux, etc. Now the DevOps engineer of the company needs to use ECS service for exploring it on applications. For ECS service they need to use ECS agent on the instance to work with Cluster. How they set up ECS agent on servers?

a. Only Amazon ECS-optimized AMIs can use ECS agent and have that agent installed. Unless those EC2 instances can be replaced with ECS-optimized AMIs, they cannot use ECS services since there is no way to install ECS agent.

b. For EC2 instances including Amazon Linux, Ubuntu, and Windows, the ECS agent can be installed. However for on-premise Redhat server, unfortunately, the ECS agent cannot be installed since Amazon ECS container agent is only supported on Amazon EC2 instances.

c. All the AWS EC2 instances and on-premise Redhat servers can install the ECS agent. The ECS agent is open sourced in Github and has detailed instructions.

d. For Amazon Linux and Ubuntu EC2 instances, the ECS agent can be installed using a package. However for Windows Server EC2 and on-premise Redhat server, unfortunately, the ECS agent cannot be installed since the agent only works on Linux.

178. A company has its DB, and they want to change its name and update the stack. On updating the CloudFormation deletes the old DB and create a new one. So all data on old DB is lost. What precautions do you need to take to prevent this in the future?

a. Create a new Change Set and use it to identify what changes may happen. Do the necessary backup before executing the Change Set. If everything is good, execute the Change Set and use the CloudFormation console to monitor.

b. Use a data pipeline to copy the data from RDS to S3 for backup before executing any stack update. By using this way, the RDS instance data is saved suitably.

c. Make sure that all RDSs are protected in the DeletePolicy by using "Keep" keyword then they are protected from deletion when stack update is happening. You could then make a snapshot of the RDS to backup data to use in the future.

d. Use Change Sets to check how your changes might impact your running resources, especially for critical resources such as RDS. Change Sets is also able to tell if the stack update is successful or not so that it can greatly help on the CloudFormation resources management.

179. An organization has CloudFormation template and now they need to change some configuration of auto-scaling. One of the employees from Developers department update the changes in template store it in S3 and then update the CloudFormation stack. Form the following option which is the best practice to use CloudFormation?

a. In the template, use more intrinsic functions such as FN::BASE64, FN::Join, etc. These functions are able to help build up a clean and efficient template.

b. The developer should update the instance regularly. On all the Amazon EC2 Linux instances and Amazon EC2 Linux instances created with AWS CloudFormation, regularly run the yum update command to update the RPM package. This ensures that you get the latest fixes and security updates.

c. The team should use revision control to manage the CloudFormation template, for example, using GitHub otherwise it is hard to track who and how the changes are made. The changes need code reviews as well to ensure the quality.

d. The developer should edit the template in the CloudFormation console directly rather than his PC as the console has provided various features to help on the edit.

180. A company uses OpsWorks for setting up short term project. Inside the project, multiple independent components need to communicate with other domains that belong to another team that their owner. From these components, one component is RDS MySQL DB which is owned and maintained by the HR department that saves its employees data. The project on OpsWork is designed on Linux Node.js Layer with specific recipes. How you as DevOps engineer provide a solution to connect to RDS MySQL DB?

a. The developer can only associate the Amazon RDS database server with an app when the app is created otherwise he has to rebuild the whole stack. After the RDS is associated, EC2 instances are able to connect with MySQL database automatically as long as proper roles have been attached to the application stack.

b. The developer can edit the app if he does not associate the database when creating the app. Under the lifecycle of Configure, AWS OpsWorks Stacks creates a file on each of the built-in application server instances containing the connection data. Then a recipe can be used to extract the connection information from the configure attributes and put it in a file that can be read by the application.

c. The developer can only associate the Amazon RDS database server with an app when the app is created otherwise he has to rebuild the whole stack. When the app is deployed, AWS OpsWorks Stacks creates a file on each of the built-in application server instances containing the connection data. The application can read the deploy attributes and use them to connect to the database server.

d. Associate the Amazon RDS database server when the developer creates the app or later by editing the app. When the app is deployed, AWS OpsWorks Stacks creates a file on each of the built-in application server instances containing the connection data. Then a custom recipe can be used to extract the connection information from the deploy attributes and put it in a file that can be read by the application.

181. A company uses CodeStar in which they create sample project of Node.js template. You deployed demo projects successfully and smoothly in Lambda. The project code is in CodeCommit, and now they want to change the Lambda resource name from ips to ipspecialist. How they do this?

   a. The CodeStar template has created resources including Lambda using its predefined name. To change the Lambda name, you have to go to the Lambda console and re-upload the code directly with the updated name.

   b. In this case, as CodeStar has used CodeCommit to manage the code repo, you can modify application resource name in the template.yml file in the CodeCommit Repo. This is also the AWS CloudFormation file that models your application's runtime environment.

   c. Unfortunately, you could not change the Lambda name as you chose to use the sample template which is read-only for demo purpose.

d. As CodeStar has used CodeCommit as its Git repo, you should pull the code from CodeCommit and make relevant changes in buildspec.yml via a Git Commit. Then CodeBuild is able to rebuild the Lambda using the updated name, and CodeStar will take care of the following deployment.

182. You want to get the SSH key as user input for SSH to EC2 instance. The EC2 instance is created by CloudFormation template as it is version controlled. How they achieve the SSH key?

   a. Design the template using YAML format. Add a parameter called "MyKeyPair" with the "Type" as "Key." For new EC2 instances, use the keyword of "Ref" to refer to this parameter in the Metadata section. Save the template in an S3 and refer to the S3 link during stack creation.

   b. In the template editor that has been provided by AWS, design the template using YAML. Add a parameter for the SSH Key such as "MyKeyPair." For new instances, use the keyword "Reference" to link to the "key" parameter.

   c. Use an editor to write a template using JSON, Add a parameter section for the SSH Key such as "MyKeyPair." For new instances, use the keyword of "Ref" to use this parameter. Save the template in S3 and upload it during stack creation.

   d. Design the template using XML format and add a parameter as the SSH Key. Refer to this parameter for new EC2 instances.

183. A company uses an Elastic BeanStalk environment for deployment, and they use the only single instance in deployment, but now they observed that need more capacity for memory and CPU utilization because application performance is now degrading. How you as DevOps engineer provide a solution for using multiple instances?

   a. Edit your environment's capacity configuration to a load balanced environment type. Make sure that all availability zones are selected. Add a scaling event when median CPU Utilization is over 85% for a period of 1 minute.

   b. Destroy the environment. Create a new environment type that has multiple instances as your old environment cannot be modified to a multiple instances environment.

   c. Change your environment type to a high available environment by editing your environment's configuration. In the Elastic BeanStalk console, select the environment, add multiple instances with autoscaling based on Memory Utilization.

d. Modify the environment's capacity settings to a load balanced environment type with autoscaling. Select all availability zones. Also, add a scaling trigger if average CPU Utilization is over 85% for 5 minutes.

184. You are using DynamoDB table to trace the usage rate or other relevant activities. In the table, there is approx. 2k new entries every day and it keeps increasing. Now you want to show this data to the CEO then how you can present it?

a. Create a new Data Pipeline to transfer the data from DynamoDB table to an S3 bucket. Add a schedule for this pipeline to activate it every day at a suitable time and then open the collected files in S3.

b. Create a new Data Pipeline to transfer the data from DynamoDB table to an S3. Add a schedule including a start time (8:00 AM) and end time (8:00 PM) for this pipeline to run every day and collect files in S3 and get them presented to PM.

c. In the DynamoDB console, select all items, use the "Export to .csv" feature to download the whole data every day. Then use a data analysis tool to manage the data.

d. Create a new Data Pipeline to transfer the data from DynamoDB table to an S3. Activate the pipeline every day and then open the files in S3 using an editor.

185. A company use AWS components and ensure that all components are monitored properly with logs, notifications, and alarms. There is the team who is continuously watching and respond accordingly. In these AWS components, they use AWS CodePipeline for deployment. How they properly monitored CodePipeline with enough logging? (Choose 2)

a. Amazon CloudWatch Events can be used to monitor the AWS Cloud resources including CodePipeline. The operation team can create a rule in Amazon CloudWatch Events based on CodePipeline metrics that you define such as "CodePipeline Pipeline Execution State Change." And then use an SNS topic as the target of this Cloudwatch Event rule.

b. Activate the CodePipeline Logging feature in the console. During the setup of that, the logs can be saved in real time to an S3 bucket that the operation team chooses. And the operation team can use an editor or analytic tool to open the text files in the S3 bucket to analyze and monitor

c. AWS Cloudwatch Metrics can be used to determine CodePipeline activities. In Cloudwatch Metrics, there are CodePipeline events in the namespace of

AWS/CodePipeline. Users can also create a dashboard to understand the CodePipeline status based on the metrics.

d. AWS CloudTrail can be used to log AWS CodePipeline API calls and related events made by or on behalf of an AWS account. By CloudTrail, users can determine the request that was made to AWS CodePipeline, the IP address from which the request was made, who made the request, when it was made, and additional details.

186. A company uses CodeDeploy, and they want to know the status of Deployment start, success, and failure of deployment of the auto scaling group. To monitor the Code Deploy activities and suitably notified Development lead. How you as a DevOps engineer meet deployment Lead requirement in the straight forward way?

a. The DevOps engineer should create a trigger in AWS CodeDeploy that publishes an Amazon Simple Notification Service (Amazon SNS) topic for the relevant AWS CodeDeploy deployment event. Then, when that event occurs, all subscribers to the associated topic will receive notifications through the endpoint specified in the topic, such as an SMS message or email message to the development lead.

b. Create a new CloudTrail and use it to record all the CodeDeploy API calls. When a CodeDeploy activity happens, the development lead will be able to see the details for the CodeDeploy status. He can then filter the CodeDeploy specific events in the CloudTrail console/CLI and understand the running status.

c. CodeDeploy is able to pass all its status to Cloudwatch metrics including CodeDeploy start, stop or pause. Create an alarm in the CodeDeploy metrics such as when a CodeDeploy failure happens. And then subscribe this alarm to an existing SNS topic. The SNS topic is responsible for notifying the development lead by email or SMS.

d. AWS Config should be used as it is able to show the status of every CodeDeploy activity. One SNS topic can be used to subscribe to the CodeDeploy activities in AWS Config to get the development lead notified.

187. An organization wants to use CodeCommit, but they need to ensure that the CodeCommit should be secure as they have very restricted security policies. Whatever the tools are added they should pass the audit security. In a security audit, the

important part is data must be encrypted then how CodeCommit pass this security audit?

    a. During the creation of new CodeCommit repo ensure that the setting of Encryption is enabled. Therefore both data in transit and at rest are encrypted, and the audit is able to pass.

    b. Nothing as data in AWS CodeCommit repositories is already encrypted in transit and at rest.

    c. The team should create a key in KMS for CodeCommit and ensure that CodeCommit uses that newly created key to encrypt all data in transit and at rest.

    d. AWS CodeCommit repositories are already encrypted at rest however the team should configure the CodeCommit to encrypt the data in transit such as during "git push."

188. An online store has its website which is used for product purchasing by the customer now they want to create feedback system, and for that, they used an Elastic BeanStalk environment. From the developer's team, one of the developer perform changes in the format of the survey and deploy into the new environment then used SwapURL for the switch to the new one. After viewing the logs and monitoring for one day, they observed that still old survey format is used after about 12 hours. What was the reason behind this?

    a. The "Swap URL" has used Route53 to change the DNS settings. It may bring in some TTL issue as DNS clients may exist at various levels and not all of them obey TTL rules.

    b. When the "Swap URL" has been utilized, Route53 is involved in adjusting the DNS Alias settings. However, Route53 may have a wrong TTL setting which is too big. As a result, the DNS clients did not expire until a long time.

    c. When the "Swap URL" has been triggered, Route53 is involved in changing the DNS settings. In this case, a wrong CNAME may be utilized, which has resulted in the wrong cases. The Route53 configurations should be checked and modified.

    d. The Elastic BeanStalk Environment has the wrong feature branch deployed. Track the Elastic BeanStalk logs to identify if the wrong code was committed. Roll back to the old environment and delete this new one.

189. You as a DevOps engineer need to build HelloWorld web service, and for that, you need to use multiple AWS services like CodeDeploy, CloudFormation, CodeCommit, ECS, and CodePipeline. How you build this?

   a. In CodePipeline, add a Source stage with CodeCommit. Add a Build stage with CodeBuild to build the new artifact which is an RPM package or an executable file and push it to ECR. Add a Deploy stage that uses CloudFormation to create a new task definition revision that points to the newly built Docker container image and updates the ECS service to use the new task definition revision.

   b. In CodePipeline, add a Source stage with CodeCommit. Add a Build stage with CodeBuild to build a new Docker container image and push it to ECR. Add a Deploy stage that uses CloudFormation to create a new task definition revision that points to the newly built Docker container image and updates the ECS service to use the new task definition revision.

   c. In CodePipeline, add a Source stage with CodeCommit. Add a Build stage with CodeBuild to build a new Docker container image and store it in S3. Add a Deploy stage that uses CloudFormation to create a new ECS Cluster that points to S3 URL with the newly built Docker container image and updates the relevant ECS service.

   d. In CodePipeline, add a Source stage with CodeCommit. Add a Staging stage with CodeBuild to build the new artifact which is an RPM package or an executable file and store it in S3. Add a Deploy stage that uses CloudFormation to create a new task definition revision that points to the installation package in S3 and updates the ECS service to use the new task definition revision.

190. An organization wants to use CloudFormation for the web service in a specific region and for that it uses AMI id to create EC2 instances with ELB in the template. How they achieve this?

   a. In the template, add a mapping section for all possible AMI IDs in all regions so that the CloudFormation does not need to remember any AMI IDs manually. Then in the Resource section, use Fn::FindInAMI to refer the correct AMI ID.

   b. In the template, add a parameter section for the AMI ID. The type of the parameter should be a String. Make sure that proper limitations are added such as the maximum length, minimum length, etc.

   c. Use a parameter for the user to input the AMI ID when the stack is created. Make sure that the parameter has the type as AWS::EC2::Image::Id.

   d. In order to use AMI Id, the template needs to have a "mapping" which is inside the "Resources" section so that the template understand which AMI ID to be

used during stack creation. The intrinsic function "FindInMap" is needed in the template to work with "mapping."

191. An organization has its legacy application which migrates to AWS by using CloudFormation. Now they want to track all API calls. The application is PHP and communicates to MySQL DB. Then how you as DevOps engineer implement CloudFormation for security audit?

   a. For CloudFormation tracking, it is suggested to use AWS Config as it is able to monitor all CloudFormation activities such as stack creation, stack update, and stack deletion.

   b. The CloudTrail actually does not support CloudFormation specific api calls. For example, when CloudFormation stack is created or updated, the relevant events are not recorded in CloudTrail. The trail only captures the API events for resources that CloudFormation has created.

   c. Create a new CloudTrail trail and configure an S3 bucket. Include the CloudFormation service for the new trail. All relevant CloudFormation API call information is recorded such as Parameter names, Parameter values, IAM roles and Tags used during stack creation.

   d. Create a new CloudTrail and configure an S3 bucket for the trail. By default, CloudFormation service is included, and all CloudFormation API calls will be recorded as CloudTrail events. The events contain lots of useful information that the security team cares about.

192. An organization has its website project that is hosted in OpsWorks. The website is already online for half a year. According to statistics, the average request volume varies sinusoidally over the day. The minimum average request volume requires five application server instances. Starting from 12 AM, the load goes up gradually with about two more instances needed every hour and reaches the highest at 12 PM. About 16 instances are needed maximum. However, there are chances for the spike that 1 or 2 more instances are required. Starting from 12 PM, the workload goes down gradually and reaches the lowest at 12 AM. Which below option is suggested to manage the instances in the OpsWorks stack?

   a. The stack should have three 24/7 instances, which are always on and handle the base load. Add 12 time-based instances and modify the number of time-based instances every two hours. Add two load-based instances to handle traffic spikes.

b. The stack should have three On-Demand instances, which are used to serve the base load. Add 12 schedule instances and modify the number of schedule instances every two hours. Add two spot instances to handle traffic spikes.

c. The stack should have three 24/7 instances, which are always on and handle the base load. Add 12 schedule instances and modify the number of schedule instances every two hours, Add two spot instances to handle traffic spikes.

d. The stack should have three 24/7 instances to handle with the base load. Add an EC2 autoscaling group to OpsWorks Stack and make sure that the launch configuration is proper. The autoscaling group is able to handle with the load change automatically. No other instances types are required.

193. A company has a project for which they use CodeStar that is able to provide a dashboard to control the project and connection of AWS services like CodeCommit, CodePipeline etc. For direct code changes, they use Eclipse and then develop software in CodeStar project. In Eclipse all Aws toolkit is installed. How you as a DevOps ensure that Eclipse properly uses CodeStar? (Choose 2)

   a. IAM users that have been added to an AWS CodeStar project as team members.

   b. Git credentials (user name and password) for the IAM users that the developers use.

   c. The developers must be members of the AWS CodeStar project team with the owner so that they are able to pull/submit the code.

   d. An IAM role that has enough AWS CodeStar permissions are added to Eclipse.

194. An organization has a project, and for that, they need to use CodeStar because the project needs high availability and scalability. A developer team head of Organization wants control of the whole project with membership. Developer team has two developers and 2 UI designer. He wants to give UI designer's read access to project board and also provide scrum master the monitoring of dashboard timely. Then how he manages the team membership?

   a. In CodeStar management console, on the "Team members" page, add the developers as Contributor, add the UI designer and the scrum master as Viewer as both of them need read-only access

   b. For each IAM user, in the IAM console, attach relevant CodeStar policies. For example, add the below policy for the admin:

      "Version": "2012-10-17",

```
"Statement": [ {
"Sid": "AdminRole",
"Effect" : "Allow" ,
"Action": [
"codestar:DisassociateTeamMember" ,
 "codestar:DisassociateTeamMember",
"codestar:UpdateTeamMember",
"codestar:CreateProject"
],
 "Resource": "*"
}]}
```

c. In CodeStar management console, on the "Team members" page, add the developers as Contributor, add the UI designer as Viewer and add the scrum master as Moderator.

d. For each IAM user, in the IAM console, attach relevant CodeStar policies. For example, add the below policy for the admin:

```
"Version": "2012-10-17",
 "Statement": [ {
"Sid": "AdminPolicy",
"Effect" : "Allow" ,
"Action": "codestar:*" ,
"Resource": "*"
}]}
```

195. An organization has its legacy product which is java application and NGINX. Now they need to use Elastic BeanStalk for this legacy product then how you as DevOps engineer deploy multi container environment in EB?

a. Use dockerrun.aws.json v1 for the multidocker environment. This file describes the containers to deploy to each container instance.

b. Use two dockerfiles for the multidocker environment. One for Java and one for Nginx.

c. Use .ebextension config files to describe the multidocker environment.

d. Use dockerrun.aws.json v2 for the multidocker environment. This file describes the containers to deploy to each container instance.

196. An organization is using Elastic BeanStalk environment for web production, and they need to read/write to RDS DB that is in use of other productions. As EB is using immutable architecture, so it creates a new instance for new deployment then how you connect to RDS for the environment?

   a. Since it is for production, it is suggested to put the RDS database outside of the Elastic BeanStalk environment. This can be done by using your application to connect to it on launch.

   b. You could not add this RDS database to Elastic BeanStalk as Elastic BeanStalk does not support PostgreSQL

   c. You could add this RDS database to Elastic BeanStalk using the database configuration card in the console. Type in the correct username, password, instance class, and other information.

   d. For the Elastic BeanStalk, it is not possible to connect to an RDS instance if it is for a production environment.

197. A company needs to use CodeCommit and CodePipeline for its development as a DevOps service. But they decided to use Jenkin as build provider as they have good hands on in this. Then how as DevOps engineer provide a solution to use CodePipeline with Jenkins?

   a. Launch an Amazon EC2 instance to host the Jenkins server and use an IAM role to grant the instance the required permissions for interacting with AWS CodePipeline. Then create a new CodePipeline. In the build stage, choose "Add Jenkins" and configure correct "Provider name" and "Server URL."

   b. Launch an Amazon EC2 instance to host the Jenkins server and using a Secret Access Key/Access Key ID to grant the instance the required permissions for interacting with AWS CodePipeline. For the new CodePipeline configuration, make sure that Jenkins is selected as the build server in the build stage. The "Server URL" should match that in the Jenkins server, however, the "Provider name" can be anything.

   c. Make sure that all of the AWS resources for this procedure are created in the same AWS Region where you create your pipeline. Then create a new CodePipeline with four mandatory stages which are "Source Stage," "Jenkins Stage," "Test Stage" and "Deploy Stage."

   d. Setup CodePipeline in one region and setup CodeCommit and Amazon EC2 instance key pair in another region. This is to address some safety concerns. Then create a new CodePipeline with four stages. In the build stage, choose "Add Jenkins" and configure correct "Provider name" and "Server URL."

198. DevOps engineer in the company uses CodeDeploy for its project. In the project, it uses EC2 instance and ELB for high availability and scalability. They use four instances minimum, and in case of extensive load, the number of instances increases to 8. Now he wants to use in-place deployment than before creating the CodeDeploy Deployment Group in AWS console what steps need to be taken? Choose 3.

    a. Make sure the correct SNS topic is created because when CodeDeploy Deployment Group is being created, one SNS topic is required to subscribe to the CodeDeploy application, which is a mandatory step

    b. Ensure that all instances under the autoscaling group have proper tags such as env/dev because when CodeDeploy Deployment Group is being created, EC2 tags are needed for CodeDeploy to understand the targets to deploy to.

    c. Make sure that you have a service role that trusts AWS CodeDeploy with correct permissions. This should be done before creating the Deployment Group in CodeDeploy. IAM should be involved for that by creating a new role, and the role type is AWS Service.

    d. Prepare an autoscaling group with Min 4 and Max 8 instances. Make sure that the autoscaling group has the correct autoscaling launch configurations attached. You can use the prebaked AMI to install some configuration packages for the instances.

199. An organization uses Github for storing the code of their project, and now they need to use CodeCommit as the project is developed and integrated into AWS. Then how Developers shifts its existing development to CodeCommit repository?

    a. To work on existing CodeCommit Repo, create an IAM user for each developer, add a CodeCommit Read policy to each user. After that, all developers are able to git clone the CodeCommit Repo and start working on their branches.

    b. Create new CodeCommit Repo when required. Git Clone the Repo in local PCs and the use git push to the new CodeCommit Repo url and after that view files in AWS CodeCommit to see if the git push is successful.

    c. In order to work on existing CodeCommit Repo for other developers, create an IAM group with a suitable CodeCommit policy. Add users to that group. Then all developers are able to git clone the CodeCommit Repo and start working on their own branches.

    d. Set up new CodeCommit Repo using AWS CLI. Find the repo url which may be an HTTPS or SSH one. Use git push to upload the repo from local to

CodeCommit server. After that, inspect if the files show properly in CodeCommit.

200. You have a project for which you create an autoscaling group with launch configuration that has recent AMI then attach this autoscaling group to existing classic ELB with health check of HTTP. Once ELB passed the health checks, they delete old Auto scaling group as they are using Bleu/Green Deployment but still new autoscaling group is not performing properly then how you minimize the issue?

    a. The health check is not configured properly. The classic ELB should be replaced using an application load balancer, and the HTTPs health check is required.

    b. After the new autoscaling group is created, wait for a longer time firstly so that the instances are ready to service the traffic. Then attach the autoscaling group to the ELB.

    c. The health check is not accurate. The classic ELB HTTP health check should point to a file that only exists after the new instances are ready to serve.

    d. The classic ELB or network ELB cannot meet the need. The application load balancer should be used as it is able to check the application status. In this case, the application is not ready yet when the ELB health check passed.

201. A company has a web application running on EC2 instances. They use 6 instances, and each instance took 45% of the resources. They want that all 6 instances are running all times and for that they use autoscaling. There is a consistent number of request. Now they want that load distribution among all instances are even and also want to use AMI for instances. How they meet this requirement?

    a. Deploy 2 EC2 instances in three regions and use Amazon Elastic Load Balancer.

    b. Deploy 3 EC2 instances in one availability zone and 3 in another availability zone and use Amazon Elastic Load Balancer.

    c. Deploy 3 EC2 instances in one region and 3 in another region and use Amazon Elastic Load Balancer.

    d. Deploy 6 EC2 instances in one availability zone and use Amazon Elastic Load Balancer.

202. A company has its environment relies on EC2 instances with pre-configured software and now they want to replicate the environment to another region for

Disaster recovery. Then how you as a DevOps engineer provide a solution to replicate?

    a. Make the EC2 instance shareable among other regions through IAM permissions.

    b. Create an AMI of the EC2 instance

    c. Create an AMI of the EC2 instance and copy the AMI to the desired region

    d. None of the above

203. A DevOps engineer assigned a task to create an environment for a production environment and development environment. For this purpose, it uses a CloudFormation template. In the template, EC2 instances are created within the same region with specific EIP and security group defined in the template. The stack of CloudFormation for development environment successfully created but the production environment is not created successfully. What was the issue of this failure?

    a. You didn't choose the Production version of the AMI you are using when creating the production stack.

    b. You hit the soft limit for security groups when creating the development environment.

    c. You hit the soft limit of 5 EIPs per region when creating the development environment.

    d. You have chosen the wrong tags when creating the instances in both environments.

204. If you have a website launched recently and experience a large amount of traffic in initial days. Now they need to set up the DNS failure to the static website in case of load failure. How they achieve this?

    a. Add more servers in case the application fails.

    b. Use Route53 with the failover option to failover to a static S3 website bucket or CloudFront distribution.

    c. Enable failover to an on-premise data center to the application hosted there.

    d. Duplicate the exact application architecture in another region and configure DNS weight-based routing

205. An organization has an application in which they review the auto scaling group, and they find an issue that their application continuously up and down in the same

hour. How you as DevOps engineer provide cost-effective solution for this with preserving its elasticity? (Choose 2)

    a. Modify the Auto Scaling group termination policy to terminate the newest instance first.

    b. Modify the Auto Scaling policy to use scheduled scaling actions

    c. Modify the Auto Scaling Group cooldown timers

    d. Modify the Amazon Cloudwatch alarm period that triggers your AutoScaling scale down policy.

206. A company wants to store its log in durable storage and after 3 months archive that logs. How the meet this requirement in AWS? (Choose 2)

    a. Use Lifecycle policies to move the data onto Amazon Simple Storage service after a period of 3 month

    b. Use Lifecycle policies to move the data onto Amazon Glacier after a period of 3 months

    c. Store the log files as they emitted from the application on to Amazon Glacier

    d. Store the log files as they emitted from the application on to Amazon Simple Storage service

207. An organization has an application in one region, and this region has 3 AZ's. The application uses 6 EC2 instances. How you as DevOps engineer provide a solution to deploy these instances in such a way that if any AZ fails there is 100% availability of all 6 instances? (Choose 2)

    a. us-west-2a with 6 instances, us-west-2b with 6 instances, us-west-2c with 0 instances

    b. us-west-2a with 3 instances, us-west-2b with 3 instances, us-west-2c with 0 instances

    c. us-west-2a with 3 instances, us-west-2b with 3 instances, us-west-2c with 3 instances

    d. us-west-2a with 2 instances, us-west-2b with 2 instances, us-west-2c with 2 instances

208. Ahmed has instances, and from these instances, one of the instances passes an unhealthy system checks, but he doesn't want to monitor this check and change it's by own. He need automate repair system check failure. How he meets this requirement?

    a. Implement a third party monitoring tool.

b. Write a script that periodically shuts down and starts instances based on certain stats.

c. Write a script that queries the EC2 API for each instance status check

d. Create CloudWatch alarms for StatuscheckFailed_System metrics and select EC2 action-Recover the instance

209. An organization has an application which takes a huge amount of data and now the organization needs to use AWS for storage. The data store in AWS support scalability in the case when the application receives the unexpected amount of data?

a. Amazon EC2, because EBS volumes can scale to hold any amount of data and when used with Auto Scaling, can be designed for fault tolerance and high availability

b. Amazon Import/Export, because Amazon assists in migrating large amounts of data to Amazon S3

c. Amazon S3, because it provides unlimited amounts of storage data, scales automatically, is highly available, and durable

d. Amazon Glacier, to keep costs low for storage and scale infinitely

210. A company has instances running in VPC. Inside VPC there are production and development instances and the company wants that production instances can't access the instances of development. How they achieve this requirement?

a. Define the tags on the test and production servers and add a condition to the IAM policy which allows access to specific tags

b. Launch the test and production instances in different Availability Zones and use Multi-Factor Authentication

c. Create an IAM policy with a condition which allows access to only instances that are used for production or development

d. Launch the test and production instances in separate VPC's and use VPC peering

211. You have three web servers for production and databases for production and development. The web server consists of EC2 instances with EBS volume and CPU load of 80%. By using ELB, traffic distribution occurs. Now they want to reduce the cost of the environment without affecting the availability. How they do this?

a. Consider removing the Elastic Load Balancer

b. Consider using spot instances instead of reserved EC2 instances

c. Consider not using a Multi-AZ RDS deployment for the development database

d. Consider using on-demand instances instead of reserved EC2 instances

212. There is CloudFormation template in which you define EC2 instances and single ELB. How you define in the template if you want DNS of ELB as a return value in the stack?

    a. Mapping

    b. Resource

    c. Parameters

    d. Output

213. If you are using EC2 instance with EBS backed volume. Now you want a backup in durable storage then how you can do this?

    a. Write a cronjob that uses the AWS CLI to take a snapshot of production EBS volumes. The data is durable because EBS snapshots are stored on the Amazon S3 standard storage class

    b. Use a lifecycle policy to back up EBS volumes stored on Amazon S3 for durability

    c. Write a cronjob on the server that compresses the data that needs to be backed up using zip compression, then use AWS CLI to copy the data into an S3 bucket for durability

    d. Configure Amazon Storage Gateway with EBS volumes as the data source and store the backups on-premise through the storage gateway

214. An organization has an application, and for that, they want a storage option that is critical. How they store data? Choose 2

    a. Encrypt the file system on an EBS volume using Linux tools

    b. With AWS you do not need to worry about encryption

    c. Enable S3 Encryption

    d. By using S3 infrequent access

215. An organization needs to create an S3 bucket with all resources in development, and for that, it uses CloudFormation template. How they create CloudFormation template?

    a. Use the metadata section in the CloudFormation template to decide on whether to create the S3 bucket or not.

b. Create separate CloudFormation templates for Development and production.

c. Create an S3 bucket from before and then just provide access based on the tag value mentioned in the CloudFormation template

d. Create a parameter in the CloudFormation template and then use the Condition clause in the template to create an S3 bucket if the parameter has a value of development

216. Consider a company has an Elastic BeanStalk environment, and now they delete this environment and create the new one. As they want to access the data on the old environment, they are unable to access it?

a. This is because the underlying EC2 Instances are created with no persistent local storage

b. This is because, before the environment termination, Elastic BeanStalk copies the data to DynamoDB, and hence the data is not present in the EBS volumes

c. This is because the underlying EC2 Instances are created with IOPS volumes and cannot be accessed once the environment has been terminated.

d. This is because the underlying EC2 Instances are created with encrypted storage and cannot be accessed once the environment has been terminated.

217. An organization has an application on AWS running on EC2 instances with auto scaling group. An application has a huge amount of load, and because of this load, they are facing loss in the request, even if the auto scaling group creates new instances they still face some loss. How you as DevOps engineer provide a solution in cost effective way so that no loss occurs.

a. Pre-warm your Elastic Load Balancer

b. Use larger instances for your application

c. Keep one extra EC2 instance always powered on in case a spike occurs

d. Use an SQS queue to decouple the application components

218. An organization has an application on AWS. The application consists of instances with ELB behind on it and auto-scaling. They are also using MySQL RDS DB. How they make this architecture more self-healing?

a. Create one more Autoscaling Group in another region for fault tolerance

b. Create one more ELB in another region for fault tolerance

c. Enable Multi-AZ feature for the AWS RDS database

    d. Enable Read Replica's for the AWS RDS database

219. A company wants log whenever the instance is added or removed from an existing Auto scaling group. How they meet their requirement? (Choose 2)
    a. Create a Cloudwatch event which will trigger the SQS queue
    b. Create a Cloudwatch event which will trigger the Lambda function
    c. Create an SQS queue which will write the event to Cloudwatch logs
    d. Create a Lambda function which will write the event to Cloudwatch logs

220. You have an Elastic BeanStalk environment, and now you want to create a new environment, but the issue arises that the old environment is terminated and you are unable to access the data of the older environment. What was the issue behind this?
    a. This is because the underlying EC2 Instances are created with no persistent local storage
    b. This is because, before the environment termination, Elastic BeanStalk copies the data to DynamoDB, and hence the data is not present in the EBS volumes
    c. This is because the underlying EC2 Instances are created with IOPS volumes and cannot be accessed once the environment has been terminated.
    d. This is because the underlying EC2 Instances are created with encrypted storage and cannot be accessed once the environment has been terminated.

221. A company has its client that is using its mobile application to access the AWS resources. The access to the resources will be given to the clients by logging via Facebook and google. Then through which mechanism company authenticates the client to access the resource?
    a. Use Web identity federation to authenticate the users
    b. Use separate IAM users that correspond to each Facebook and Google user
    c. Use AWS Policies to authenticate the users
    d. Use separate IAM Roles that correspond to each Facebook and Google user

222. What is the duration of response from the instance in OpsWorks stack before declaring the instance as a failed instance?
    a. 20 minute
    b. 30 second
    c. 1 minute

d. 5 minute

223. An organization needs to use OpsWorks stack in AWS. They have some custom recipes that are part of their on-premises Chef configuration. Now they want that whenever an instance is launched in OpsWorks uses this Chef configuration. How they achieve this? (Choose 2)
   a. Ensure the recipe is placed as part of the Setup Lifecycle event as part of the Stack setting.
   b. Ensure the recipe is placed as part of the Setup Lifecycle event as part of the Layer setting.
   c. Ensure the custom cookbooks option is set in Opswork layer.
   d. Ensure the custom cookbooks option is set in Opswork stack.

224. An institute has multiple CloudFormation templates in AWS, and they want to know that who from its teaching staff use the CloudFormation stacks from their AWS account because of security reasons. How they achieve this requirement?
   a. Connect SQS and CloudFormation so that a message is published for each resource created in the CloudFormation stack.
   b. Enable Cloudwatch logs for each CloudFormation stack to track the resource creation events.
   c. Enable CloudTrail logs so that the API calls can be recorded
   d. Enable CloudWatch events for each CloudFormation stack to track the resource creation events.

225. A company using auto scaling group with 4 instances and now they need to change the type of instance that is running and also want that service is not interrupted during this change as they want 2 instances in service always. How they do this?
   a. AutoScalingIntegrationUpdate
   b. AutoScalingReplacingUpdate
   c. AutoScalingScheduledAction
   d. AutoScalingRollingUpdate

226. To create a current application in a specific environment which command is used in Elastic BeanStalk CLI?
   a. eb app

b. eb create

c. eb env

d. eb start

227. You want to deploy the .NET application in AWS for continuous integration and deployment. The code of this application is in the Git repository. What are the steps need to be taken to deploy this application? (Choose 2)

    a. Use a chef recipe to deploy the code and attach it to the Elastic BeanStalk environment.

    b. Use the CodePipeline service to provision an IIS environment to host the application.

    c. Use the Elastic Beanstalk service to provision an IIS platform web environment to host the application.

    d. Create a source bundle for the .Net code and upload it as an application revision.

228. For the creation of Stack resources in CloudFormation which command is sued for coordination of creation? (Choose 2)

    a. CreationPolicy attribute

    b. HoldPolicy attribute

    c. AWS::CloudFormation::HoldCondition

    d. AWS::CloudFormation::WaitCondition

229. An organization has multiple application which now they want to shift to AWS by using Elastic BeanStalk. But the application supported platform is not available in Elastic BeanStalk. Then how they move their applications to AWS using EB?

    a. Create a docker container for the custom application and then deploy it to Elastic BeanStalk.

    b. Use custom CloudFormation templates to deploy the application into Elastic BeanStalk

    c. Use custom chef recipe's to deploy your application in Elastic BeanStalk.

    d. Use the Opswork service to create a stack. In the stack, create a separate custom layer. Deploy the application to this layer and then attach the layer to Elastic BeanStalk

230. How in Elastic BeanStalk environment you deployed a new version of the application with the fastest approach whenever the changes occur?
    a. Rolling
    b. Rolling with batch
    c. All at once
    d. Immutable

231. A company using DynamoDB and want to keep track of all the calls that are made from source IP address. How they do this?
    a. AWS Cloudwatch
    b. AWS CloudTrail
    c. AWS CodePipeline
    d. AWS CodeCommit

232. A company wants to create a CI/CD model for application in the organization then how they achieve this in AWS?
    a. AWS SQS
    b. AWS CodeDeploy
    c. AWS IAM
    d. AWS CodePipeline

233. When you use CodeDeploy to deploy application and application use EC2/on-premises compute platform then which file need to be added along with source code?
    a. appconfig.yml
    b. appconfig.json
    c. appspec.json
    d. appspec.yml

234. An organization has multiple CloudFormation stacks in AWS and them continuously as part of cleaning delete number of the stack, but from these stacks, few of them are not deleted. What was the issue behind this?
    a. The stack consists of an EC2 resource which was created with a custom AMI.
    b. The stacks were created with the wrong template version. Since the standard template version is now higher, it is preventing the deletion of the stacks. You need to contact AWS support.

c. The stack has an S3 bucket defined which has objects present in it.

d. The stack has an EC2 Security Group which has EC2 Instances attached to it.

235. A company has continuous releases cycles of application and to deploy this application they need to use AWS service in which application deployed quickly, and rollback occurs quickly to the previous version of the application. How they do this in AWS? (Choose 2)

a. Use the CloudFormation service. Create separate templates for each application revision and deploy them accordingly.

b. Use the Elastic BeanStalk service. Use Application versions and upload the revisions of your application. Deploy the revisions accordingly and rollback to prior versions accordingly.

c. Use the Opswork service to deploy the web instances. Deploy the app to the Opswork web layer. Rollback using the Deploy app in Opswork.

d. Use the Elastic BeanStalk service. Create separate environments for each application revision. Revert back to an environment incase the new environment does not work.

236. How you as DevOps engineer deploy Docker container in OpsWorks? (Choose 2)

a. In the App for Opswork deployment, specify the git url for the recipes which will deploy the applications in the docker environment.

b. Use Elastic BeanStalk to deploy docker containers since this is not possible in Opswork. Then attach the Elastic BeanStalk environment as a layer in Opswork.

c. Use custom cookbooks for your Opswork stack and provide the Git repository which has the chef recipes for the Docker containers.

d. Use CloudFormation to deploy docker containers since this is not possible in Opswork. Then attach the CloudFormation resources as a layer in Opswork.

237. An organization is using CodeBuild service of AWS for build process as they need to automate the build process. From the following option which is needed to be defined as a file of build command?

a. appspec.json

b. appspec.yml

c. buildspec.yml

d. buildspec.xml

238.   A company uses CloudFormation for the provision of resources of application then how they create a nested stack in CloudFormation?

    a. AWS::CloudFormation::StackNest

    b. AWS::CloudFormation::Stack

    c. AWS::CloudFormation::Nested

    d. AWS::CloudFormation::NestedStack

239.   How you make sure that your data is secured in transit while using ELB? (Choose 2)

    a. Use an HTTPS front end listener for your ELB

    b. Use an HTTP front end listener for your ELB

    c. Use an SSL front end listener for your ELB

    d. Use a TLS front end listener for your ELB

240.   A company has a web application that is hosted in AWS EC2 instances but the application changes on a quarterly basis then from the following options which are best for Blue/Green Deployment? (Choose 2)

    a. Deploy the application to an Elastic BeanStalk environment. Use the Rolling updates feature to perform a Blue Green deployment.

    b. Place the EC2 instances behind an ELB. Have a secondary environment with EC2 Instances and ELB in another region. Use Route53 with geo-location to route requests and switch over to the secondary environment.

    c. Deploy the application to an Elastic BeanStalk environment. Have a secondary Elastic BeanStalk environment in place with the updated application code. Use the swap URL's feature to switch onto the new environment.

    d. Deploy the application using Opswork stacks. Have a secondary stack for the new application deployment. Use Route53 to switch over to the new stack for the new application update.

241.   A company is designing a CloudFormation template which deploys a LAMP stack. Once you deployed the stack and CREATE_COMPLETE status is showing, but the apache server is still not up and running and is experiencing issues while starting up. Now they want that CREATE_COMPLETE status is shown only when all resources are completely up and running? (Choose 2)

a. Use lifecycle hooks to mark the completion of the creation and configuration of the underlying resource.

b. Use the CFN helper scripts to signal once the resource configuration is complete.

c. Define a stack policy which defines that all underlying resources should be up and running before showing a status of CREATE_COMPLETE.

d. Use the CreationPolicy to ensure it is associated with the EC2 Instance resource.

242. An organization is using AWS OpsWorks stacks for automated resources, and now they want to associate their custom recipes to the running stack, but they are unable to do that. What was the issue behind this?

a. The stack layers were created without the custom cookbooks option. Just change the layer settings accordingly.

b. Once you create layers in the stack, you cannot assign custom recipe's; this needs to be done when the layers are created.

c. The stacks were created without the custom cookbooks option. Just change the stack settings accordingly.

d. Once you create a stack, you cannot assign custom recipe's; this needs to be done when the stack is created.

243. A company is using CodeDeploy service of AWS for deploying an application. What pre-requisites that need to be used to ensure that EC2 instance can work with CodeDeploy? (Choose 2)

a. Ensure that the CodeDeploy agent is installed on the EC2 Instance

b. Ensure the EC2 Instance is placed in the default VPC

c. Ensure the EC2 Instance is configured with Enhanced Networking

d. Ensure an IAM role is attached to the instance so that it can work with the Code Deploy Service.

244. An organization wants a reliable and durable logging solution for tracking the changes to occur in resources of AWS. How they do this?

a. Create three new CloudTrail trails with three new S3 buckets to store the logs one for the AWS Management console, one for AWS SDKs and one for command line tools. Use IAM roles and S3 bucket policies on the S3 buckets that store your logs.

b. Create a new CloudTrail trail with an existing S3 bucket to store the logs and with the global services option selected. Use S3 ACLs, and Multi Factor Authentication (MFA) Delete on the S3 bucket that stores your logs.

c. Create a new CloudTrail with one new S3 bucket to store the logs. Configure SNS to send log file delivery notifications to your management system. Use IAM roles and S3 bucket policies on the S3 bucket that stores your logs.

d. Create a new CloudTrail trail with one new S3 bucket to store the logs and with the global services option selected. Use IAM roles S3 bucket policies and Multi Factor Authentication (MFA) Delete on the S3 bucket that stores your logs.

245. A company has an application hosted in AWS. The application is using EC2 instances with ELB and S3. Now they want encryption of data at rest and in transit. How they do this? (Choose 3)

a. Use IOPS volumes when working with EBS volumes on EC2 Instances

b. Use server side encryption for S3

c. Encrypt all EBS volumes attached to EC2 Instances

d. Use SSL/HTTPS when using the Elastic Load Balancer

246. A company needs to build a layer in software sack on AWS that need to be able to scale depend on demand as quickly as possible. The code is running on an EC2 instance in auto scaling group with ELB. Then through which deployment method, they can do this?

a. Create a new Auto Scaling Launch Configuration with UserData scripts configured to pull the latest code at all times.

b. Create a Dockerfile when preparing to deploy a new version to production and publish it to S3. Use UserData in the Auto Scaling Launch configuration to pull down the Dockerfile from S3 and run it when new instances launch.

c. Bake an AMI when deploying new versions of code, and use that AMI for the Auto Scaling Launch Configuration.

d. SSH into new instances that come online, and deploy new code onto the system by pulling it from an S3 bucket, which is populated by code that you refresh from source control on new pushes.

247. A company using EC2 instances for application and now they want to use AWS tool which automates the process of collection of software inventory from instances and also helps in applying OS patches. Which AWS service they use for this purpose?

a. AWS CodePipeline
b. AWS AMI's
c. EC2 system manager
d. AWS CodeDeploy

248. Ali has its online store for which a web application is hosted on AWS that contains a number of web servers. Now he wants to monitor the error which occurs when users are using application. How he performs this requirement? (Choose 2)
    a. Increment a metric filter in CloudTrail whenever the pattern is matched.
    b. Send the logs from the instances onto Cloudwatch logs.
    c. Search for the keyword "ERROR" in the log files on the server.
    d. Search for the keyword "ERROR" in Cloudwatch logs.

249. A company is using Jenkins tool for application, and now they need AWS service to which they integrate it. From the following option which is a good option?
    a. Amazon EC2
    b. Elastic BeanStalk
    c. Amazon ECS
    d. All of the above

250. An organization using Blue/Green Deployment technique for deploying its application new version. As a DevOps engineer, you need to monitor the health of an application then which AWS service you can use for this purpose?
    a. AWS CloudTrail
    b. AWS CloudWatch
    c. AWS CodeDeploy
    d. AWS CodeCommit

251. An organization has its web application on AWS running on instances of auto scaling group with ELB. Now they need to create new AMI on each application version for deployment. The deployment technique is Blue/Green Deployment, but in this technique, they need that size of the fleet is constant over a period of 3 hours to get assures that new version is working well. Then which technique they used to rollback easily? (Choose 2)
    a. Configure Elastic Load Balancing to vary the proportion of requests sent to instances running the two application versions.

b. Create an Auto Scaling launch configuration with the new AMI to use the new launch configuration and to register instances with the new load balancer

c. Create an Auto Scaling launch configuration with the new AMI to use the new launch configuration and to register instances with the existing load balancer

d. Use Amazon RouteS3 weighted Round Robin to vary the proportion of requests sent to the load balancers.

252. You as DevOps engineer use an auto scaling group to which lifecycle hooks. Then in case of scale in and scale out what is the wait state? (Choose 2)

   a. Terminating:Wait
   b. Launching:Wait
   c. Exiting:Wait
   d. Pending:Wait

253. An organization has AD on its on-premises and now they need to extend its footprint on AWS with the use of on-premises AD for authentication then which AWS service can be used for connecting on-premises AD to AWS?

   a. Use the ClassicLink feature on AWS
   b. Use the AWS Simple AD service
   c. Use the Active Directory service on AWS
   d. Use the Active Directory connector service on AWS

254. Ahmed is using EC2 instances on AWS with ELB. Launching of EC2 instances has occurred via auto scaling group. Now he wants that logs from the server are stored in durable storage so that it will be used in future by him. How he performs this requirement? (Choose 2)

   a. Use AWS Data Pipeline to move log data from the Amazon S3 bucket to Amazon SQS in order to process and run reports

   b. On the web servers, create a scheduled task that executes a script to rotate and transmit the logs to an Amazon S3 bucket.

   c. On the web servers, create a scheduled task that executes a script to rotate and transmit the logs to Amazon Glacier.

   d. Use AWS Data Pipeline to move log data from the Amazon S3 bucket to Amazon Redshift in order to process and run reports

255. A company using CloudFormation template for testing an application. Now they need that when the stack is deleted the DB is still there for future use. How that was possible?

    a. In the AWS CloudFormation template, set the AWS::RDS::DBInstance's DBInstanceClass property to be read-only.

    b. In the AWS CloudFormation template, set the WaitPolicy of the AWS::RDS::DBInstance's WaitPolicy property to "Retain."

    c. In the AWS CloudFormation template, set the DeletionPolicy of the AWS::RDS::DBInstance's DeletionPolicy property to "Retain."

    d. Ensure that the RDS is created with Read Replica's so that the Read Replica remains after the stack is torn down.

256. An organization has an application based on PHP language that uses MySQL as DB. Now they need AWS service through which they deploy code in single command simply?

    a. AWS OpsWorks

    b. AWS Elastic BeanStalk

    c. AWS EC2+ELB

    d. AWS CloudFormation

257. Which Blue/Green deployment option is best to deploy an application running on EC2 instance behind an ELB and launching of instance occurs as a part of Auto Scaling?

    a. Use the OpsWorks service to deploy your resources. Use 2 Opswork layers to deploy 2 versions of your application. When the time comes for the switch, change to the alternate layer in the Opswork stack

    b. Re-deploy your application behind a load balancer that uses Auto Scaling groups, create a new identical Auto Scaling group, and associate it to the load balancer. During deployment, set the desired number of instances on the old Auto Scaling group to zero, and when all instances have terminated, delete the old Auto Scaling group.

    c. Use the Elastic BeanStalk service to deploy your resources. Use 2 Elastic BeanStalk environments. Use Rolling deployments to switch between the environments.

d. Use a CloudFormation stack to deploy your resources. Use 2 CloudFormation stacks. Whenever you want to switch over, deploy and use the resources in the second CloudFormation stack.

258. A company is using Elastic BeanStalk for deploying the application. Application consist of web and application server. In webserver when the application version is deploying, it first needs to run some Python scripts. How they do this?

   a. Make use of the custom resource
   b. Make use of Docker containers
   c. Make use of container command
   d. Make use of multiple Elastic BeanStalk environments

259. An organization has read intensive application which is consist of a set of webservers and RDS. Because this read intensive nature on DB the response time of application is decreased. How they overcome this issue? (Choose 2)

   a. Use ElastiCache in front of your Amazon RDS DB to cache common queries
   b. Use SQS to cache the database queries
   c. Create Amazon DB Read Replicas. Configure the application layer to query the readreplica's for query needs
   d. Use Autoscaling to scale out and scale in the database tier

260. Which AWS service is used to get the current configuration snapshot?

   a. AWS Trusted Advisor
   b. AWS CloudWatch
   c. AWS Config
   d. AWS CodeDeploy

261. An organization has an application hosted on AWS. The application contains a set of EC2 instances with ELB and RDS instance. How you as DevOps engineer make this application architecture self-healing and cost effective? (Choose 2)

   a. Use CloudWatch metrics to check the utilization of the databases servers. Use Autoscaling Group to scale the database instances accordingly based on the CloudWatch metrics.
   b. Utilize the Read Replica feature for the Amazon RDS layer

c. Use CloudWatch metrics to check the utilization of the web layer. Use Autoscaling Group to scale the web instances accordingly based on the CloudWatch metrics.

d. Utilize the Multi-AZ feature for the Amazon RDS layer

262. You want logs of your application running on EC2 instances for real time processing and analyzing. How you can achieve this?

    a. Use another EC2 Instance with a larger instance type to process the logs

    b. Use Amazon S3 to store the logs and then use Amazon Kinesis to process and analyze the logs in real time

    c. Use Amazon Glacier to store the logs and then use Amazon Kinesis to process and analyze the logs in real time

    d. Use Cloudwatch logs to process and analyze the logs in real time

263. A company hosts its NGINX server and web application on AWS EC2 instances. Its users use both but when a company updates version of application the instances face some technical issue and they need urgent restart as they donot have time to identify the issue. How they could do this?

    a. Install Cloudwatch logs agent on the instance and send all the logs to Cloudwatch logs.

    b. Stream all the data to Amazon Kinesis and then analyze the data in real time.

    c. Create a snapshot of the EBS volume before the restart, attach it to another instance as a volume and then diagnose the issue.

    d. Enable detailed monitoring and check the Cloudwatch metrics to see the cause of the issue.

264. A company wants to deploy its application using AWS CodeDeploy then how many types of deployment they can use in AWS CodeDeploy? (Choose 2)

    a. Immutable

    b. In-place

    c. Blue/Green

    d. None of the above

265. How you as a DevOps Engineer deploy multi container Docker environment on EB?

    a. Dockerfile

b. DockerMultifile
c. Docekrrun
d. Dockerrun.aws.json

266. An organization performs processing on AWS. The processing occurs in this way that EC2 instances process the message from SQS queue. In the message the location of the file defines which is S3. EC2 instances are placed with Autoscaling group, but they observed that when the instance is processing the message, it got terminated. How you as DevOps engineer resolve this issue?
    a. Increase the minimum and maximum size for the Auto Scaling group, and change the scaling policies, so they scale less dynamically.
    b. Use lifecycle hooks to ensure the processing is complete before the termination occurs
    c. Suspend the AZRebalance termination policy
    d. Change the CoolDown property for the Autoscaling Group

267. A company wants a cost effective solution for continuous integration and deployment pipeline. Jenkins is used for continuous integration. How they achieve their requirement? (Choose 2)
    a. Ensure the Instances are created beforehand for faster turnaround time for the application builds to be placed.
    b. Ensure the Instances are launched only when the build tests are completed.
    c. Ensure that all build tests are conducted on the newly launched EC2 Instances.
    d. Ensure that all build tests are conducted using Jenkins before deploying the build to newly launched EC2 Instances

268. How you as DevOps engineer automate the creation of EBS snapshot?
    a. Use Cloudwatch Events to trigger the snapshots of EBS Volumes
    b. Use the AWS CodeDeploy service to create a snapshot of the AWS Volumes
    c. Use the AWSConfig service to create a snapshot of the AWS Volumes
    d. Create a powershell script which uses the AWS CLI to get the volumes and then run the script as a cron job.

269. An organization uses a set of EC2 Instances sitting behind an Elastic Load Balancer. Now they want to create an Opswork stack to host the newer version of this application. The idea is to first get the stack in place, carry out a level of testing and

then deploy it at a later stage. The Opswork stack and layers have been setup. To complete the testing process, the current ELB is being utilized. But they observed that current application has stopped responding to requests. What was the issue behind this?

    a. This is because the Opswork web layer is utilizing the current instances after the ELB was attached as an additional layer.

    b. The ELB would have deregistered the older instances

    c. You have configured the Opswork stack to deploy new instances in the same domain the older instances.

    d. This is because the Opswork stack is utilizing the current instances after the ELB was attached as a layer.

270. You have an application running on EC2 instances. Now the instances need to write data to DynamoDB table with sharing any keys. How that can be achieved?

    a. Add an IAM User to a running EC2 instance

    b. Create an IAM Role that allows write access to the DynamoDB table

    c. Create an IAM User that allows write access to the DynamoDB table

    d. Add an IAM Role to a running EC2 instance

271. An organization has applications which rely on multiple dependencies as they belong to different programming languages. These applications are on the company's premises, and now they want to move them on AWS. How they could do this?

    a. Launch separate EC2 Instances to host each application type for the developer community

    b. Use the Opswork service, create a stack and create separate layers for each application environment for the developer community

    c. Use the Elastic BeanStalk service and use Docker containers to host each application environment for the developer community

    d. Use the CloudFormation service to create docker containers for each type of application

272. An organziation hired DevOps engineer who is responsible for an AWS Elastic BeanStalk application. They want to move a continuous deployment model, releasing updates to the application multiple times per day with zero downtime. How DevOps engineer could do this with immediate roll back to the previous verion?

a. Create a second Elastic BeanStalk environment with the new application version, and configure the old environment to redirect clients, using the HTTP 301 response code, to the new environment.

b. Develop the application to poll for a new application version in your code repository; download and install to each running Elastic BeanStalk instance.

c. Create a second Elastic BeanStalk environment running the new application version, and swap the environment CNAMEs.

d. Enable rolling updates in the Elastic BeanStalk environment, setting an appropriate pause time for application startup.

273.   A company wants to give access to its premium client on AWS account to read the message on private S3 bucket. How they give this?

a. Generate a signed S3 PUT URL and a signed S3 PUT URL, both with wildcard values and 2 year durations. Pass the URLs to the vendor.

b. Create a cross-account IAM Role with permission to access the bucket, and grant permission to use the Role to the vendor AWS account.

c. Create an EC2 Instance Profile on your account. Grant the associated IAM role full access to the bucket. Start an EC2 instance with this Profile and give SSH access to the instance to the vendor.

d. Create an IAM User with API Access Keys. Grant the User permissions to access the bucket. Give the vendor the AWS Access Key ID and AWS Secret Access Key for the User.

274.   You have a fleet of EC2 instances that need access to S3 bucket in a secure way with maintaining the integrity of objects stored in S3. How they could do this? (Choose 2)

a. Use an S3 bucket policy that ensures that MFA Delete is set on the objects in the bucket

b. Create an IAM Role and ensure the EC2 Instances uses the IAM Role to access the data in the bucket.

c. Create an IAM user and ensure the EC2 Instances uses the IAM user credentials to access the data in the bucket.

d. Use S3 Cross Region replication to replicate the objects so that the integrity of data is maintained.

275.   Which of the following option you can use to define as source repository in AWS CodeDeploy?

    a. Bitbucket repositories
    b. S3 buckets
    c. GitHub repositories
    d. Subversion repositories

276.   If you want to define user data to EC2 instances in the CloudFormation template then where you define it in the template?

    a. In the Metadata section of the EC2 Instance in the Output section
    b. In the Metadata section of the EC2 Instance in the resources section
    c. In the properties section of the EC2 Instance in the Output section
    d. In the properties section of the EC2 Instance in the resources section

277.   From the following option which is the best option to monitor the cost of AWS resource and also look for cost optimization? (Choose 2)

    a. Consider using the Trusted Advisor
    b. Create budgets in billing section so that budgets are set before hand
    c. Use the Cost Explorer to see the costs of AWS resources
    d. Send all logs to CloudWatch logs and inspect the logs for billing details

278.   A company is using its own log analysis application takes more than four hours to generate a report of the top 10 users of your web application. You have been asked to implement a system that can report this information in real time, ensure that the report is always up to date, and handle increases in the number of requests to your web application. Choose the option that is cost-effective and can fulfill the requirements.

    a. Configure an Auto Scaling group to increase the size of your Amazon EMR cluster.
    b. Post your log data to an Amazon Kinesis data stream, and subscribe your log-processing application, so that is configured to process your logging data.
    c. Publish your data to CloudWatch Logs, and configure your application to autoscale to handle the load on demand.
    d. Publish your log data to an Amazon S3 bucket. Use AWS CloudFormation to create an Auto Scaling group to scale your post-processing application which is configured to pull down your log files stored in Amazon S3.

279. An organization has multiple applications in AWS account, and they want to identify the cost per month to operate for a good understanding of business as they donot want to expend initial development time. How they do this?

   a. Use the AWS Price API and constantly running resource inventory scripts to calculate total price based on multiplication of consumed resources over time.

   b. Use AWS Cost Allocation Tagging for all resources which support it. Use the Cost Explorer to analyze costs throughout the month.

   c. Use custom CloudWatch Metrics in your system, and put a metric data point whenever cost is incurred.

   d. Create an automation script which periodically creates AWS Support tickets requesting detailed intra-month information about your bill.

280. Your application is running behind a load balancer on Amazon EC2 instances. Your company has decided to use a strategy for the blue / green deployment. How do you do this for every deployment?

   a. Create a new load balancer with new Amazon EC2 instances, carry out the deployment, and then switch DNS over to the new load balancer using Amazon Route53 after testing.

   b. Launch more Amazon EC2 instances to ensure high availability, de-register each Amazon EC2 instance from the load balancer, upgrade it, and test it, and then register it again with the load balancer.

   c. Set up Amazon Route53 health checks to fail over from any Amazon EC2 instance that is currently being deployed to.

   d. Using AWS CloudFormation, create a test stack for validating the code, and then deploy the code to each production Amazon EC2 instance.

281. You configure the continuous integration (CI) system to create AMIs in your deployment process. You want to build them in a cost- effective, automated way. What method are you supposed to use?

   a. Upload all contents of the image to Amazon S3 launch the base instance, download all of the contents from Amazon S3 and create the AMI.

   b. Have the CI system launch a new instance, bootstrap the code and apps onto the instance and create an AMI out of it.

c. Attach an Amazon EBS volume to your CI instance, build the root file system of your image on the volume, and use the CreateImage API call to create an AMI out of this volume.

d. Have the CI system launch a new spot instance bootstrap the code and apps onto the instance and create an AMI out of it.

282. Your web application is running on three M3 instances in three AZs. A group of three to thirty instances are scaled using Autoscaling group. When you review the CloudWatch metrics, you see that there are sometimes 15 instances in your Auto Scaling group. The web application reads and writes to a DynamoDB-configured backend with 800 Write and read capacity units. The company ID is your DynamoDB main key. In your web application you receive 25 TB of data. You have one customer who complains delay in load time when his employees arrive at the office at 9:00 am and load the website consisting of content drawn out by DynamoDB. Other customers use the web application routinely. Select the response to ensure high availability and reduce access times for the customer.

   a. Double the number of Read Capacity Units in your DynamoDB instance because the instance is probably being throttled when the customer accesses the website and your web application.

   b. Add a caching layer in front of your web application by choosing ElastiCache Memcached instances in one of the AZs.

   c. Implement an Amazon SQS queue between your DynamoDB database layer and the web application layer to minimize the large burst in traffic the customer generates when everyone arrives at the office at 9:00AM and begins accessing the website.

   d. Change your Auto Scaling group configuration to use Amazon C3 instance types, because the web application layer is probably running out of compute capacity.

   e. Use data pipelines to migrate your DynamoDB table to a new DynamoDB table with a primary key that is evenly distributed across your dataset. Update your web application to request data from the new table

283. Your company assigns you the management of application that uses Amazon SDK and Amazon EC2 roles to store and retrieve Amazon S3 data, access multiple tables of DynamoDB and exchange messages using Amazon SQS queues. Your Compliance Vice- President is concerned that your security practices is not outstanding. He asked you to check that the application AWS access key is not older than six months, and to

provide control evidence that these keys are rotated at least once every six months. Which option suits the best to provide the required information to VP?

    a. Update your application to log changes to its AWS access key credential file and use a periodic Amazon EMR job to create a compliance report for your VP

    b. Create a script to query the IAM list-access keys API to get your application access key creation date and create a batch process to periodically create a compliance report for your VP.

    c. Create a new set of instructions for your configuration management tool that will periodically create and rotate the application's existing access keys and provide a compliance report to your VP.

    d. Provide your VP with a link to IAM AWS documentation to address the VP's key rotation concerns.

284. During a deployment cycle, you recently found a major error in your web application. It took the team four hours during this unsuccessful deployment to return to a previously functional state, which left customers poor user experience. Your team discussed the need to roll back failed deployments quicker and more robust. Your web application is running on Amazon EC2 and is using Elastic Load Balancing to balance your load. How do you solve the problem?

    a. Using Elastic BeanStalk redeploy your web application and use the Elastic BeanStalk API to trigger a FailedDeployment API call to initiate a rollback to the previous version.

    b. Create deployable versioned bundles of your application. Store the bundle on Amazon S3. Use an AWS OpsWorks stack to redeploy your web application and use AWS OpsWorks application versioning to initiate a rollback during failures.

    c. Use an AWS OpsWorks stack to re-deploy your web application and use AWS OpsWorks DeploymentCommand to initiate a rollback during failures.

    d. Create deployable versioned bundles of your application. Store the bundle on Amazon S3. Re-deploy your web application on Elastic BeanStalk and enable the Elastic BeanStalk auto-rollback feature tied to CloudWatch metrics that define failure.

285. A company creates a two-tier web application for the dynamic content of transactions. The data tier is utilizing an Online Transactional Processing (OLTP) database. To enable an elastic and scalable web tier, what services should you use?

    a. Elastic Load Balancing, Amazon RDS with Multi-AZ, and Amazon S3

b. Amazon EC2, Amazon Dynamo DB, and Amazon S3

c. Elastic Load Balancing, Amazon EC2, and Auto Scaling

d. Amazon RDS with Multi-AZ and Auto Scaling

286. You have an OpsWork stack on Linux instances. Your recipe execution failed. How can you diagnose the reason of failure?

   a. Deregister the instance and check the EC2 Logs

   b. Use AWS CloudTrail and check the OpsWorks logs to diagnose the error

   c. Log into the instance and check if the recipe was properly configured.

   d. Use AWS Config and check the OpsWorks logs to diagnose the error

287. As a DevOps Engineers, you have to host a custom application with custom dependencies for a development team by using AWS service. Choose the perfect way from the following options.

   a. Package the application and dependencies with Docker, and deploy the Docker container with Elastic BeanStalk.

   b. Package the application and dependencies within Elastic BeanStalk, and deploy with Elastic BeanStalk

   c. Package the application and dependencies with Docker, and deploy the Docker container with CloudFormation.

   d. Package the application and dependencies in an S3 file, and deploy the Docker container with Elastic BeanStalk.

288. In CloudWatch, containers for metrics are called

   a. Packages

   b. Metric Collection

   c. Namespaces

   d. Locale

289. A multi-level architecture is being operated on AWS with the Nginx web server instances. The application is having bugs when operated by users. How can you quickly and effectively identify those errors?

   a. Send all the errors to AWS Lambda for processing.

   b. Send all the errors to AWS Config for processing

c. Install the CloudWatch Logs agent and send Nginx access log data to CloudWatch. From there, pipe the log data through to a third party logging and graphing tool.

d. Install the CloudWatch Logs agent and send Nginx access log data to CloudWatch. Then, filter the log streams for searching the relevant errors.

290. When a lifecycle hook is implemented in Autoscaling, how much time will the instance take by default in proceeding to a pending state?

   a. 120 minutes
   b. 60 minutes
   c. 5 minutes
   d. 1 minute

291. Choose the invalid statement regarding the application deployment if you want to deploy applications to ELB.

   a. The application can be bundled in a zip file
   b. Should not exceed 512 MB in size
   c. Can include parent directories
   d. Can be a war file which can be deployed to the application server

292. You are using AWS Elastic BeanStalk to run social media marketing application for which you have written a component in Ruby. To support different marketing campaigns, this application component sends messages to social media sites. Your management needs to record responses to these messages from social media to analyze the marketing campaign's effectiveness compared to past and future efforts. A new application component has already been developed for the social media site API to read the replies.

Which method should you use to record social media responses for analytical historical data in a sustainable data storage that can be accessed at any time?

   a. Deploy the new application component as an Elastic BeanStalk application, read the data from the social media sites, store it in DynamoDB, and use Apache Hive with Amazon Elastic MapReduce for analytics.

   b. Deploy the new application component in an Auto Scaling group of Amazon EC2 instances, read the data from the social media sites, store it with Amazon Elastic Block Store, and use AWS Data Pipeline to publish it to Amazon Kinesis for analytics.

  c. Deploy the new application component in an Auto Scaling group of Amazon EC2 instances, read the data from the social media sites, store it in Amazon Glacier, and use AWS Data Pipeline to publish it to Amazon RedShift for analytics.

  d. Deploy the new application component as an Amazon Elastic BeanStalk application, read the data from the social media site, store it with Amazon Elastic Block store,and use Amazon Kinesis to stream the data to Amazon CloudWatch for analytics

293. What advantages does the Blue Green deployment have when changing your infrastructure or application level? Choose 3 options from the following.

  a. Ability to deploy with higher risk
  b. Near zero-downtime release for new changes
  c. Better rollback capabilities
  d. Good turnaround time for application deployments

294. You are working in a company where CloudFormation stack resources are creating some problems. Select the options from the following which will help you in debugging.

Choose 2 answers

  a. Use the AWS CloudFormation console to view the status of your stack.
  b. Use AWSConfig to debug all the API call's sent by the CloudFormation stack.
  c. Use CloudTrail to debug all the API call's sent by the CloudFormation stack.
  d. See the logs in the /var/log directory for Linux instances

295. You want to avoid SSH or RDP into the instances. Which of the following tools can be used for EC2 to administrate the instances?

  a. Run command
  b. EC2Config
  c. AWS CodePipeline
  d. AWS Config

296. You are developing a cloud stack involving the development of a web server and a database server. You have to make sure the web server is created in the stack after you create the database server. How can you do that?

a. Ensure that the database server is defined as a child of the web server in the CloudFormation template.

b. Ensure that the database server is defined first and before the web server in the CloudFormation template. The stack creation normally goes in order to create the resources.

c. Use the DependsOn attribute to ensure that the database server is created before the web server.

d. Ensure that the web server is defined as a child of the database server in the CloudFormation template.

297. Your company makes you responsible for the development of a number of cloud templates. During a stack update, you must be careful that no one can update production- based resources accidentally on the stack. How can this be done most effectively?

a. Use S3 bucket policies to protect the resources.

b. Use MFA to protect the resources

c. Create tags for the resources and then create IAM policies to protect the resources.

d. Use a Stack-based policy to protect the production-based resources.

298. You are operating a document management software that includes Go as the front end, MongoDB and is hosted on a Web server. You pre-bake AMI's with the latest version of the Web server, then for setup of application, you use User Data section. You now have an amendment to the underlying version of the Operating System and must, therefore, deploy it. How to do that as easily as possible?

a. Create a CloudFormation stack with the new AMI and then deploy the application accordingly.

b. Create a new pre-baked AMI with the new OS and use the User Data section to deploy the application.

c. Create a CloudFormation stack with the new AMI and then deploy the application accordingly.

d. Create an OpsWorks stack with the new AMI and then deploy the application accordingly.

299. For sending log data to EC2, you can use which of the following tools?

a. CloudWatch Agents

b. Logs Stream
c. Logs Console
d. CloudWatch Logs Agents

300. In a project, a Linux- based instance stack in OpsWorks has been defined. Further, you want to attach a database to it. Which of the following is an important step towards ensuring that the Linux application can communicate with the database?
   a. Configure SSL so that the instance can communicate with the database
   b. Configure database tags for the OpsWorks application layer
   c. Add another stack with the database layer and attach it to the application stack.
   d. Add the appropriate driver packages to ensure the application can work with the database

301. You are starting to create an application. This application mandate requirements for security and compliance are that protected health information that belongs to your application should be encrypted both at rest and transit. The data flowed through the load balancer and stored on Amazon EBS volumes using three-architecture for processing. The outputs are stored in S3 using AWS SDK service. Choose the two options which allow fulfilling the security requirements.
   a. Use SSL termination with a SAN SSL certificate on the load balancer. Amazon EC2 with all Amazon EBS volumes using Amazon EBS encryption, and Amazon S3 with server-side encryption with customer-managed keys.
   b. Use TCP load balancing on the load balancer. SSL termination on the Amazon EC2 instances. OS-level disk encryption on the Amazon EBS volumes and Amazon S3 with server-side encryption.
   c. Use SSL termination on the load balancer, Amazon EBS encryption on Amazon EC2 instances and Amazon S3 with server-side encryption.
   d. Use TCP load balancing on the load balancer. SSL termination on the Amazon EC2 instances and Amazon S3 with server-side encryption.
   e. Use SSL termination on the load balancer an SSL listener on the Amazon EC2 instances, Amazon EBS encryption on EBS volumes containing PHI and Amazon S3 with server-side encryption.

302. A website is running in a virtual private cloud, using a load balancer and an autoscaling group. Your Head of Security has asked you to set up a system of

monitoring that will rapidly detect and notify your team when there is a sudden increase in traffic. How would you configure that?

a. Set up a cron job to actively monitor the AWS CloudTrail logs for increased traffic and use Amazon SNS to alert your team.

b. Use an Amazon EMR job to run every thirty minutes analyze the CloudWatch logs from your application Amazon EC2 instances in a batch manner to detect a sharp increase in traffic and then use the Amazon SNS SMS notification to alert your team

c. Use an Amazon EMR job to run every thirty minutes, analyze the Elastic Load Balancing access logs in a batch manner to detect a sharp increase in traffic and then use the Amazon Simple Email Service to alert your team.

d. Set up an Amazon CloudWatch alarm for the Elastic Load Balancing NetworkIn metric and then use Amazon SNS to alert your team.

e. Set up a cron job to actively monitor the AWS CloudTrail logs for increased traffic and use Amazon SNS to alert your team.

303.   An application is running on a custom application server, but now a developer team of your company wants to transfer the application into Elastic BeanStalk. They want to avail Elastic Load balancing and Amazon SQS services in their application. What would you do to deploy the application in Elastic BeanStalk, if you are the part of developer team?

a. Use a Docker container that has the third party application server installed on it and that creates the load balancer and an Amazon SQS queue using the application source bundle feature.

b. Configure an Elastic BeanStalk platform using AWS OpsWorks deploy it to Elastic BeanStalk and run a script that creates a load balancer and an Amazon SQS queue.

c. Configure an AWS OpsWorks stack that installs the third party application server and creates a load balancer and an Amazon SQS queue and then deploys it to Elastic BeanStalk.

d. Create a custom Elastic BeanStalk platform that contains the third party application server and runs a script that creates a load balancer and an Amazon SQS queue.

304. You are working on an application for which you need long term storage for backups and other information. That storage should be readily available. Which S3 storage option will be suitable at low cost?
    a. Glacier
    b. S3 Standard
    c. Reduced Redundancy Storage
    d. Amazon S3 Standard- Infrequent Access

305. Which one can be configured for CloudWatch Events as targets? Choose 3 answers
    a. AWS Lambda Functions
    b. Amazon ECS Tasks
    c. Amazon EC2 Instances
    d. Amazon CodeCommit

306. Choose the services along with CloudFormation from the following options which assist in building a Continuous Delivery release practice.
    a. AWS Lambda
    b. AWS CodePipeline
    c. AWS CloudTrail
    d. AWS Config

307. You want to deploy code that is hosted on your GitHub repository using Code Deploy. Which additional services can contribute to meeting this requirement?
    a. Use the CodeCommit Service
    b. Use the CodeBatch Service
    c. Use the SQS Service
    d. Use the CodePipeline Service

308. You are creating templates using CloudFormation that has a parameter which intakes database password. How can you make sure that if anybody describes the stack, they will not get the password?
    a. Use the hidden property for the parameter value
    b. Use the NoEcho property for the parameter value
    c. Set the hidden attribute for the CloudFormation resource.
    d. Use the password attribute for the resource

309. The AWS Elastic BeanStalk application is in charge of your team. The company needs to move to a continuous deployment model to release updates several times a day with zero downtime for the application. What should be done to do this and can still roll back in an emergency to the previous version almost immediately?

    a. Create a second Elastic BeanStalk environment running the new application version, and swap the environment CNAMEs.

    b. Enable rolling updates in the Elastic BeanStalk environment, setting an appropriate pause time for application startup.

    c. Create a second Elastic BeanStalk environment with the new application version, and configure the old environment to redirect clients, using the HTTP 301 response code, to the new environment

    d. Develop the application to poll for a new application version in your code repository; download and install to each running Elastic BeanStalk instance.

310. A company creates CloudFormation Template that passes user data to the underlying EC2 Instance. Choose the function that is normally used in the CloudFormation template to transfer data into the UserData section?

    a. "UserData": {   "Fn::Ref": {

    b. "UserData": {   "Fn::GetAtt": {

    c. "UserData": {   "Fn::FindInMap": {

    d. "UserData": { "Fn::Base64": {

311. Choose 3 answers from the following options which are true about the OpsWorks Stack Instances.

    a. You can use instances running on your own hardware.

    b. You can start and stop instances manually.

    c. A stacks instances can be a combination of both Linux and Windows-based operating systems.

    d. You can use EC2 Instances that were created outside the boundary of OpsWorks.

312. When using an Elastic Load Balancer with OpsWorks stacks, which one is incorrect?

    a. Each load balancer can handle only one layer.

    b. You can attach only one load balancer to a layer.

    c. A Classic Load Balancer can span across AWS OpsWorks Stacks layers.

d. You need to create the load balancer beforehand and then attach it to the OpsWorks stack.

313. You're DevOps Engineer in a Multi-national Company. In order to start building its resources in AWS, the company wants to use CloudFormation templates. The templates for different departments, such as networking, security, apps, etc. are required. What is the best way to develop these templates for CloudFormation?

   a. Create separate logical templates, for example, a separate template for networking, security, application, etc. Then nest the relevant templates.
   b. Consider using Elastic BeanStalk to create your environments since CloudFormation is not built for such customization.
   c. Consider using OpsWorks to create your environments since CloudFormation is not built for such customization.
   d. Use a single CloudFormation template, since this would reduce the maintenance overhead on the templates itself.

314. Choose the option from the following which is not the lifecycle event in OpsWorks.

   a. Setup
   b. Configure
   c. Uninstall
   d. Shutdown

315. You developed a new feature using AWS services. You want to test it from inside a staging VPC. How should you do it with the fastest turnaround time?

   a. Use an Amazon EC2 instance that frequently polls the version control system to detect the new feature, use AWS CloudFormation and Amazon EC2 user data to run any testing harnesses to verify application functionality and then use Amazon SNS to notify the development team of the results.
   b. Use an Elastic BeanStalk application that polls the version control system to detect the new feature, use AWS CloudFormation and Amazon EC2 user data to run any testing harnesses to verify application functionality and then use Amazon Kinesis to notify the development team of the results.
   c. Launch an Amazon Elastic Compute Cloud (EC2) instance in the staging VPC in response to a development request, and use configuration management to set up the application. Run any testing harnesses to verify application

functionality and then use Amazon Simple Notification Service (SNS) to notify the development team of the results.

    d. Use AWS CloudFormation to launch an Amazon EC2 instance using Amazon EC2 user data to run any testing harnesses to verify application functionality and then use Amazon Kinesis to notify the development team of the results.

316. You want to allow automated testing of your AWS CloudFormation template as part of your deployment pipeline. What tests need to be carried out so that feedback can be faster while reducing costs and risk? Choose 3 answers

    a. Use the AWS CloudFormation Validate Template to validate the properties of resources defined in the template.

    b. Validate the template is syntax using a general JSON parser.

    c. Update the stack with the template. If the template fails, rollback will return the stack and its resources to exactly the same state.

    d. Use the AWS CloudFormation Validate Template to validate the syntax of the template

    e. Validate the AWS CloudFormation template against the official XSD scheme definition published by Amazon Web Services.

    f. When creating the stack, specify an Amazon SNS topic to which your testing system is subscribed. Your testing system runs tests when it receives notification that the stack is created or updated.

317. Up to how many application versions you can rollback by default in AWS?

    a. 1

    b. 2

    c. 3

    d. 4

318. In the context of your ongoing application, an I / O load performance test is performed before it is deployed to production with new AMIs. The app is running with one EBS PIOPS volume per instance and requires consistent I / O performance.

To ensure that I / O load performance tests produce the correct results repeatably, which of the following option must be carried out?

    a. Ensure that the I/O block sizes for the test are randomly selected.

    b. Ensure that snapshots of the Amazon EBS volumes are created as a backup.

    c. Ensure that the Amazon EBS volume is encrypted.

d. Ensure that the Amazon EBS volumes have been pre-warmed by reading all the blocks before the test.

319. You are responsible for designing a number of CloudFormation templates. You must change the stack resources sometimes on the basis of the requirement. How can you monitor the impact of resource change in a CloudFormation stack before stack changes are implemented?

   a. Use CloudFormation changesets to check for the impact to the changes.
   b. Use CloudFormation Stack Policies to check for the impact to the changes.
   c. There is no way to control this. You need to check for the impact beforehand.
   d. Use CloudFormation Rolling Updates to check for the impact to the changes.

320. A report of the top 10 users in your web application is generated in more than 4 hours in your current log analysis application. You were asked to implement a system to report this information in real time, to ensure that the report is up to date and to deal with the increase in your web application requests. Choose the cost-effective solution from the options.

   a. Publish your log data to an Amazon S3 bucket. Use AWS CloudFormation to create an AutoScaling group to scale your post-processing application which is configured to pull down your log files stored in Amazon S3.
   b. Publish your data to CloudWatch Logs, and configure your application to autoscale to handle the load on demand.
   c. Configure an Auto Scaling group to increase the size of your Amazon EMR cluster
   d. Post your log data to an Amazon Kinesis data stream, and subscribe your log-processing application, so that is configured to process your logging data.

321. A number of instances are running on your OpsWorks stacks. If you want to install security updates, what is the AWS recommendation in accordance with this task? Choose 2 answers.

   a. Create a CloudFormation template which can be used to replace the instances.
   b. Create and start new instances to replace your current online instances. Then delete the current instances.
   c. On Linux-based instances in Chef 11.10 or older stacks, run the Update Dependencies stack command.
   d. Create a new OpsWorks stack with the new instances.

322. After the launching of EC2 instance in an Auto Scaling Group, you have implemented a system to dynamically automate configuration deployment and application. Your system uses a configuration management tool in which the master node is not available. This tool works in a standalone configuration. Because of the application load volatility, new instances should be launched within 3 minutes of the launching of instance operating system. The following times are required for the completion of deployment stages:
   - Configuration management agent installation: 2 minutes
   - The configuration of an instance using artifacts : 4 minutes
   - Application framework installation : 15 minutes
   - Deployment of application code : 1 minute

How do you automate deployment with this type of standalone agent configuration?

   a. Build a custom Amazon Machine Image that includes the configuration management agent and application framework pre-installed. Configure your Auto Scaling launch configuration with an Amazon EC2 UserData script to pull configuration artifacts and application code from an Amazon S3 bucket, and then execute the agent to configure the system.

   b. Configure your Auto Scaling launch configuration with an Amazon EC2 UserData script to install the agent, pull configuration artifacts and application code from an Amazon S3 bucket, and then execute the agent to configure the infrastructure and application.

   c. Build a custom Amazon Machine Image that includes all components pre-installed, including an agent, configuration artifacts, application frameworks, and code. Create a startup script that executes the agent to configure the system on startup.

   d. Create a web service that polls the Amazon EC2 API to check for new instances that are launched in an Auto Scaling group. When it recognizes a new instance, execute a remote script via SSH to install the agent, SCP the configuration artifacts and application code, and finally execute the agent to configure the system

323. You work for your business as a DevOps Engineer. A number of environments are currently hosted through Elastic BeanStalk. It is necessary to ensure that changes to the Elastic BeanStalk environment are carried out using the fastest deployment method. Choose the Elastic BeanStalk 's fastest deployment method?

   a. Rolling with an additional batch

b. Blue/Green
c. Rolling
d. All at once

324. A client of your company uses Chef Configuration in his data center. The company assigns you to work with him. What is the service that allows customers to take advantage of existing Chef AWS recipes?
   a. AWS OpsWorks
   b. AWS Elastic BeanStalk
   c. AWS CloudFormation
   d. Amazon Simple Workflow Service

325. An application is written in Go Programming language which has to be deployed to AWS. The application code is stored on a Git repository. Choose 2 options for this deployment.
   a. Write a Dockerfile that installs the Go base image and fetches your application using Git, Create an AWS CloudFormation template that creates and associates an AWS::EC2::Instance resource type with an AWS::EC2::Container resource type.
   b. Write a Dockerfile that installs the Go base image and uses Git to fetch your application. Create a new AWS OpsWorks stack that contains a Docker layer that uses the Dockerrun.aws.json file to deploy your container and then use the Dockerfile to automate the deployment.
   c. Create a new AWS Elastic BeanStalk application and configure a Go environment to host your application, Using Git check out the latest version of the code, once the local repository for Elastic BeanStalk is configured using "eb create" command to create an environment and then use "eb deploy" command to deploy the application.
   d. Write a Dockerfile that installs the Go base image and fetches your application using Git, Create a new AWS Elastic BeanStalk application and use this Dockerfile to automate the deployment.

326. How can you run and manage Docker-enabled applications easily across a cluster of EC2 instances? Choose the suitable service from the following options.
   a. Elastic Container Service
   b. CloudWatch

  c. OpsWorks

  d. Elastic BeanStalk

327. What is not a supported Elastic BeanStalk service platform?

  a. PHP

  b. AngularJS

  c. .Net

  d. Java

328. Your development team uses Elastic BeanStalk. Deploying multiple versions of your application is your responsibility. How do you ideally ensure that you do not cross Elastic BeanStalk 's application version limit?

  a. Create a script to delete the older versions.

  b. Use lifecycle policies in Elastic BeanStalk

  c. Create a Lambda function to delete the older versions.

  d. Use AWSConfig to delete the older versions

329. Choose CloudFormation helper scripts that can help install packages on EC2 resources.

  a. cfn-get-metadata

  b. cfn-signal

  c. cfn-hup

  d. cfn-init

330. In your company, you are a DevOps Engineer. You were instructed to make sure that EBS Volumes have an automated backup solution. These snapshots should be removed after 20 days. How can you efficiently meet this requirement?

  a. Use Lifecycle policies to push the EBS Volumes to Amazon Glacier. Then use further lifecycle policies to delete the snapshots after 20 days.

  b. Use Lifecycle policies to push the EBS Volumes to Amazon S3. Then use further lifecycle policies to delete the snapshots after 20 days.

  c. Use Amazon Data Lifecycle Manager to automate the process.

  d. Use the aws ec2 create-volume API to create a snapshot of the EBS Volume. The use the describe-volume to see those snapshots which are greater than 20 days and then delete them accordingly using the delete-volume API call.

331. You want to describe the stack resources. Which of the following CLI command you will choose?

    a. aws cloudformation describe-stack-resources

    b. aws cloudformation describe-stack

    c. aws cloudformation list-stack

    d. aws cloudformation list-stack-resources

332. You are creating a DynamoDB application for the storage of JSON data. The read and write capability of the DynamoDB table has already been set. The amount of traffic received during the deployment period by the application is not known. You IT officer asks you to ensure that DynamoDB is not throttled and is not an application bottleneck? Choose 2 answers.

    a. Monitor the SystemErrors metric using CloudWatch

    b. Create a CloudWatch alarm which would then send a trigger to AWS Lambda to increase the Read and Write capacity of the DynamoDB table.

    c. Monitor the ConsumedReadCapacityUnits and ConsumedWriteCapacityUnits metric using CloudWatch.

    d. Create a CloudWatch alarm which would then send a trigger to AWS Lambda to create a new DynamoDB table.

333. Amazon SQS and Auto Scaling are used by your application for background work. The Auto Scaling policy is based on the number of messages in the queue with a maximum instance count of 100. The group has never exceeded 50 since the application was launched. The Auto Scaling Group is now up to 100, the queue size is up, and very few tasks are done. The numbers of messages are at a normal level that is sent to the queue. How do you know why it's an unusual increase in queue size and how should you decrease it?

    a. Analyze the application logs to identify possible reasons for message processing failure and resolve the cause for failures.

    b. Temporarily increase the AutoScaling group's desired value to 200. When the queue size has been reduced,reduce it to 50.

    c. Analyze CloudTrail logs for Amazon SQS to ensure that the instances Amazon EC2 role have permission to receive messages from the queue.

    d. Create additional Auto Scaling groups enabling the processing of the queue to be performed in parallel.

334.   You have very high traffic in your application, which means that autoscaling in multi- availability areas to meet the requirements of your application but in the result, one of the availability zone have no traffic. What could be the reason?
    a.   Availability zone is not added to Elastic load balancer
    b.   Autoscaling only works for a single availability zone
    c.   Autoscaling can be enabled for multi-AZ only in northern Virginia region
    d.   Instances need to manually add to an availability zone

335.   Which of the following solution can be used to monitor changes made to your AWS resources is a reliable and durable logging solution?
    a.   Create a new CloudTrail with one new S3 bucket to store the logs. Configure SNS to send log file delivery notifications to your management system. Use IAM roles and S3 bucket policies on the S3 bucket that stores your logs.
    b.   Create three new CloudTrail trails with three new S3 buckets to store the logs one for the AWS Management console, one for AWS SDKs and one for command line tools. Use IAM roles and S3 bucket policies on the S3 buckets that store your logs.
    c.   Create a new CloudTrail trail with an existing S3 bucket to store the logs and with the global services option selected. Use S3 ACLs, and Multi-Factor Authentication (MFA) Delete on the S3 bucket that stores your logs.
    d.   Create a new CloudTrail trail with one new S3 bucket to store the logs and with the global services option selected. Use IAM roles S3 bucket policies and Multi-Factor Authentication (MFA) Delete on the S3 bucket that stores your logs.

336.   You plan to use CloudWatch to monitor AWS- hosted resources. What can you do ideally with CloudWatch logs? Choose 3 answers.
    e.   Stream the log data into Amazon Elasticsearch for any search analysis required.
    f.   Stream the log data to Amazon Kinesis for further processing
    g.   Send the data to SQS for further processing.
    h.   Send the log data to AWS Lambda for custom processing

337.   A large number of DynamoDB records in a given region are currently being written by an application. A secondary application must make changes every 2 hours to the DynamoDB table and process the updates accordingly. Which of the following is the ideal way to ensure that the DynamoDB table provides the applications with the appropriate changes?

a. Create another DynamoDB table with the records modified in the last 2 hours.

b. Transfer the records to S3 which were modified in the last 2 hours

c. Use DynamoDB streams to monitor the changes in the DynamoDB table.

d. Insert a timestamp for each record and then scan the entire table for the timestamp as per the last 2 hours.

338. You have an application to support thousands of users, therefore, you have created a DynamoDB table. You must make sure every user can access his or her own information only at a particular table. Most of the user's accounts are with a third-party ID provider, including Facebook, Google or Amazon Login. How would you implement this? Choose 2 options

a. Use a third-party identity provider such as Google, Facebook or Amazon so users can become an AWS IAM User with access to the application.

b. Create an IAM User for all users so that they can access the application.

c. Use Web identity federation and register your application with a third-party identity provider such as Google, Amazon, or Facebook.

d. Create an IAM role which has specific access to the DynamoDB table.

339. Your Company uses a third-party configuration management tool for web application development environment in order to create a Docker container on a local developer's machine.

What are you supposed to do for checking your application is not affected by the web application, supporting network storage and security infrastructure after the deployment for staging and production environments in AWS occurs.

a. Define an AWS CloudFormation template to place your infrastructure into version control and use the same template to deploy the Docker container into Elastic BeanStalk for staging and production.

b. Because the application is inside a Docker container, there are no infrastructure differences to be taken into account when moving from the local development environments to AWS for staging and production.

c. Write a script using the AWS SDK or CLI to deploy the application code from version control to the local development environments staging and production using AWS OpsWorks.

d. Define an AWS CloudFormation template for each stage of the application deployment lifecycle –development, staging, and production –and have tagged in each template to define the environment.

340. You have just developed an application for analytical workloads on large data sets stored on Amazon Redshift. Amazon Redshift Tables must be accessible to the application. Choose the best practically possible option in terms of security to access table?

   a. Create an IAM user and generate encryption keys for that user. Create a policy for RedShift read-only access. Embed the keys in the application.
   b. Use roles that allow a web identity federated user to assume a role that allows access to the RedShift table by providing temporary credentials.
   c. Create a RedShift read-only access policy in IAM and embed those credentials in the application.
   d. Create an HSM client certificate in Redshift and authenticate using this certificate.

341. In several Amazon EC2 instances, you have an I / O and a network- intensive application that can not handle a large ongoing increase in traffic. Two volumes of Amazon EBS PIOPS are used in the Amazon EC2 instances, each with the identical instance.

   Choose the right approach in order to reduce the load on instances with the least interference with the application.

   a. Stop each instance and change each instance to a larger Amazon EC2 instance type that has enhanced networking enabled and is Amazon EBS-optimized. Ensure that RAID striping is also set up on each instance.
   b. Add an instance-store volume for each running Amazon EC2 instance and implement RAID striping to improve I/O performance.
   c. Create an AMI from each instance, and set up Auto Scaling groups with a larger instance type that has enhanced networking enabled and is Amazon EBS-optimized.
   d. Create an AMI from an instance, and set up an Auto Scaling group with an instance type that has enhanced networking enabled and is Amazon EBS-optimized.
   e. Add an Amazon EBS volume for each running Amazon EC2 instance and implement RAID striping to improve I/O performance.

342. You are working on an application that has three EC2 instances in the auto scaling group behind an Elastic Load Balancer. You find that the autoscaling group was updated with a new launch configuration that refers to an updated AMI. Your ELB

health checks were successful still you have received complains of error from users. What will you do for preventing this situation again?

    a. Create a new launch configuration with the updated AMI and associate it with the AutoScaling group. Increase the size of the group to six and when instances become healthy revert to three.

    b. Update the launch configuration instead of updating the Autoscaling Group'

    c. Create a new ELB and attach the Autoscaling Group to the ELB

    d. Manually terminate the instances with the older launch configuration.

343. For your application, initially, you have created an Autoscaling group with a set of t2.small instances. Now the requirement of the instances is changed to a larger type instance. How will you change your instance type ideally?

    a. Create another Autoscaling Group and attach the new instance type.

    b. Create a new launch configuration with the new instance type and update your Autoscaling Group.

    c. Change the Instance type in the current launch configuration to the new instance type.

    d. Change the Instance type of the Underlying EC2 instance directly.

344. Choose 3 options from the following which represents the basic stages of a CI/CD Pipeline.

    a. Build

    b. Production

    c. SourceControl

    d. Run

345. An organization has a number of the web on ELB. They have to do two things:

    • The SSL key used for data encryption should be secure.

    • Only a subset of users should decrypt the ELB logs.

Which architecture fulfills all both of the requirements?

    a. Use Elastic Load Balancing to distribute traffic to a set of web servers. Configure the load balancer to perform TCP load balancing, use an AWS CloudHSM to perform the SSL transactions, and write your web server logs to an ephemeral volume that has been encrypted using a randomly generated AES key.

b. Use Elastic Load Balancing to distribute traffic to a set of web servers. To protect the SSL private key, upload the key to the load balancer and configure the load balancer to offload the SSL traffic. Write your web server logs to an ephemeral volume that has been encrypted using a randomly generated AES key.

c. Use Elastic Load Balancing to distribute traffic to a set of web servers. Use TCP load balancing on the load balancer and configure your web servers to retrieve the private key from a private Amazon S3 bucket on boot. Write your web server logs to a private Amazon S3 bucket using Amazon S3 server-side encryption.

d. Use Elastic Load Balancing to distribute traffic to a set of web servers, configure the load balancer to perform TCP load balancing, use an AWS CloudHSM to perform the SSL transactions, and write your web server logs to a private Amazon S3 bucket using Amazon S3 server-side encryption.

346. You decided to change the instance type of your production instances that run in the Autoscaling Group. To launch our architecture, we used the CloudFormation template and currently used 4 instances in production. The service cannot be interrupted therefore two instances should always run during the update. Which of the following options can be applicable?

a. AutoScalingReplacingUpdate
b. AutoScalingScheduledAction
c. AutoScalingRollingUpdate
d. AutoScalingIntegrationUpdate

347. You are responsible for creating a LAMP stack CloudFormation template. Once you've deployed a stack, you can see that the stack status is CREATE COMPLETE, but the apache server is still not up and running and has problems in starting up. How can you find that the status of CREATE_COMPLETE only appears when all the defined resources in the stack are up and running? (Choose 2 answers)

a. Use lifecycle hooks to mark the completion of the creation and configuration of the underlying resource.
b. Use the CreationPolicy to ensure it is associated with the EC2 Instance resource.
c. Use the CFN helper scripts to signal once the resource configuration is complete.

d. Define a stack policy which defines that all underlying resources should be up and running before showing a status of CREATE_COMPLETE.

348. In your organization, you have set up the following AWS services: Auto Scaling Group, Elastic Load Balancer, and EC2 instances. If the utilization of CPU is less than 30%, you have to terminate an instance from the Autoscaling Group. How can you do that?

    a. Create a CloudWatch alarm to send a notification to the Auto Scaling group when the aggregated CPU utilization is less than 30% and configure the Auto Scaling policy to remove one instance.

    b. Create a CloudWatch alarm to send a notification to SQS. SQS can then remove one instance from the Autoscaling Group.

    c. Create a CloudWatch alarm to send a notification to the admin team. The admin team can then manually terminate an instance from the Autoscaling Group.

    d. Create a CloudWatch alarm to send a notification to the ELB. The ELB can then remove one instance from the Autoscaling Group.

349. You are running 6 instances for your web application which consume approximately 45 percent of the resources. To ensure that six instances always run you have an Autoscaling group. There are no spikes in the number of requests that are received in this application procedure. You want this application to be highly available all the times. You want to distribute the load evenly across all instances. For every instance, you want to use the same Amazon Machine Image (AMI). What architectural decisions should you make from the following?

    a. Deploy 3 EC2 instances in one region and 3 in another region and use Amazon Elastic Load Balancer.

    b. Deploy 6 EC2 instances in one availability zone and use Amazon Elastic Load Balancer.

    c. Deploy 3 EC2 instances in one availability zone and 3 in another availability zone and use Amazon Elastic Load Balancer.

    d. Deploy 2 EC2 instances in three regions and use Amazon Elastic Load Balancer.

350. You have created a web application based on Autoscaling group of web servers using ELB. You create a new AMI for every application version deployment. You are releasing a new version of the application in which you want a controlled migration of

users with the A / B deployment technique, while the fleet is constant 12 hours long, to ensure that the new version is functioning. What option do you want to enable this technique while easily rolling back when required?

    a. Create an Autoscaling launch configuration with the new AMI. Configure Auto Scaling to vary the proportion of instances launched from the two launch configurations.

    b. Create a load balancer. Create an Auto Scaling launch configuration with the new AMI to use the new launch configuration and to register instances with the new load balancer. Use Amazon Route53 weighted Round Robin to vary the proportion of requests sent to the load balancers.

    c. Launch new instances using the new AMI and attach them to the Auto Scaling group. Configure Elastic Load Balancing to vary the proportion of requests sent to instances running the two application versions.

    d. Create an Autoscaling launch configuration with the new AMI. Configure the AutoScaling group with the new launch configuration. Use the Auto Scaling rolling updates feature to migrate to the new version.

    e. Create an Auto Scaling launch configuration with the new AMI. Create an Auto Scaling group configured to use the new launch configuration and to register instances with the same load balancer. Vary the desired capacity of each group to migrate.

351.   You are working for a startup that has developed a new mobile app for photo sharing. Your application has grown in popularity in recent months, resulting in a decrease in application performance due to the increase in load. Your application features a two-tier architecture consisting of an Auto Scaling PHP application tier and MySQL RDS instance initially deployed with CloudFormation. Auto Scaling group has a min value of 4 and a max value of 8. Due to the high CPU usage of the instances, the desired capacity is now 8. Once analyzed, you are confident that performance problems stem from a CPU capacity restriction, while memory use is low. You thus decide to move from M3 instances to C3 instances that are computer- optimized.

How would you deploy this change to reduce interruptions for your end- users as minimum as possible?

    a. Update the launch configuration specified in the AWS CloudFormation template with the new C3 instance type. Run a stack update with the new template. Auto Scaling will then update the instances with the new instance type.

b. Update the launch configuration specified in the AWS CloudFormation template with the new C3 instance type. Also, add an UpdatePolicy attribute to your Auto Scaling group that specifies an AutoScalingRollingUpdate. Run a stack update with the new template

c. Sign in to the AWS Management Console, copy the old launch configuration, and create a new launch configuration that specifies the C3 instances. Update the AutoScaling group with the new launch configuration. Auto Scaling will then update the instance type of all running instances

d. Sign in to the AWS Management Console and update the existing launch configuration with the new C3 instance type. Add an UpdatePolicy attribute to your AutoScaling group that specifies an AutoScaling rolling update.

352. You are responsible for an application which is using EC2, ELB, and Autoscaling. The ELB access logs were requested by your manager. You don't find any log in S3 bucket. Why is that happening?

a. The Autoscaling service is not sending the required logs to ELB

b. You don't have the necessary access to the logs generated by ELB.

c. The EC2 Instances are not sending the required logs to ELB

d. By default ELB access logs are disabled.

353. You have a Chef Version 11.10 running on AWS OpsWorks Stack. Your company has its own cookbook hosted on Amazon S3, and this is specified in the stack as a custom cookbook. A cookbook located in an external Git repository is required which is an open source cookbook. How could you use both of the custom books?

a. In the OpsWorks stack settings add the open source project's cookbook details in addition to your cookbook.

b. In your cookbook create an S3 symlink object that points to the open source project's cookbook.

c. In the AWS OpsWorks stack settings, enable Berkshelf. Create a new cookbook with a Berksfile that specifies the other two cookbooks. Configure the stack to use this new cookbook.

d. Contact the open source project's maintainers and request that they pull your cookbook into theirs. Update the stack to use their cookbook.

354. You work for your business as a DevOps Engineer. Currently, Elastic BeanStalk hosted several environments. There is a need to ensure that the rollback time must

less for deployment of new version application. Which Elastic BeanStalk deployment method you will use to meet this requirement?

a. All at once
b. Blue/Green
c. Rolling
d. Rolling with an additional batch

355. You have an ample multi-level architecture that uses a load balancer and is supported by a web tier within an Amazon EC2 Auto Scaling group. This architecture serves public facing web traffic. During a traffic peak, you notice that the amount of incoming traffic and auto-scaling policy that you set up is adding new instances disproportionately. How to stop the Auto Scaling Group in reaction to incoming traffic from scaling incorrectly?

a. Using a custom CloudWatch metric insert the elapsed time since the instance launch to the time the instance responds to an Elastic Load Balancing health check, and periodically adjust the Pause Time of the UpdatePolicy and reduce the Scaling Adjustment property by 50%

b. Using CloudWatch and the instance BootTime metric, increase the PauseTime and CoolDown property on the Auto Scaling group to be over the value of the metric.

c. Using a custom CloudWatch metric insert the elapsed time since the instance launch to the time the instance responds to an Elastic Load Balancing health check, and periodically adjust the Pause Time and the CoolDown property on the AutoScaling group to be over the value of the metric.

d. Using a third-party configuration management tool and the AWS SDK suspend all ScheduledActions of the Auto Scaling group until after the traffic peak and then resume all scheduled actions.

356. Choose the two intervals from the following options at which logs get produced by the Elastic Load Balancer service.

a. 30 seconds
b. 1 minute
c. 5 minutes
d. 60 minutes

357. An organization wants to deploy its infrastructure by using standard templates. In this respect, which AWS service can be used? Choose the correct option.
    a. AWS OpsWorks
    b. Amazon Simple Workflow Service
    c. AWS Elastic BeanStalk
    d. AWS CloudFormation

358. You are active in an accounting company and need to store customer's important financial data. Initial frequent access to data is necessary, but data may be archived and reported after a period of 2 months only in the event of an audit. How do you achieve this most economically?
    a. Store data in Amazon S3 and use lifecycle management to move data from S3 to Glacier after 2 months.
    b. Store all data in a Glacier
    c. Use lifecycle management to store all data in Glacier
    d. Store all data in a private S3 bucket

359. Choose the file which is can be used to deploy multi-container Docker environment on to Elastic BeanStalk
    a. DockerMultifile
    b. Dockerfile
    c. Dockerrun
    d. Dockerrun.aws.json

360. You have to set up a solution that incorporates single sign-on from your corporate AD or LDAP directory and do not allow access to each user to a designated user folder in a bucket. Choose 3 answers to fulfill the given scenario
    a. Configuring IAM role
    b. Setting up a federation proxy or identity provider
    c. Tagging each folder in the bucket
    d. Setting up a matching IAM user for every user in your corporate directory that needs access to a folder in the bucket
    e. Using AWS STS service to generate temporary tokens

361. Select the components of the AWS Data pipeline service. (Choose 2 answers)
    a. Task History
    b. Task Runner
    c. Workflow Runner
    d. Pipeline Definition

362. You are working in a company where they are going to do a major public announcement of a social media site in AWS. The website is running on EC2 instances launched in multiple availability zones with a Multi-AZ RDS MySQL Extra Large DB Instance. The site executes high number of small reads and writes per second and depends on an eventual consistency model. After complete tests you observe that there is read contention on RDS MySQL. Which approaches would you choose to meet these requirements? Choose 2 answers.
    a. Deploy ElasticCache in-memory cache running in each availability zone
    b. Increase the RDS MySQL Instance size and implement provisioned IOPS
    c. Add an RDS MySQL read replica in each availability zone
    d. Implement sharding to distribute load to multiple RDS MySQL instances

363. Which of the following steps would you follow when there is an audit of your AWS account in the coming days to provide right access?
    a. Enable S3 and ELB logs. Send the logs as a zip file to the IT Auditor
    b. Enable CloudWatch Logs. Create a user for the IT Auditor and ensure that full control is given to the user for the CloudWatch Logs.
    c. Ensure CloudTrail is enabled. Create a user account for the Auditor and attach the AWSCloudTrailReadOnlyAccess Policy to the user.
    d. Ensure that CloudTrail is enabled. Create a user for the IT Auditor and ensure that full control is given to the user for CloudTrail.

364. An online web store adopted AWS CloudFormation to automate load-testing of their online products details. They created two templates of CloudFormation, one is for their products details and the other one for load testing stack. Load-testing stack creates RDS Postgres database and two web servers running on EC2 instance that measures response time, send HTTP requests, and record the results into the database. A test time is usually 15 – 30 minutes. The AWS CloudFormation stacks are torn down immediately after the test completion. The recorded test results of Amazon RDS database must remain accessible for virtualization and analysis.

If the AWS CloudFormation load-testing stack is deleted then what could be the possible solutions that allows access to the test results. (Choose 2 answers)
   a. Define an update policy to prevent deletion of the Amazon RDS database after the AWS CloudFormation stack is deleted.
   b. Define a deletion policy of type Retain for the Amazon RDS resource to assure that the RDS database is not deleted with the AWS CloudFormation stack.
   c. Define a deletion policy of type Snapshot for the Amazon RDS resource to assure that RDS database can be restored after the AWS CloudFormation stack is deleted.
   d. Define automated backups with a backup retention period of 30 days for the Amazon RDS database and perform point-in-time recovery of the database after the AWS CloudFormation stack is deleted.
   e. Define an Amazon RDS Read-Replica in the load-testing AWS CloudFormation stack and define a dependency relation between master and replica via the Depends On attribute.

365. You are working in a company where there are multiple AWS accounts. Currently two accounts are active, one is of development and one for production. You have to provide access to the production team for S3 bucket of development account. What would you do for this purpose?
   a. Create an IAM cross-account role in the development account that allows user from production account to access the S3 bucket in the Development account.
   b. Create an IAM user in the Development account that allow users from the Production account (the trusted account) to access the S3 bucket in the development account.
   c. When creating the role, define the development as a trusted entity and specify a permissions policy that allows trusted users to update the S3 bucket.
   d. Use web identity federation with a third-party identity provider with AWS STS to grant temporary credentials and membership into the production IAM user.

366. A company is using auto-scaling group to scale out and scale in EC2 instances. The traffic peak occurs every Monday at 8 am and it comes down before weekend on Friday 5 pm. You have to configure Autoscaling group in this scenario, what should you do?
   a. Create a scheduled policy to scale up on Friday and scale down on Monday.
   b. Create a scheduled policy to scale up on Monday and scale down on Friday.

c. Create dynamic scaling policies to scale up on Monday and scale down on Friday.

d. Manually add instances in Autoscaling group on Monday and remove them on Friday.

367. Your company's owner asked you to show all of the CloudFormation stacks which have a completed status. Which command would you use?
    a. stacks-complete
    b. list-templates
    c. list-stacks
    d. describe-stacks

368. You have launched multiple instances in different availability zones in an autoscaling group as you are running a high traffic application. You noticed that one availability zone is not receiving any traffic. What could be the reason?
    a. Autoscaling can be enabled for multi-AZ only in North Virginia region
    b. Autoscaling only works in single region
    c. Instances need to be manually added to the availability zones
    d. Availability zone is not added to Elastic Load Balancer

369. You are configuring a new Autoscaling group. Which of the following features you will add to ensure that additional instances are neither launched not terminated before the previous scaling activity takes effect
    a. Termination policy
    b. Cool down period
    c. Creation policy
    d. Ramp up period

370. A company is using AWS CodeDeploy in AWS environment. They want to specify scripts to be run on each instance at various stages of the deployment process. Which feature will provide this?
    a. CodeDeploy file
    b. Config file
    c. Deploy file
    d. AppSpec file

371. You are working in a company that has recently extended its data center into a VPC on AWS. The on-premise users are required to manage AWS resources from the AWS console. You are restricted not to re-create IAM users. Which of the options below will fit your authentication needs?

    a. Use your on-premises SAML 2 O-compliant identity provider (IDP) to grant the members federated access to the AWS Management Console via the AWS single-sign-on (SSO) endpoint.

    b. Use your on-premises SAML2.0-compliant identity provider (IDP) to retrieve temporary security credentials to enable members to sign in to the AWS management console.

    c. Use Auth 2.0 to retrieve temporary AWS security credentials to enable your members to sign in to the AWS Management Console.

    d. Use your on-premises SAML2.0-compliant identity provider (IDP) to retrieve temporary security credentials to enable members to sign in to the AWS management console.

372. While using CloudFormation, How can you resolve a dependency error?
    a. Use the DependsOn attribute
    b. Use the perimeter attribute
    c. Use the mapping attribute
    d. Use the error attribute

373. You want to store a large amount of data which should be readily accessible for a short period, but after that it should be indefinitely archived. Which cost-effective solution you will choose?

    a. Store your data in an EBS volume, and use lifecycle policies to archive to Amazon Glacier.

    b. Store your data in Amazon S3, and use lifecycle policies to archive to S3-infrequently Access.

    c. Store your data in Amazon S3, and use lifecycle policies to archive to Amazon Glacier.

    d. Store all the data in S3 so that it can be most cost-effective

374. A user has launched an EC2 instance using CloudFormation. He wants that Autoscaling and ELB stack creation starts after the EC2 instance launched and configured properly. What should be the possible way of configuration?

   a. The user can use the WaitCondition resource to hold the creation of the other dependent resources.
   b. The user can use the HoldCondition resource to wait for the creation of the other dependent resources.
   c. It is not possible that the stack creation will wait until one service is created and launched.
   d. The user can use the DependentCondition resource to hold the creation of the other dependent resources.

375. Elastic BeanStalk doesn't support all platforms, choose which one is not the supported platform?

   a. Go
   b. Node.js
   c. Java SE
   d. Kubernetes
   e. Packer Builder

376. A company created an application which provides RDS access to the user. Using MySQL RDS DB, the user enables Multi-AZ feature. How will AWS checks that if they shut down their servers, the switching between DB to a standby Replica will not affect the application access?

   a. The switchover changes Hardware so RDS does not need to worry about access.
   b. RDS uses DNS to switch over to standby replica for seamless transition.
   c. RDS will have an internal IP which will redirect all requests to the new DB
   d. RDS will have both the DBs running independently and the user has to manually switch over.

377. You are using an EC2 instance on which web and worker role infrastructure is defined. Jobs send by the web role are managed through SQS. Now what way will be suitable to check that the jobs send by the web role.

   a. Use CloudWatch monitoring to check the size of the queue and then scale out SQS to ensure that it can handle the right number of jobs

b. Use CloudWatch monitoring to check the size of the queue and then scale out using Autoscaling to ensure that it can handle the right number of jobs.

c. Use ELB to ensure that the load is evenly distributed to the set of web and worker instances.

d. Use Route53 to ensure that the load is evenly distributed to the set of web and worker instances.

378. Which of the following option will not save the cost on the AWS services?

a. Release the elastic IP if not required once the instance is terminated

b. Delete the unutilized EBS volumes once the instance is terminated

c. Delete the AWS ELB after the instances are terminated

d. Delete the Autoscaling launch configuration after the instances are terminated.

379. Select the best possible way to automate the creation of EBS snapshot

a. Create a PowerShell script which uses the AWS CLI to get the volumes and then run the script as a cron job.

b. Use the AWS CodeDeploy service to create a snapshot of AWS volumes.

c. Use CloudWatch Events to trigger the snapshots of EBS volumes.

d. Use the AWS Config service to create a snapshot of AWS volumes.

380. The company has extended their footprints on AWS, but they still want to use their previous on-premise active directory for authentication. Choose the AWS service which allows them to use the existing credentials stored in the on-premise directory.

a. Use the Active Directory connector service on AWS

b. Use the ClassicLink feature on AWS

c. Use the AWS simple AD service

d. Use the Active Directory service on AWS

381. Recently a company started using Docker Cloud. A Solution provider give suggested to use SaaS platform to manage Docker containers in the AWS cloud. He is also is on the same cloud platform. The SaaS solution requires access to AWS resources. Which of the following would satisfy the requirement to enable the SaaS solution to work securely with AWS resources?

a. Create an IAM role for EC2 instances, assign it a policy mat allows only the actions required tor the Saas application to work, provide the role ARM to the SaaS provider to use when launching their application instances.

b. Create an IAM role for cross-account access allows the SaaS provider's account to assume the role and assign it a policy that allows only the actions required by the SaaS application.

c. Create an IAM user within the enterprise account assign a user policy to the IAM user that allows only the actions required by the SaaS application. Create a new access and secret key for the user and provide these credentials to the SaaS provider.

d. From the AWS Management Console, navigate to the Security Credentials page and retrieve the access and secret key for your account.

382. Choose three lifecycle events options provided by OpsWorks
   a. Decommission
   b. Deploy
   c. Shutdown
   d. Setup

383. You are running an application globally. You have multiple EC2 instances running in different regions. You want to monitor performance of each instance using CloudWatch. What will you do?
   a. Create separate dashboard in each region
   b. This is not possible
   c. Register instances running on different region to CloudWatch
   d. Have one single dashboard to report metrics to CloudWatch from different regions

384. Which system architecture is best for a company who is working on automatic photograph tagging by using artificial neural networks (ANNs), which have C++ format and it processes on GPU. The images loaded in S3 bucket are million but on average, 3 images per day. You control the S3 bucket for you in a batch. You have a control on one more S3 bucket in which a customer publishes JSON formatted manifest. Bootstrap time of your neural network software is 5 minutes, and image takes 10 milliseconds to process using full GPU. Tags are JSON formatted which must be published to S3 bucket.
   a. Make an S3 notification configuration which publishes to AWS Lambda of the manifest bucket. Make the Lambda CloudFormation stack which contains the logic to construct an Autoscaling worker tier EC2 G2 instances with the

artificial neural network code on each instance. Handle the CloudFormation Stacks creation success or failure using another Lambda function. Create an SQS queue of the images in the manifest. Tear the stack down when the queue is empty.

b. Deploy your artificial neural network code to AWS Lambda as a bundled binary for the C++ extension. Make an S3 notification configuration on the manifest, which publishes to another AWS Lambda running controller code. This controller code publishes all the images in the manifest to AWS Kinesis. Your ANN code Lambda function uses the Kinesis as an Event source. The system automatically scales when the stream contains the images.

c. Create an OpsWorks stack with two layers. The first contains lifecycle scripts for launching and bootstrapping an HTTP API on G2 instances for image processing, and the second has an always-on instance which monitors the S3 manifest bucket for new files. When a new file is detected, requests instances to boot on the new artificial neural network layer. When the instances are booted and the HTTP APIs are up, submit processing requests to individual instances.

d. Create an Autoscaling, Load Balanced Elastic BeanStalk worker tier Application and Environment. Deploy the artificial neural network code to G2 instances in this tier. Set the desired capacity to 1. Make the code periodically check S3 for new manifests. When a new manifests is detected, push all of the images in the manifest into the SQS queue associated with the Elastic BeanStalk worker tier.

385. A company has given you the task to configure an AWS Elastic BeanStalk work tier for easy debugging, but you are facing problems in finishing queue jobs, what will you configure?
    a. Configure Enhanced Health Reporting
    b. Configure Blue-Green Deployments
    c. Configure Rolling Deployments
    d. Configure a Dead Letter Queue

386. Select the components which is not exist in Elastic BeanStalk
    a. Docker
    b. Environment
    c. Application
    d. ApplicationVersion

387. The service used to get the snapshot of the current configuration of the resources in AWS account is:
    a. AWS Trusted Advisor
    b. AWS Config
    c. AWS IAM
    d. AWS CodeDeploy

388. You want to use intrinsic functions to assign values to properties that will not be available until runtime. You are working on CloudFormation template. Choose the best description to use intrinsic functions.
    a. You can use intrinsic functions only in the resource properties part of a template
    b. You can use intrinsic functions in any part of a template, except AWS TemplateFormatVersion and Description.
    c. You can use intrinsic functions in any part of a template.
    d. You can only use intrinsic functions in specific part of a template. You can use intrinsic functions in resource properties, metadata attributes, and update policy attributes.

389. You want to use the instance in OpsWorks stack. Which of the following tasks you can't able to do?
    a. You can start and stop instances manually in a stack
    b. In a stack you can use a mix of both Linux and windows operating systems
    c. You can use custom AMI's as long as they are based on one of the AWS OpsWorks Stacks-supported AMIs
    d. You can use time-based automatic scaling with any stack

390. A company is designing loosely coupled system, which of the following design strategies are ideal? Choose 2 answers
    a. Having the web and worker roles running on the same set of EC2 instances
    b. Having the web and worker roles running on separate EC2 instances
    c. Using SQS to establish communication between the web and worker roles
    d. Using SNS to establish communication between the web and worker roles

391. You have a task to spin up a new EC2 instance using CLI. Which command you will use?

    a. aws ec2 create-instances

    b. aws ec2 new-instances

    c. aws ec2 run-instances

    d. aws ec2 launch-instances

392. CloudFormation template offers 6 section i.e., Template Description Declaration, Template Format Version Declaration, Parameters, Resources, Outputs and Mappings. Which is the compulsory section for CloudFormation Template to be accepted?

    a. Resources

    b. Mappings

    c. Outputs

    d. Parameters

393. A company is running a legacy application on m4.large instance size, only 5% of CPU is utilized. You are a senior technical manager and wants to make a cost-effective solution through which you can change the instance without stopping the application. Choose the following by which you will be able to achieve your task.

    a. Use a C4.large instance with enhanced networking

    b. Use two t2.nano instances that have single root I/O Virtualization

    c. Use t2.nano instance and add spot instances when required

    d. Use a T2 burstable performance instance

394. In Elastic BeanStalk service which of the following rolling type update doesn't exist for configuration update?

    a. Immutable

    b. Rolling based on instances

    c. Rolling based on health

    d. Rolling based on time

395. An IT company Technical assistant come to know that Elastic BeanStalk service provides Managed update facility which are minor and patch version updates. The company starts hosting a production environment in Elastic BeanStalk. The Technical assistant come to you to ask the effect of updates on the system, because the system

requires these updates periodically. What would you tell him about managed update facility?

a. Elastic BeanStalk applies managed updates with no downtime
b. Elastic BeanStalk applies managed updates with no reduction capacity
c. Package updates can be configurable weekly maintenance window
d. All of the above

396. You are working in a company's data security unit. You want to ensure the encryption of your both at rest and in transit. Which of the following you will not apply for the encryption?

a. Enable SSL termination on the ELB
b. Enabling proxy protocol
c. Using S3 Server Side Encryption (SSE) to store the information
d. Enabling sticky sessions on your load balancer

397. An organization hires you to work on AWS for their Production RollOut. They ask you to implement automation for deployment which will automatically create a LAMP stack, deploy an RDS MySQL DB instance, download the latest PHP installable from S3 and set up the ELB. Which of the following AWS service you will use to deploy the software orderly?

a. AWS DevOps
b. AWS CloudFormation
c. AWS Elastic BeanStalk
d. AWS CloudFront

398. A company is using OpsWorks with several stacks for dev, staging, and production to deploy and manage the application. They want to start using python instead of Ruby, they have already Ruby on Rail content management platform. Choose the correct solution to manage the new deployment.

a. Create a new stack that contains a new layer with the Python code. To cut over the new stack the company should consider using Blue/Green deployment
b. Update the existing stack with Python application code and deploy the application using the deploy life-cycle action to implement the application code

c. Create a new stack that contains Python application code and manage separate deployments of the application via the secondary stack using the deploy life-cycle action to implement the application code

d. Create a new stack that contains Python application code and manage separate deployments of the application via the secondary stack

399. Select the 2 environment types that are available in Elastic BeanStalk environment
   a. SQS, Autoscaling
   b. Single instance
   c. Multi-instance
   d. Load balancing, Autoscaling

400. An IT administrator has a responsibility to create development environment which would confirm to the LAMP development stack. Whenever a new instance is launched, the development team should be updated with the latest version of the LAMP stack. Choose 2 answers which will satisfy the requirements in a best way.
   a. Use the User data section and use a custom script which will be used to download the necessary LAMP stack packages.
   b. Create a CloudFormation template and use the cloud-init directives to download and install the LAMP stack packages.
   c. Create an EBS volume with the LAMP stack and attach it to an instance whenever it is required.
   d. Create an AMI with all the artifacts of the LAMP stack and provide an instance to the development team based on AMI.

401. Your company IT supervisor is interested in optimizing the cost of running AWS resources. Which of the 2 options are suitable for this purpose?
   a. Use the Trusted advisor to see the underutilized resources
   b. Create a script which monitors all the running resources and calculates the cost accordingly. It analyse those resources and see which can be optimized.
   c. Create CloudWatch alarms to monitor underutilized resources and either shut down or terminate resources which are not required.
   d. Create CloudWatch logs to monitor underutilized resources and either shut down or terminate resources which are not required.

402. You have an instance in Autoscaling group in which lifecycle hooks are enabled. Due to lifecycle hooks initially the instance is put into Pending: Wait state, which means that instance cannot handle the traffic in this state. In wait state, other scaling actions are also suspended. Then the instance is put into Pending: Proceed and then it changes to InService, which means that instances in Autoscaling group can now serve the traffic, but you have observed that bootstrapping process finishes earlier than the status Pending: Proceed is updated.

What can you do to check that the instances status are updated correctly after the bootstrapping process?

   a. Use the complete-lifecycle-action call to complete the lifecycle action. Run this command from another EC2 instance.
   b. Use the complete-lifecycle-action call to complete the lifecycle action. Run this command from Command Line Interface.
   c. Use the complete-lifecycle-action call to complete the lifecycle action. Run this command from a SQS queue.
   d. Use the complete-lifecycle-action call to complete the lifecycle action. Run this command from the Simple Notification Service.

403. Your company has a partnership with another company. They want access to your AWS account by using their own AWS account in order to read protected messages in a private S3 bucket. Select the best solution.

   a. Allow them to ssh into your EC2 instance and grant them an IAM role with full access to the bucket.
   b. Create an S3 bucket policy that allows the Partner Company to read from the bucket from their AWS account.
   c. Create a cross-account IAM role with permission to access the bucket, and grant permission to use the role to the vendor AWS account.
   d. Create an IAM user with API Access Keys. Give your partner company the AWS Access Key ID and AWS Secret Access Key for the user.

404. You created an Encrypted EBS volume and attach it to a supported instance type. Choose 3 data types from the following which are encrypted.

   a. All data moving between the volume and instance
   b. All snapshots created from the volume
   c. Data at rest inside the volume
   d. All data copied from EBS volume to S3

405. A company has given you the task of designing CloudFormation template. You have to look up that the CloudFormation stack is deleted and a snapshot of the Relational database is created which is the part of stack. What will you do to complete this task?

    a. Create a new CloudFormation template to create a snapshot of the relational database

    b. Create a snapshot of relational database beforehand so that when the CloudFormation stack is deleted, the snapshot of database is present.

    c. Use the Update policy of the CloudFormation template to ensure a snapshot is created of the relational database.

    d. Use the Deletion policy of the CloudFormation template to ensure a snapshot is created of the relational database.

406. Your company assigned you a task to create a CloudFormation template that should be able to spin up the resources in different regions. Which of the following aspects allow you to create such template?

    a. Use the output sections in CloudFormation template, so that based on the relevant region, the relevant resource can be spinned up

    b. Use the parameters sections in CloudFormation template, so that based on the relevant region, the relevant resource can be spinned up

    c. Use the mappings sections in CloudFormation template, so that based on the relevant region, the relevant resource can be spinned up

    d. Use the metadata sections in CloudFormation template, so that based on the relevant region, the relevant resource can be spinned up

407. You have designed a critical application with the requirement of least downtime of rollback (if required). You want to roll out updates to your application introduced on Elastic BeanStalk Environment. Which of the following deployment action is best suitable for this purpose?

    a. Create another parallel environment in Elastic BeanStalk. Use the swap URL feature.

    b. Create a CloudFormation template with the same resources as those in the Elastic BeanStalk environment

    c. Create another parallel environment in Elastic BeanStalk. Create a new Route53 Domain name for the new environment and release that URL to the users.

d. Use Rolling updates in Elastic BeanStalk so that if the deployment fails, the rolling update feature would roll back to the last deployment.

408. Select the available run command types for OpsWorks stacks. Choose 3 answers.
    a. UnDeploy
    b. Configure
    c. Execute Recipes
    d. Update Custom Cookbooks

409. A company wants to use a SaaS third-party app running on AWS. The SaaS application must be able to issue several API commands to detect Amazon EC2 resources in the company's account. The company has internal security policies that require external access to its environment and must ensure with the minimum privilege principles and controls must controls which ensure that the credentials used by the SaaS vendor cannot be accessed by third party. Which of the following would satisfy all these requirements?
    a. Create an IAM user within the enterprise account assign a user policy to the IAM user that allows only the actions required by the SaaS application. Create a new access and secret key for the user and provide these credentials to the SaaS provider.
    b. From the AWS Management Console, navigate to the Security Credentials page and retrieve the access and secret key for your account.
    c. Create an IAM role for EC2 instances, assign it a policy that allows only the actions required tor the Saas application to work, provide the role ARN to the SaaS provider to use when launching their application instances.
    d. Create an IAM role for cross-account access allows the SaaS provider's account to assume the role and assign it a policy that allows only the actions required by the SaaS application.

410. Your company has announced a new IT procedure for EC2 instances which states that EC2 instance must be of particular instance type. You want to find out the list of instances that doesn't match the demanded instance type. Choose from the following option which would you use to obtain the list?
    a. Use TrustedAdvisor to check which EC2 instances don't match the intended instance type.

b. Use VPC Flow Logs to check which EC2 instances don't match the intended instance type.

c. Use AWS CloudWatch alarms to check which EC2 instances don't match the intended instance type.

d. Use AWS Config to create a rule to check EC2 instance type

411. You are running a Video processing application launched in AWS. Users upload videos on site which are then processed by using built-in custom program in case there are any failure in processing, that program is able to balance the situation. Now considering the minimum cost budget, which of the following mechanism should you use to deploy the instance for running video processing activities?

a. Create a launch configuration with Dedicated Instances. Ensure the user section data details the installation of the custom software. Create an Autoscaling group with the launch configuration.

b. Create a launch configuration with Spot Instances. Ensure the user section data details the installation of the custom software. Create an Autoscaling group with the launch configuration.

c. Create a launch configuration with On-Demand Instances. Ensure the user section data details the installation of the custom software. Create an Autoscaling group with the launch configuration.

d. Create a launch configuration with Reserved Instances. Ensure the user section data details the installation of the custom software. Create an Autoscaling group with the launch configuration.

412. IT department of a company wants to launch instances in Autoscaling group. They need to setup lifecycle hooks for setting custom based software and do the required configuration on the instances. This setting would maximum take an hour. Considering the scenario what will you suggest to setup lifecycle hooks? Choose 2 answers

a. Configure the lifecycle hook to record heartbeats. If the hour is up, choose to terminate the current instance and start a new one.

b. Configure the lifecycle hook to record heartbeats. If the hour is up, restart the timeout period.

c. If the software installation and the configuration is complete, then send the signal to complete the launch of the instance.

d. If the software installation and the configuration is complete, then restart the time period.

413. The company for which you are working has an enormous infrastructure built on AWS. However, there are some security concerns regarding this infrastructure and an external auditor has been given the task of thoroughly checking all the AWS assets of your company. Your company is located in the Asia-Pacific (Sydney) region of AWS whereas auditor is in USA. You have been assigned the task of providing the auditor with a login in order to check all your VPC assets, in particular, security groups and NACLs. Choose the best and secured solution for initiating this investigation.
    a. Give him root access to your AWS Infrastructure, because he is an auditor he will need access to every service.
    b. Create an IAM user who will have read-only access to your AWS VPC infrastructure and provide the auditor with those credentials.
    c. Create an IAM user tied to an administrator role. Also provide an additional level of security with MFA.
    d. Create an IAM user with full VPC access but set a condition that will not allow him to modify anything if the request is from any IP other than his own.

414. You are a finance supervisor of a company. You have to maintain and keep yourself notified when the AWS resources cost reaches the borderline of the budget i.e. 3000 USD. Which of the following strategy would be the simplest to apply in order to get notified?
    a. Use the CloudWatch billing alarm to notify you when you reach the threshold value.
    b. Use CloudWatch events to notify you when you reach the threshold value
    c. Use SQS queues to notify you when you reach the threshold value
    d. Use CloudWatch logs to notify you when you reach the threshold value

415. Using ELB, an autoscaling group of Java/Tomcat application servers and DynamoDB as data store in EC2 instance, A web-startup is running its successful social news app. Web applications requires high memory therefore m2x large is the most suitable instance. The semi-automated creation and testing of a new AMI for the application servers is required by each new deployment, which takes some time and is done only once a week. A new chat feature was recently introduced in nodejs and is waiting to be integrated into the architecture. The new component is shown CPU

bound in the first test because the company has some experience using Chef, they have decided to streamline the deployment process and use AWS OpsWorks as an application life cycle tool to simplify application management and reduce deployment cycles. What configuration is needed in AWS OpsWorks to integrate the new chat module into the most cost-effective?

 a. Create one AWS OpsWorks stack create two AWS OpsWorks layers create one custom recipe

 b. Create two AWS OpsWorks stacks create two AWS OpsWorks layers create one custom recipe

 c. Create two AWS OpsWorks stacks create two AWS OpsWorks layers create two custom recipe

 d. Create one AWS OpsWorks stack, create one AWS OpsWorks layer, create one custom recipe

416. A company wants to access the On-premise LDAP server from an application launched on a VPC. The connection of VPC and On-premise location are established through an IPSec VPN. Choose 2 correct options for application user authentication.

 a. The application authenticates against LDAP and retrieves the name of an IAM role associated with the user. The application then calls the IAM Security Token Service to assume that IAM role. The application can use the temporary credentials to access any AWS resources.

 b. Develop an identity broker that authenticates against LDAP and then calls IAM Security Token Service to get IAM federated user credentials. The application calls the identity broker to get IAM federated user credentials with access to the appropriate AWS service.

 c. Develop an identity broker that authenticates against IAM Security Token Service to assume an IAM role in order to get temporary AWS security credentials. The application calls the identity broker to get AWS temporary security credentials.

 d. The application authenticates against LDAP and then calls the IAM Security Service to log in to IAM using the LDAP credentials. The application can use IAM temporary credentials to access the appropriate AWS service.

417. Technical team of your company is concerned with AWS account security. What will you suggest to prevent the account from hackers?

a. Don't write down or remember the root account password after creating the AWS account.

b. Use short but complex password on the root account and any administrators.

c. Use AWS IAM Geo-Lock and disallow anyone from logging in except for in your city.

d. Use MFA on all users and accounts, especially on the root account.

418. For your task, you can host your own source code repository system or you can use AWS CodeCommit. What are the advantages from the following to prefer CodeCommit over your own source code?

a. No specific restriction on files and branches

b. Reduction in fees paid over licensing

c. Reduction in hardware maintenance costs

d. All of the above

419. A company is sending messages to EC2 instance using SQS. The message size is increased greater than 5 MB. Which of the following way they should choose?

a. Use the Amazon SQS Extended Client Library for Java and Amazon S3 as a storage mechanism for message bodies.

b. Use Kinesis as a buffer stream for message bodies. Store the checkpoint ID for the placement in the Kinesis Stream in SQS.

c. Use SQS's support for message partitioning and multi-part uploads on Amazon S3.

d. Use AWS EFS as a shared pool storage medium. Store file system pointers to the files on disk in the SQS message bodies.

420. You are running a set of resources on your AWS account. You want to be notified whenever your resources cost reaches the threshold value you have set. For this purpose which would be the suitable way?

a. Create a consolidated billing report and see if the costs are going beyond the threshold.

b. Download the cost reports and analyze the reports to see if the costs are going beyond the threshold

c. Create a billing alarm which can alert you when the costs are going beyond a certain threshold.

d. Create a script which monitors all the running resources and calculates the costs accordingly.

421. Your company CTO assigns you to connect a MySQL Database to a WordPress application keeping concern that the environment must be fault tolerant and highly available. Choose 2 options from the following which would individually plays their role to perform the required task.
   a. Create a MySQL RDS environment and create a Read Replica
   b. Create Multiple EC2 instances in the same AZ. Host MySQL and enable replication via scripts between instances.
   c. Create a MySQL RDS environment with Multi-AZ feature enabled
   d. Create Multiple EC2 instances in the separate AZ. Host MySQL and enable replication via scripts between instances.

422. You have created an Autoscaling group with t2.micro instance type. You have set Min Capacity: 2, Desired Capacity: 2 and Max Capacity: 2, now you are facing issues in running your application. A friend give you advice to change the instance type, which of the following would be the solution for doing this?
   a. Make a copy of the Launch Configuration. Change the instance type in the new launch configuration. Attach that to the Autoscaling group. Change the maximum and desired size of the Autoscaling group to 4. Once the new instances are launched, change the desired and max size back to 2.
   b. Change the instance type in the current launch configuration. Change the desired value of Autoscaling group to 4. Ensure that the new instances are launched.
   c. Delete the current launch configuration. Create a new launch configuration with the new instance type and add it to the Autoscaling group. This will then launch the new instance.
   d. Change the desired and maximum size of the Autoscaling group to 4. Make a copy of the Launch Configuration. Change the instance type in the new launch configuration. Attach that to Autoscaling group and change the max and desired capacity size to 2.

423. AWS DevOps admins are working on building the infrastructure of company's development team through CloudFormation which includes the VPC and networking

components, installing a LAMP stack and securing the created resources. For designing this template choose the best way among the following options.

   a. Create multiple CloudFormation templates based on the number of development groups in the environment.
   b. Create multiple CloudFormation templates for each set of logical resources, one for networking, and the other for LAMP stack creation.
   c. Create multiple CloudFormation templates based on the number of VPC's in the environment.
   d. Create a single CloudFormation template to create all the resources since it would be easier from the maintenance perspective.

424. You have to fire up different instance sizes based of environment type (i.e If this is for prod, use m4.large instead of t2.micro) for that purpose, which of the following would you set?

   a. Conditions
   b. Resources
   c. Mappings
   d. Outputs

425. You are working in a company where you have to record all the activities occurring in AWS account and provide the access of the loggings of events to the security officer across all regions in a simple and secure way that no one else would be able to access those events other than the security officer. Select the best solution from the given options.

   a. Use CloudTrail to log all events to an Amazon Glacier vault. Make sure the vault access policy only grant access to the security officer's IP address.
   b. Use CloudTrail to log all events to separate S3 bucket in each region as CloudTrail cannot write to a bucket in different region. Use MFA and bucket policies on all the different buckets.
   c. Use CloudTrail to log all events to one S3 bucket. Make this S3 bucket only accessible by your security officer with a bucket policy that restricts access to his user only and also add MFA to the policy for a further level of security.
   d. Use CloudTrail to send all API calls to CloudWatch and send an email to security officer every time an API call is made. Make sure the emails are encrypted.

426. An Autoscaling group is created with the following settings:

Min capacity – 2

Max capacity – 4

Desired capacity – 2

Due to some reason the IT team is notified to prevent launching of any new instance for two hours. Currently 2 instances are running. Which of the 2 options will allow you to achieve your purpose?

   a. Change the desired capacity to 4
   b. Change the Max capacity to 2
   c. Suspend the launch process of the Autoscaling group
   d. Change the min capacity to 2

427. If you are asked to build a social media mobile application which needs permission for every user login and storing their data in DynamoDB. What would you choose from the following options in order to grant access to DynamoDB to your application users when required?

   a. Create an active directory server and an AD user for each mobile application user. When the user signs in to the AD sign-on, allow the AD server to federate using SAML 2.0 to IAM and assign a role to the AD user which is the assumed with AssumeRoleWithSAML.
   b. During the install configuration process, for each user create an IAM credential and assign the IAM user to a group with proper permissions to communicate with DynamoDB.
   c. Create an IAM group that only gives access to your application and to the DynamoDB tables. Then, when writing to DynamoDB, simply include the unique device ID to associate the data with that specific user.
   d. Create an IAM role with the proper permission policy to communicate with the DynamoDB table. Use web identity federation, which assumes the IAM role using AssumeRoleWithWebIdentity, when the user signs in, granting temporary security credentials using STS.

428. You want to design a .Net front end and DynamoDB back end application. You know that the application runs with heavy load. How will you ensure the scalability of application for minimum DynamoDB database load?

   a. Launch DynamoDB in Multi-AZ configuration with a global index to balance writes.

b. Use SQS to assist and let the application pull messages and then perform the relevant operation in DynamoDB.

c. Increase write capacity of DynamoDB to meet the peak loads

d. Add more DynamoDB databases to handle the load

429. While viewing your user reviews, your company decides to upgrade the application that was running on instances in an Autoscaling group. They suggested to use new instances if possible without any downtime. You are not allowed to swap any environment URLs. Which of the following options IS suitable to deploy the new version of application?

a. Using "Blue Green" deployment method

b. Using "Rolling Updates" deployment method

c. Using "Blue Green" with "All at once" deployment method

d. Using "All at once" deployment method

430. You were hired for a startup as a DevOps engineer. Your company uses AWS for 100% of its infrastructure. Currently the deployment is not automated and have experienced many failures while trying to deploy to production. The company has told you that the risk mitigation process is the most important thing now, and you have a lot of money for tools and AWS resources.

Depending on the type, company stack includes a 2-tier API with data stored in DynamoDB or S3. In Auto Scaling Groups, the compute layer is EC2. company use Route53 for DNS to an ELB. Load of an ELB balances over EC2 instances. The scaling group varies properly from 4 to 12 EC2 servers. Which of the following approaches, given the stack of this company and its priorities, best meets the needs of the company?

a. Model the stack in AWS OpsWorks as a single Stack, with 1 compute layer and its associated ELB. Use Chef and App Deployments to automate Rolling Deployment.

b. Model the stack in three CloudFormation templates: Data layer, compute layer, and networking layer. Write stack deployment and integration testing automation following Blue-Green methodologies.

c. Model the stack in AWS Elastic BeanStalk as a single Application with multiple Environments. Use Elastic BeanStalk's Rolling Deploy option to progressively roll out application code changes when promoting across environments.

d. Model the stack in 1 CloudFormation template, to ensure consistency and dependency graph resolution. Write deployment and integration testing automation following Rolling Deployment methodologies.

431. When considering AWS Elastic BeanStalk, the 'Swap Environment URLs includes most directly helps in what?
    a. Immutable Rolling Deployments
    b. Blue-Green Deployments
    c. Canary Deployments
    d. Mutable Rolling Deployments

432. Which of the following 3 things would you be able to accomplish with the CloudWatch logs benefit?

Pick 3 answers

    a. Send the log data to AWS Lambda for custom processing or to load into other systems
    b. Record API calls for your AWS account and delivers log files containing API calls to your Amazon S3 bucket.
    c. Stream the log data to Amazon Kinesis
    d. Stream the log data into Amazon Elasticsearch in near real-time with CloudWatch logs subscriptions.

433. You are working for an organization that has an on-premise foundation. There is presently a choice to move to AWS. The arrangement is to move the development environment first. There are number of custom based applications that should be deployed for the development community. Which of the following can actualize the application for the development group? (Choose 2 answers)
    a. Create Docker containers for the custom application components
    b. Use OpsWorks to deploy the docker containers
    c. Use CloudFormation to deploy the docker containers
    d. Use Elastic BeanStalk to deploy the docker containers

434. Choose the best possible answer which explains the working of following resource in the CloudFormation template.

"SNS Topic" :{

       "Type" :"AWS::SNS::Topic",

```
        "Properties" :{

            "Subscription" :[{

                "Protocol": "sqs"

                "Endpoint" :{"Fn::GetAtt" :["SQSQueue","Arn"]}

            }]

}
```

a. Creates an SNS topic that allows SQS subscription endpoints
b. Creates an SNS topic which allows SQS subscription endpoints to be added as a parameter on the template
c. Creates an SNS topic and adds a subscription ARN endpoint for the SQS resource created under the logical name SQSQueue
d. Creates an SNS topic and then invokes the call to create an SQS queue with a logical resource name of SQSQueue

435. A large number of aerial image data has been uploaded to S3 by your company. In the past, you used a dedicated group of servers in your local environment to process these data and used Rabbit MQ– an open source message system to get job information to the servers. The data would go to the tape and be shipped offsite once processed. Your manager told you to use the current design and use AWS archive storage and messaging to reduce costs. Which option is right?

a. Setup Auto-scaled workers triggered by queue depth that use spot instances to process messages in SQS. Once data is processed, change the storage class of the S3 objects to Glacier.
b. Use SNS to pass job messages and use CloudWatch alarms to terminate spot worker instances when they become idle. Once data is processed, change the storage class of the S3 object to Glacier.
c. Use SQS for passing job messages. Use CloudWatch alarms to terminate EC2 worker instances when they become idle. Once data is processed, change the storage class of the S3 objects to Reduced Redundancy Storage.
d. Change the storage class of the S3 objects to Reduced Redundancy Storage. Setup Auto-scaled workers triggered by queue depth that use spot instances to process messages in SQS. Once data is processed, change the storage class of the S3 objects to Glacier.

436. You plan to launch instances that have an application installed with Autoscaling. Which of the following methods will help to ensure that the instances are up and running for traffic from users in the shortest possible time?
    a. Use user data to launch scripts to install the software.
    b. Log in to each instance and install the software
    c. Use AMI's which already have the software installed.
    d. Use Docker container to launch the software.

437. A company wants to pass a custom script to a new Amazon Linux instance. What feature does enable them to achieve this?
    a. IAM roles
    b. EC2Config service
    c. AWS Config
    d. User data

Answers

1. **A** (AutoScalingRollingUpdate)

Explanation:

The AutoScalingRollingUpdate is a common approach for updating the auto scaling group. The replaces the old auto-scaling group with the new ones with the specified features ad parameter.

2. **C** (Re-deploy your infrastructure using AWS CloudFormation, Elastic BeanStalk and auto-scaling. Set up your auto-scaling group policies to scale based on the number of requests per second as well as the current customer load time).

Explanation:

Auto-scaling is used to ensure that there will be a valid number of EC2 instances which can handle the load of the application. The desired number of instances can be specified at the time of the creation of the group and after that. Options A and B are invalid because auto-scaling is required to solve the issue that application can handle the traffic. Option D is also invalid because there is no auto-scaling template.

3. **D** (Modify the application running on the instances to put itself into an auto-scaling standby state while it processes a task and return itself to Inservice when the processing is complete.)

Explanation:

You can put the instances into stand by state. After the processing is completed the instances put back to the state where the auto-scaling group governs them.

4. **C** (Develop each app in a separate docker container and deploy using Elastic BeanStalk.)

Explanation:

By using dockers you can define your runtime environment, you can choose your own application dependencies and programming languages and own platform too. The entire idea of docker is that you have a separate environment for each application and Elastic Beanstalk supports the deployment of the web application from dockers container.

5. **C** (Place each developer own public key into a private S3 bucket, use instance profile and configuration management to create a user account for each developer on all instances, and place the user's public keys into the appropriate account.)

Explanation:

An instance profile basically works as the container for an IAM role which is used to pass the role information when the instance starts. The key can be created in a private S3 bucket and assigned to the instance profile.

6. **B** (Create a custom resource type using template developer, custom resource template, and CloudFormation)

Explanation:

Custom resources allow custom provisioning logic in order to create, update or delete stack at any time in AWS CloudFormation.

7. **D** (Assign an IAM role to your Amazon EC2 instances, and use this IAM role to access the Amazon RDS DB from your Amazon EC2 instances)

Explanation:

Roles are basically used to delegate access to the users and application that don't have access to your aws resource. To connect DB instance or DB cluster with IAM user or roles, the IAM policy must be created.

8. **A** (Terminating)

Explanation:

The lifecycle in an EC2 instance starts when you launch an instance and terminates when the life cycle ends. The auto-scaling group takes the instance out of service and terminate it.

9. **C** (Create a new load balancer with new Amazon EC2 instances, carry out the deployment, and then switch DNS over to the new load balancer using Amazon Route53 after testing.)

Explanation:

Create an ELB which is used to point all new production changes. Use the weighted route policy to distribute the traffic, and when all the changes have been tested, Route53 can be set as the new ELB.

10. **C** (Deliver custom metrics to Amazon CloudWatch per application that breaks down application data transfer into multiple, more specific data point)

Explanation:

The metrics can be published to CloudWatch using CLI and API and can be viewed statistically with the AWS management console.

11. **A** (Create separate templates based on functionality, create nested stacks with CloudFormation.)

Explanation:

Common pattern includes components which contain the same components in a template. You can separate these components and create dedicated templates for them. By this, you can mix and move different templates, but nested stacks are used to create a single unified-stack. Nested stacks are stacks that created other stacks.

12. **C** (Update the template and then update the stack with the new template. Only those resources that need to be changed will remain as they are.)

Explanation:

When there is a need to update a stack or changes the resources in a stack you need to update the stack only rather deleting it and creating anew stack.

13. **A** (Write a script that is run by a daily cron job on an Amazon EC2 instance and that executes API describe calls of the EC2 auto scaling group and removes terminated instances from the configuration management system.)

   D (Write a small script that is run during Amazon EC2 instance shutdown to de-register the resource from the configuration management system.)

Explanation:

If you specify one or more instance ID's, EC2 returns information of those instances. If do not, EC2 returns information of all the relevant instances.

14. **A** (Create an auto-scaling group life cycle hook to hold the instance in the pending: wait state until your bootstrapping is complete. Once bootstrapping is complete, notify auto-scaling to complete the life cycle hook and move the instance into pending: proceed state.)

Explanation:

Auto-scaling life cycle enables to perform custom actions on an auto-scaling group. After adding life cycle in an auto-scaling group, the auto-scaling respond to scale out an event while launching an instance and scale in the event while terminating the instance.

15. **A** (Develop models of your entire cloud system in CloudFormation. Use this model in staging and production to achieve greater parity).

Explanation:

After resources and stack set up, the templates can be reused to replicated the infrastructure in multiple environments.

16. **B** (AWS OpsWorks)

Explanation:

The chef is used by OpsWorks which is a configuration management service. It is an automation platform that treats configuration of the server as a code.

17. **D** (Access logging is an optional feature of ELB that is disabled by default)

Explanation:

ELB provides access log that captured the detailed information about the request sent to load balancer. Access logging is disabled by default but can be enabled, it captures the logs and stores them in S3 bucket.

18. **C** (Install the CloudWatch logs agent on your AMI, and configure CloudWatch logs agent to stream your logs)

Explanation:

CloudWatch logs are used to monitor applications and system using log data. It can track the number of errors occurred in the application and sent the notification when the errors are exceeded from the specified threshold value. CloudWatch log uses log data, therefore, no changes in code are required.

19. **A** (Add Amazon RDS DB read replicas, and have your application direct read queries to them.)
    D (Use ElastiCache in front of your Amazon RDS DB to cache common queries)
    E (Shard your data set among multiple Amazon RDS DB instances)

Explanation:

Read replicas of Amazon RDS enhanced the performance and scalability. The replication feature made it easy to scale out beyond the capacity of database instance for read-heavy workloads.

Amazon ElastiCache is web service that made it easy to operate, deploy, and scale an in-memory data stored or cache in a cloud.

20. **B** (Ensure that the Amazon EBS volumes have been pre-warmed by reading all the blocks before the test.)

Explanation:

During the AMI creation process, The EC2 instance creates the snapshot of instance's root volume and any other EBS attached to the instance. The new volumes receive maximum performance and do not require initialization also known as pre-warming. The storage blocks from volume, restored from snapshots must be initialized. This process took time but increased the latency of an I/O operation for every time the first block is accessed.

21. **A** (Install an Amazon CloudWatch log agent on every web server during the bootstrap process. Create a CloudWatch log group and define metric filters to create custom metrics that track unique visitors from the streaming web server logs. Create a scheduled task on an Amazon EC2 instance that runs every hour to generate a new report based on the CloudWatch custom metrics)

C (On the web servers, create a scheduled task that executes a script to rotate and transmit the logs to an Amazon S3 bucket. Ensure that the operating system shutdown procedure triggers a logs transmission when the Amazon EC2 instance is stopped/ terminated. Use AWS data pipeline to move log data from the Amazon S3 bucket to Amazon redshift in order to process and run reports every hour.)

Explanation:

CloudWatch log agent installer can install and configure the CloudWatch logs agent on an existing EC2 instance. Amazon RedShift is a data warehouse that analyzes all your data using standard SQL and business intelligence tools.

22. **B** (Using AWS CloudFormation templates, creates one Elastic BeanStalk application and all AWS resources (in the same template) for each web application. The new version would be deployed using AWS CloudFormation templates to create new Elastic BeanStalk environments, and traffic would be balanced between them using weighted round robin (WRR) records in Amazon Route53)

Explanation:

In Amazon Route53, you can define a percentage of traffic for a green environment and gradually update the weight until the green environment carries full traffic production.

23. **A** (Use a parameter of the environment, and add a condition on the Route53 resource in the template to create the record only when the environment is not production)

Explanation:

The optional condition section includes the statement that defines when the resource is created, and property is defined.

24. **C** (When using AWS SDK's and Amazon EC2 roles, you do not have to explicitly retrieve API keys, because the SDK handles retrieving them from the Amazon EC2 metadata service)

Explanation:

IAM roles are designed in such a manner that application can be made requests for API securely in the instances without requiring application usage and security credentials.

25. **C** (Copy the unencrypted snapshot and check the box to encrypt the new snapshot. Volumes restored from this encrypted snapshot will also be encrypted)

   D (Create and mount a new encrypted Amazon EBS volume. Move the data to the new volume. Delete the old Amazon EBS volume.)

Explanation:

To migrate data from encrypted to un-encrypted volume create a destination volume and attach the destination volume to the instance that host the data to migrate. Copy the data from the source directory to the destination volume. Encrypt volume data utilizing the snapshot.

26. **B** (Separate the AWS CloudFormation template into a nested structure that has individual templates for the resources that are to be governed by different departments, and use the outputs from the networking and security stacks for the application template that you control.)

Explanation:

As the infrastructure grows, common patterns emerge in which you declare the same components in your template. You can separate the common components and can create dedicated templates for them.

27. A (Manages an Amazon SQS queue and running a daemon process on each instance).

Explanation:

Elastic BeanStalk is used to simplify this process by managing the Amazon SQS queue and running daemon process on each instance which read and writes messages for you from the queue.

28. B (Install a CloudWatch logs agent on your servers to stream web application logs to CloudWatch)

    D (Create a CloudWatch logs group and define metric filters that capture 500 internal server error. Set a CloudWatch alarm on that metric)

    E (Use Amazon simple notification service to notify an on-call engineer when a CloudWatch alarm is triggered)

Explanation:

CloudWatch is used to monitor those applications and systems that are using log data. It takes logs from log data; therefore, no code changes are required.

29. A (Develop the application in Docker containers, and then deploy them to Elastic BeanStalk environments with auto-scaling and elastic load balancing.

Explanation:

Elastic Beanstalk supports deployment in Docker containers. Docker containers have their run time environment; you can choose your platform, programming language and application dependencies that are not supported by other platforms.

30. C (Saved Configurations)

Explanation:

You can change your configuration as an object in an Amazon S3 bucket, and this can be applied during running environment or environment creation. To define platform configurations, saved configuration options, tiers, and tags, saved configuration use YAML template.

31. C (2 servers in each of availability zones a through 2, inclusive)

Explanation:

The best way to distribute availability zones across instances is to avoid more disastrous scenarios. In this case, there will always a minimum of more than eight servers, if one AZ goes down.

32. **D** (Fn::Parse)

Explanation:

Intrinsic functions Fn::If, Fn::Not, Fn::Equal is used conditionally to create stack resources. These conditions are evaluated based on the input parameters which are declared while creating the stack resources.

33. **B** (Enable access logs on the load balancer)

Explanation:

To capture the detailed information for the requests sent to the load balancer, log access is generated by the elastic load balancer. And each log contains some information such as the time when the request is received, the clients IP address, latencies, request paths, and server response. These access logs are used to analyze traffic pattern and to troubleshoot the issues.

34. **D** (Create an IAM role that allows write access to the DynamoDB table)

Explanation:

IAM roles are designed in such a manner that your application can make API request from your instance without requiring to manage security credentials.

35. **A** (Use a "Container Command" within an Elastic BeanStalk configuration file to execute the script, ensuring that the "leader only" flag is set to true.)

Explanation:

Container Command runs after the application and web server have been set up, and the application version archive has been extracted before the application version is deployed. The command container-command key is used to execute commands that affect application source code

36. **A** (Terminate the instance and launch a new instance)

Explanation:

Auto-Scaling performs health checks periodically and identifies when an instance is unhealthy. It is used to determine the health check status of an instance using EC2 status checks, elastic load balancing health checks or custom health checks.

37. **A** (You need to create an instance profile and associate it with that specific role).

Explanation:

An instance profile is like a container which is used to pass the role information when the instance starts.

38. **A** (Amazon CloudWatch)

   B (Amazon Simple Notification Service)

Explanation:

Amazon CloudWatch monitors applications that run in real time on AWS. It can be used to collect and track metrics. CloudWatch sends notification alarms and makes changes automatically to the resources that you are monitoring based on the defined rules. CloudWatch use Amazon SNS to send emails.

39. **D** (Implement a Route53 weighted routing policy that distributes the traffic between your on-premises application and the AWS application depending on weight).

Explanation:

Weighted Routing associates you with multiple resources with a single domain name and subdomain name and chooses how much traffic route from each resource.

40. **D** (DynamoDB table with roughly equal read and write throughput, with ElastiCache caching).

Explanation:

Because the 100x ratio is mostly driven by the small subset, with caching, only a roughly equal read and writes will miss the cache., the supermajority will hit the 1% score.

41. **B** (Increase the minimum number of instances in the auto-scaling group)

Explanation:

If you increase the minimum number of instances, this will be running when the load on the website is not even high.

42. **D** (Create an Amazon SNS topic for each on-call group, and configure each of these with the team member emails as a subscriber. Create another Amazon SNS topic and configure your CloudWatch alarms to notify this topic when triggered. Create an HTTP subscriber to this topic that notifies your application via HTTP post when an alarm is triggered. Use the AWS SDK tools to integrate your application with Amazon SNS and send messages to the correct team topic when on shift.)

Explanation:

This option fulfills all the requirement. First is to create SNS group so that each member gets the email address and ensure that the application uses HTTP endpoint and SDK for publishing messages.

43. **B** (Re-deploy with a CloudFormation template, define update policy on autoscaling groups in your CloudFormation template.)

 C (Use update policy attribute to specify how CloudFormation handles updates to auto-scaling group resource.)

Explanation:

Auto-scaling group resource supports update policy attribute. This defines how an auto-scaling group policy updates when there is an update in CloudFormation stack is occur.

44. **A** (Dockerrun.aws.json)

Explanation:

Thee Dockerrun.aws.json file is an Elastic BeanStalk json specified file that describes how to deploy docker container as an Elastic BeanStalk application.

45. **B** (The health check is place is not sufficiently evaluating the application function.)

Explanation:

The custom health check is used to evaluate the functionality of the application. If the application functionality is not running and you do not have custom health checks, the instances will still be seemed as healthy.

46. **C** (Use a "Container Command" within an Elastic BeanStalk configuration file to execute the script, ensuring that the "leader only" flag is set to true.)

Explanation:

Container Commands key is used to execute commands that affect application source code. You can use leader only to run the command on a single instance or configure a test to run only the command when a test command evaluates to true.

47. **C** (Configure a web identity federation role within IAM to enable access to the correct Dynamo DB resources and retrieve temporary credentials.)

Explanation:

WIF can let users sign-in utilizing a well-known third-party identity provider such as Login with Amazon, Facebook, Google, or any OpenID Connect (OIDC) 2.0 compatible provider. You can exchange the credentials from that provider for temporary permissions to use resources in your AWS account.

48. **D** (Begin using CloudWatch logs on every service. Stream all log groups into an AWS elastic search service domain running kibana 4 and perform log analysis on a search cluster.)

Explanation:

Amazon Elasticsearch service makes it easy to operate, deploy and scale elastic search for log analytics, full-text search, application monitoring, and many more. It is a service which delivers elastic search easy-to-use API's and real-time capabilities along with availability, scalability and production security required by the workload.

49. **A** (Create a second ELB, and a new auto-scaling group assigned a new launch configuration. Create a new AMI with an updated app. Use Route53 weighted round robin records to adjust the proportion of traffic hitting the two ELBs)

Explanation:

The weighted routing policy of Route53 is used to direct the proportion of traffic to your application. The best policy is to create new ELB, attach to the auto-scaling group and then divert the traffic by using Route53.

50. **B** (Increase your auto-scaling group's number of max servers)

D (Push custom metrics to CloudWatch for your application that include more detailed information about your web application, such as how many requests it is handling and how many are waiting to be processed.)

Explanation:

Option B is valid because the max server is low. Therefore, the application cannot handle the peak load.

Option D ensures that auto-scaling can scale the group to right metrics

51. **C** (Authenticate your users at the application level, and use AWS security token service (STS) and grant token-based authorization to S3 object.)

   E (Use a key-based naming scheme comprised from the user IDs for all user objects in a single Amazon S3 bucket.)

Explanation:

The AWS STS is the web service that enables you to request temporary and limited credentials to IAM users and for users that you want to authenticate.

52. **C** (Post your log data to an Amazon Kinesis data stream, and subscribe your log processing application so that is configured to process your logging data.)

Explanation:

Amazon Kinesis data stream provides collection and analyzing of data in real time which made it easier to respond quickly to the new information.

53. **C** (Create a new auto-scaling group with the new launch configuration and desired capacity same as that of the initial auto-scaling group and associate it with the same load balancer. Once the new auto-scaling group instances got registered with ELB modify the desired capacity of the initial auto-scaling group to zero and gradually delete the old auto-scaling group.)

Explanation:

The blue group is used to carry the production load, and the green group is used for stage and deploy with the new code. When it's time to deploy, you attach the green group to the load balancer to introduce the traffic to the new environment.

54. **D** (Update the launch configuration specified in the AWS CloudFormation template with the new C3 instance type. Also, add an update policy attribute to your auto-scaling group that specifies auto-scaling rolling update. Runa stack update with the new template.)

Explanation:

The auto-scaling group resources support an update policy attribute. This is used to define how auto-scaling resources updated when there is an update in the CloudFormation stack occurs.

55. **B** (Update the launch configuration in the AWS CloudFormation template with the new C3 instance type. Add an update policy attribute to the auto-scaling group that specifies an auto-scaling rolling update. Run a stack update with the updated template.)

Explanation:

Firstly, ensure that the CloudFormation template is updated with the new instance type.

The auto-scaling group resource contains an update policy attribute. Which is used to define that the auto-scaling group is updated when there is the update in the CloudFormation stack occurs. Common approach for updating an auto-scaling group is rolling update, which is done by specifying the auto-scaling rolling update policy.

56. **A** (Use CloudWatch logs agent to send log data from the app to CloudWatch logs from Amazon EC2 instances.)

   C (Once a CloudWatch alarm is triggered, use SNS to notify the senior DevOps engineer.)

   D (Set the threshold your application can tolerate in a CloudWatch logs group and link a CloudWatch alarm on that threshold.)

Explanation:

CloudWatch Logs are used to monitor application and system using log data. It can track the number of errors and notify when the errors reached a defined threshold. It uses logs data for monitoring. Therefore, no code changes are required.

57. **D** (The health check is not checking the application process.)

Explanation:

In the case of the custom health check, you can send information from your health check to auto-scaling. So that auto-scaling can utilize this information.

58. **D** (Set up an auto-scaling group for the web server tier along with an auto-scaling policy that uses the Amazon EC2 CPU utilization CloudWatch metric to scale the instances.)

   G (Use an Amazon RDS multi-AZ deployment.)

Explanation:

The scaling of EC2 instance in an auto-scaling group is usually done with the metric of the CPU utilization of the instance of the auto-scaling group.

Amazon RDS multi-AZ provides durability and availability of database instances and makes hem fit for production database workloads.

59. **D** (Auto-Scaling will select the AZ with 4 EC2 instances and terminate an instance.)

Explanation:

To ensure that the network architecture spans availability zones evenly, the default termination policy is designed.

60. **C** (Using Amazon SNS, create a notification on any Amazon S3 objects that automatically updates a new DynamoDB table to store all metadata about the new object. Subscribe the application to the Amazon SNS topic to update its internal Amazon S3 object metadata cache from the DynamoDB table.)

Explanation:

The best option is to have a notification which then triggers an update to the applicate to update the DynamoDB accordingly.

61. **A** (Create a chef recipe to update this configuration file, configure your AWS OpsWorks stack to use custom cookbooks, and assign this recipe to the configure life cycle event of the specific layer.)

Explanation:

In AWS OpsWorks stacks lifecycle event, each set has a layer of 5 lifecycle events, and each one is associated with set f recipes that are specific to that layer.

62. **C** (Create an Amazon S3 lifecycle configuration to move log files from Amazon S3 to Amazon Glacier after seven days.)

E (Configure your application to write logs to a separate Amazon EBS volume with the "delete or termination" field set to false. Create a script that moves the logs from the instance to Amazon S3 once an hour.)

F (Create a housekeeping script that runs on T2 micro instance managed by an auto-scaling group for high availability. The script uses the AWS API to identify any unattached Amazon EBS volumes containing log files. Your housekeeping script will

mount the Amazon EBS volume, upload all logs to Amazon S3, and then delete the volume.)

Explanation:

To store all logs indefinitely, so glacier is the best option. You can also use the script to put the logs on to a new volume and then move the logs to S3. The EC2 uses the EBS volumes, and the logs are stored in EBS volumes marked for non-termination.

63. **B** (Use of an identity provider like Google or Facebook to exchange for temporary AWS security credentials.)

Explanation:

In WIF, you don't need to create a custom sign-in code or you can manage your own user identity. Users of the app can sign-in using their own IdP, receive an authentication token and exchange that token with temporary security credentials which maps to an IAM role with permission to use the AWS resources in AWS account.

64. **C** (Ship the logs to an Amazon Kinesis Stream and have the consumers analyze the logs in a live manner.)

Explanation:

Kinesis data stream is used for continuous data aggregation and intake. The data intake and processing are in real time, so the processing is typically lightweight.

65. **C** (Create a new launch configuration with the new instance type.)

Explanation:

Create a new configuration, attach it with the existing auto-scaling group and then terminate the running instances.

66. **B** (Add an Amazon S3 bucket policy with a condition statement that requires multi-factor authentication in order to delete objects and enable bucket versioning.)

D (Create an Amazon identity access and management role with authorization to access the Amazon S3 bucket, and launch all of your application's Amazon EC2 instances with this role.)

Explanation:

MFA delete is enabled on versioning bucket by adding another layer of protection.

IAM roles are assigned so that application can be made API requests from the instance securely.

67. **B** (Perform syntax and build test on the continuous integration system before launching the new Amazon EC2 instance units and integration tests.)

Explanation:

Continuous Integration is a developer's practice which requires developers to integrate the code into a shared repository level several times a day. Each of the check-ins is verified by an automated build which allows the team to detect problems early.

68. **B** (Create multiple separate templates for each logical part of the system, create a nested stack in AWS CloudFormation, and maintain several templates to version-control.)

Explanation:

As the infrastructure grows, a common pattern emerges in which you declared the same components in each of the template. Common components can be separate out, and dedicated templates can be created for them. By this way, you can mix and match different templates. Use a nested stack to create a single, unified stack.

69. **C** (Create a docker file to install Node.js and gets the code from git. Use the docker files to perform the deployment on a new AWS Elastic BeanStalk application.)

D (Create an AWS CloudFormation template which creates an instance with the AWS::EC2::Instance resource type and an AMI with docker pre-installed. With user data, install Git to download the Node.js application and then set it up.)

Explanation:

Elastic Beanstalk supports the deployment of the web application by using Docker container. In docker, you can define your own run time and platform.

On launching a new instance on EC2, you have the option of passing user data on the instance that can be used to perform a common automated task and can run the scripts even after the instance starts.

70. **D** (Have the CI system launch a new instance, then bootstrap the code and dependencies on that instance, and create an AMI using the CreateImage API call.)

Explanation:

There is a number of open source system such as Jenkins which can be used as a CI based system. Since the number of calls is fewer in a week.

71. **A** (Use Elastic BeanStalk and re-deploy using application versions.)

Explanation:

AWS Elastic BeanStalk application is perfect for developers to maintain the application version. With Elastic BeanStalk, you can quickly deploy and maintain application without worrying about the infrastructure that runs the application.

72. **A** (AWS Elastic BeanStalk)

Explanation:

With Elastic BeanStalk, you can quickly deploy and maintain application without worrying about the infrastructure that runs the application. It reduces management complexity without restricting choice or control.

73. **D** (Suspend the process AddToLoadBalancer.)

Explanation:

In case if you suspend the AddToLoadBalancer, the auto-scaling launches the instances but does not add them to the target group or load balancer. And if to resume the AddToLoadBalancer, auto-scaling resumes the addition of instance in the target group or load balancer.

74. **A** (Using AWS CloudFormation, create a CloudWatch Log, log group and send the operating system and application logs of interest using the CloudWatch logs agent.)

    C (Using configuration management, set up remote logging to send events to Amazon Kinesis and insert these into Amazon cloud search or Amazon RedShift, depending on the available analytic tool.)

Explanation:

Amazon CloudWatch logs are used to monitor, store or access your log files from Amazon EC2 instances, CloudTrail and other sources. You can also retrieve the associated log data from the CloudWatch Log.

75. **C** (The instances will not be registered with ELB. You must manually register when the process is resumed.)

Explanation:

In case if you suspend the AddToLoadBalancer, the auto-scaling launches the instances but does not add them to the target group or load balancer. And if to resume the

AddToLoadBalancer, auto-scaling resumes the addition of instance in the target group or load balancer.

76. **C** (Use a Creation Policy to wait for the creation of the other dependent resources.)

Explanation:

The Creation Policy instructs the CloudFormation to wait on an instance until unless CloudFormation receives a specified number of signals.

77. **E** (Update the stack using Change Sets.)

Explanation:

When you are updating a stack, you need to understand how changes will affect the running resources. Change Sets allow you to preview how proposed changes affect the running resources.

78. **C** (Use Oldest Launch Configuration to phase out all instances that use the previous configuration.)

   D (Attach an additional auto-scaling configuration behind the ELB and phase in newer instances while removing older instances.)

Explanation:

Auto-scaling terminates the instances that have old configuration policy while using the Old Launch Configuration. This is helpful when you are updating a group and phasing out the instances from the previous configuration.

79. **C** (Applications have many environments, environments have many deployments.)

Explanation:

In EBS, an application serves as a container for the environment that runs your web app, version of web app source codes, saved the configuration, logs and other artifacts which were created while using EBS.

80. **C** (Store your logs in Amazon S3, and use lifecycle policies to archive to Amazon Glacier.)

Explanation:

Life cycle configuration rules are defined for the object that has a well-defined lifecycle.

Life Cycle Configuration is the set of rules that defines action subjected by the S3 to a group of objects.

81. A (io1)

Explanation:

Provisioned IOPS SSD is used in critical business applications that require sustained IOPS performance.

82. D (Configure a Dead Letter Queue)

Explanation:

Elastic BeanStalk worker environment supports Amazon SQS queue service dead letter queues. In dead letter queue, other queues can send messages that for some reasons could not be processed. Messages that are unsuccessful in processing are targeted from source queue to the dead-letter queue. you can gather these type of messages in dead-letter queue to find the reason of their failure.

83. A (Some of the new jobs coming in are malformed and un-processable.)

Explanation:

You have to define how to scale in response to the changing demand while configuring the Dynamic Scaling.

84. B (Use AWS Directory Service AD Connector.)

Explanation:

AD Connector is a directory gateway by which you can redirect the directory request to your existing Microsoft Active Directory without caching any information in the cloud. It is available in two sizes, large and small. Small AD Connector is designed for the organization up to 500 users while the larger supports up to 5000 users organization.

85. A (Install an Amazon CloudWatch Logs agent on every web server during the bootstrap process. Create a CloudWatch Log Group and define a metric filter to create custom metrics that track unique visitors for the streaming web server logs. Create a scheduled task on an Amazon EC2 instance that runs every hour to generate a new report based on the CloudWatch custom metrics.)

C (On the web servers, create a scheduled task that executes a script to rotate and transmit the logs to an Amazon S3 bucket. Ensure that the operating system shut down procedure triggers a log transmission when the EC2 instance is stopped/terminated. Use AWS data pipeline to move log data from the Amazon S3 bucket to Amazon Redshift to process and run reports every hour.)

Explanation:

Use CloudWatch Logs Agent installer to run CloudWatch logs agent on EC2 instances. Amazon Redshift is a standard data warehouse service that is used to analyze data using standard SQL and business intelligence tools.

86. C (There will always be a few seconds of downtime before the application is available.)

Explanation:

The Elastic BeanStalk uses a drop-in upgrade process. There might be a few seconds of downtime. Use rolling deployment to minimize the deployment effects on the production environment.

87. A (Git Credentials.)

B (SSH Keys)

D (AWS Access Keys)

Explanation:

The IAM supports AWS CodeCommit with three types of credentials. Git Credentials is used to communicate with the AWS CodeCommit repositories over HTTPS. SSH Key is a public-private key generated that is used to communicate with the AWS CodeCommit repositories over SSH.

88. C (Elastic BeanStalk)

Explanation:

You can create a docker environment that can support multiple containers per EC2 instance with multi-container docker platform for EBS.

89. A (A second, standby database is deployed and maintain in a different availability zone from the master, using synchronous replication)

Explanation:

Amazon RDS multi-AZ model provides enhanced availability and durability of database instances by making them naturally fit for production database workloads.

90. **A** (Purchase standard reserve instances to run the accounting software. Use scheduled reserved instances to run the batch jobs.)

Explanation:

Standard Reserved Instances provides the best sufficient discount and best suited for steady-state usage. Scheduled reserved instances are available to be launch within the time windows you reserve. By you allow to match your capacity reservation to a predictable recurring schedule which requires a fraction of days, week or a month.

91. **C** (Use MFA on all users and accounts, especially on the root account.)

Explanation:

MFA add more security layer to your account. When you go to the security credential dashboard one of the items is to enable MFA on your root account.

92. **B** (Set-up a DynamoDB global table. Create an auto-scaling group behind an ELB in each of the two regions for your application layer in which the DynamoDB is running in. Add a Route53 latency DNS record with DNS failover, using the ELBs in the two regions as the resource records.)

Explanation:

DynamoDB global tables provide fully-managed solutions for the deployment of multi-region, multi-master database. And you need to maintain and build your own replication solution in DynamoDB global table.

93. **D** (Create a CloudFormation custom resource type by implementing create, update and delete functionality, either by subscribing a custom resource provider to an SNS topic, or by implementing the logic in AWS Lambda.)

Explanation:

Custom resources enable you to write custom provision logic in the templates that AWS CloudFormation can run anytime you create, update or delete stacks.

94. **B** (Use a script which will query the data the keys are created. If older than 2 months, delete them and create new keys.)

Explanation:

CLI command-list-access keys can be used to get the access keys. This command can also return the create date of the key. If create date is older than the 2 months then it will be deleted. The CLI return-list-access key command is used to return the information about the access key ID associated with the specific IAM user. If there are none, the action returns with the empty list.

95. **A** (Adjust the cool down period set for the auto-scaling group.)

    B (Set a custom metric which monitors a key application functionality for the scale-in and scale-out process.)

Explanation:

The auto-scaling cooldown period is a configuration setting that makes sure that auto-scaling does not launch or terminate any additional instance until the previous activity takes place.

96. **C** (3,4,1 and 2)

Explanation:

That is the correct sequence initiated to creating an application, specify the deployment group, specify the deployment configuration, upload the version and then deploy.

97. **B** (Bake an AMI when deploying new versions of code, and use that AMI for the auto-scaling launch configuration.)

Explanation:

The time required to spin-up an instance should be fast. It's better to create an AMI rather than use User data. When using user data, the instance will be run during boot up. An AMI provides the information that is required to launch an instance.

98. **B** (Create a cloud front distribution and direct Route53 to the distribution. Use the ELB as an origin and specify cache behaviors to proxy cache requests which can be served late.)

Explanation:

Cloud Front distribution is used to distribute heavy reads for your application.

99. **C** (Use AWS cost allocation tagging for all resources which support it. Use the cost explorer to analyze costs throughout the month)

Explanation:

The tag is a label that you assign on AWS resource. Each tag consists of a key and a value. Tags are used to organize the resource and, and cost allocation tags are used to track the AWS cost on a detailed level of an application.

100.   **B** (Model your stack in one template, so you can leverage CloudFormation's state management and dependency resolution to propagate all changes)

Explanation:

CloudFormation's best practices are created a nested stack and re-use templates.

101.**A** (Using AWS CloudFormation, create a CloudWatch logs, log group and send the operating system and application logs of interest using the CloudWatch logs agent.)

C (Using configuration management, set up remote logging to send events to Amazon Kinesis and insert these into Amazon Cloud Search or Amazon Redshift, depending on available analytic tools.)

Explanation:

CloudWatch logs are used to monitor, store or access your log files from Amazon EC2 instances, CloudTrails and other AWS resources.

102.   **C** (Swap URL's)

Explanation:

By Swap URL version you can just keep your environment ready. And when you are ready to cut over you can just use the swap URL feature to swap to your new environment.

103.   **A** (In-place Deployment.)

D (Blue/Green Deployment)

Explanation:

In In-place Deployment, the application on each instance in the application group is stopped, the latest application version is installed, and the new version application is started and launched.

In Blue/Green Deployment, the instances of deployment group are replaced by the other set of instances.

104.   **C** (Develop each app in a separate docker container and deploy using Elastic BeanStalk.)

Explanation:

EBS supports the deployment of a web application from docker container. In docker, you can define your run time environment where you can choose your platform, programming language and application dependencies that are not supported by other platforms.

105.   **C** (AWS CloudTrail; CloudWatch Events)

Explanation:

AWS CloudTrail is used to get the history of API calls and other related events. History includes the calls with the AWS management console, AWS CLS, AWS SDK and other services of AWS.

106.   **D** (Blue/Green Deployment.)

Explanation:

EBS performs an in-place update. When you update an application, the application became unavailable to the user for a short period. This can be avoided by using blue/green deployment where you can create a new version in a separate environment and then swap CNames of the two environments to redirect the traffic to new version instantly.

107.   **A** (Use 9001 MTU instead of 1500 for jumbo frames, to raise packet body to packet overhead ratios.)

Explanation:

Jumbo packet allows the data more than 1500 bytes by increasing the payload size per packets. And increasing the percentage of the packet that is not the packet overhead.

108.   **A** (Use a DynamoDB stream specification and stream all changes to AWS Lambda. Log the changes to AWS CloudWatch logs, removing sensitive information before logging.)

Explanation:

In DynamoDB table you can use Lambda function as triggers. Triggers are the responses that received after updating the Dynamo DB table.

109.   **D** (Create a Route53 latency-based routing record with failover and point it to two identical deployments of your stateless API in two different regions. Make sure both regions use auto-scaling group behind ELBs.)

Explanation:

Failover route let you route the traffic to the resource where the resource is healthy or to a different resource when the first resource is unhealthy.

110. **D** (Create some custom CloudWatch metrics which are pertinent to the key features of your application.)

Explanation:

The issue could be relevant to the few features. Enabling CloudWatch all the API calls of all services. The monitoring of CPU utilization will reverify that there is some issue but will not resolve the issue. ELB logs do the same things.

111. D (Blue/Green)

Explanation:

In blue/green deployment you always have the previous version of your application available. If there is an issue with the new version, you can switch back to the older one.

112. **B** (Put the instance in a standby state.)

Explanation:

Auto-scaling enables you to put an instance into the standby state that is in the In-service state, update or troubleshoot the instance and then return the instance into the service.

113. A (AWS Elasticsearch Service)

Explanation:

Elasticsearch is a completely managed service that delivers elastic search easy to use API and real-time capabilities along with the availability, security, and scalability which is required by the production's workload.

114. **B** (Kinesis Firehose + Redshift)

Explanation:

Kinesis Firehose is the easiest way to load streaming data into AWS. It can capture, transform and load the streaming data into Kinesis analytics, S3, Redshift, and

Elasticsearch service. Whereas Redshift is a fully managed, petabyte-scale data warehouse service in the cloud.

115. **B** (S3 is unavailable, so you can't create EBS volumes from a snapshot you use to deploy new volumes.)

Explanation:

The EBS snapshots are stored in S3. If you the script which deploy EC2 instances, then the EBS volume need to be constructed from snapshot stored in S3.

116. **D** (AWS Elastic BeanStalk)

Explanation:

Elastic BeanStalk is capable of deploying the application without worrying about the infrastructure that runs those applications.

117. **C** (Create a new launch configuration with the new instance type.)

Explanation:

The best solution is to create a new launch configuration. Attach it with the auto-scaling group and then terminate the running instance.

118. **A** (Amazon Kinesis)

   B (Amazon S3)

   D (Amazon Lambda)

Explanation:

These are the products which can be integrated with the CloudWatch Logs. In Kinesis data can be fed for real-time analysis. In S3 you can use CloudWatch logs to store your log data in highly durable storage. And the Lambda function is designed to work with CloudWatch Logs.

119. **B** (CodeDeploy)

Explanation:

AWS CodeDeploy is a deployment service that automates the application deployment to on-premises instances or EC2 instances.

120.   **D** (All of the above)

Explanation:

All these three services are used to implement DevOps in a company. AWS EBS is used for deploying and scaling the web application and services developed with Java, PHP, Node.js and Docker, etc. with servers such as Apache, passenger, IIS, and Nginx. OpsWorks is a configuration system that is used to configure and operate applications by using chef. And CloudFormation is an easy way to create and manage AWS resources collection.

121. **C** (You hit the soft limit of 5 EIPs per region and requested a 6th.)

Explanation:

By default, AWS accounts are limited to 5 Elastic IP addresses per region. You can hit a maximum of 5 EIPs per region.

122.   **A** (Route53 Health Checks)

Explanation:

Route53 health checks monitor the health and performance of the web application and servers. The health check that is created is monitor by the health of the specified resource such as web server, the status of Amazon CloudWatch alarms, and the status of our health checks.

123.   **B** (Calculate the bottleneck or constraint on the computer layer, then select that as the new metric, and set the metric thresholds to the bounding values that begin to affect the response latency.)

Explanation:

In the ideal case, the right metric is not used for scale up and down.

124.   **C** (Subscribe your continuous delivery system to an SNS topic that you also tell your CloudFormation stack to publish events into.)

Explanation:

The progress of stack update is monitor by reviewing the stack's event. The start of the stack update process is marked as UPDATE-IN-PROGRESS event for the stack.

125.   **B** (Review CloudWatch metrics for one-minute interval graphs to determine which component(s) slowed the system down.)

Explanation:

If the data points are of the one-minute interval, the graph will not be available in the CloudWatch.

126. **B** (It takes time for the ELB to register the instances, hence there is a small time frame before your instances can start receiving traffic.)

Explanation:

Before start receiving the traffic on EC2 instance, they checked by the ELB health checks, and if the health checks are successful, the EC2 instance changes their state to In-service state, and then the instances start receiving the traffic.

127. **C** (Create a cross-account role for the vendor account and grant that role access to the S3 bucket.)

Explanation:

You share resources in one account with the users in the different account. By cross-account access, you don't need to create individual IAM users in each account. The users don't have to sign out and then sign in in another account to get access to the AWS resources.

128. **A** (Create and start new instances to replace your current online instances. Then delete the current instances.)

   C (On Linux-based instances in Chef 11.10 or older stacks, run the Update Dependencies stack command.)

Explanation:

AWS OpsWorks Stack does not automatically install an update after an instance is online to avoid the interruptions. Instead, you need to manage updates to your online instance by yourself. On Linux-based instance in chef 11.10 or older stack, run the Update Dependencies Stack Command, this installs the current security patches and updates to the specified instances.

129. **C** (ROLLBACK-IN-PROGRESS)

Explanation:

AWS CloudFormation provision and configures the resources by making the call to AWS services that are prescribed in the template. After the resource has been created, AWS CloudFormation reports that stack is created. If stack creation fails, the CloudFormation rolls back the changes by deleting the resources that it created.

130.   **B** (Game ID as the hash key, Highest score as the range key.)

Explanation:

It is best to choose the hash key as the column which has a wide range of values.

131. **A** (AWS Config.)

Explanation:

You can monitor your stack by the following ways. AWS OpsWorks Stack uses Amazon CloudWatch to provide 13 custom metrics with detailed monitoring for each on the instance in the stack.

Similarly, Amazon CloudWatch Logs are used to monitor stacks system, application and custom logs. AWS OpsWorks Stack integrated with CloudTrail to log every API call and store data in S3 bucket.

132.   **A** (Build the application out using AWS Cognito and web identity federation to allow users to log in using Facebook or Google accounts. Once they are logged in, the secret token passed to that user is used to directly access resources on AWS, like AWS S3.)

Explanation:

AWS Cognito easily adds user sign-up and sign-in and manage permissions for your mobile and web app. You can create your on-user identity in Amazon cogito.

133.A (Bid on spot instances just above the asking price as soon as new commits come in, perform all instances configuration and setup, then create an AMI based on the spot instance.)

Explanation:

Amazon EC2 spot instances allow you to bid on spare Amazon EC2 computing capacity. Spot instances are often available on a discount **to** compare to on-demand pricing.

134.   **B** (The ELB stops sending traffic to the instance that failed its health check.)

Explanation:

The load balancer route requests only from the healthy instance. When the instance is unhealthy, it stops routing the request to that instance. It resumes its routing request when the instance becomes again healthy.

135.   **B** (Prebuilt images stored in public or private online image repository.)

Explanation:

Building the custom images during deployment using the docker file is not supported by the multi-container docker platform or EBS. You have to build your images and deploy them to the online repository before creating an Elastic BeanStalk environment.

136.   **A** (Create separate templates based on functionality, create nested stacks with CloudFormation.)

Explanation:

The common pattern can emerge in the same component in each of the template as the infrastructure grows. You can create dedicated templates by separate out common components. You can mix and match different templates by using a nested stack to create a single unified stack.

137.   **B** (Use a Cloud Front distribution with access log delivery to S3. Clicks should be recorded as query string GETs to the distribution. Reports are built and sent by periodically running EMR jobs over the access logs in S3.)

Explanation:

The ideal approach of getting the data onto EMR is to use S3. Since the data is extremely spikey, highly-scaled using edge location through cloud front distribution is the best way to fetch the data. When you are building or analyzing the report of data from a large data set, you need to define EMR because this service is built on Hadoop framework which is used to process a large set of data.

138.   **C** (Create Read Replicas for RDS since the load is mostly read.)

Explanation:

The Amazon RDS Read Replicas provides the enhanced durability and performance for the database instance. This feature makes it elastically easier to scale out beyond the capacity constraint of the single-DB instance for heavy-read workloads.

139.   **B** (Use CloudFormation Nested Stack templates, with three child stacks to represent the three logical layers of your cloud.)

Explanation:

The common pattern can emerge in the same component in each of the templates as the infrastructure grows. You can create dedicated templates by separate out common components. You can mix and match different templates by using a nested stack to create a single unified stack.

140.   **D** (Use a placement group for your instances, so the instances are physically near each other in the same availability zone.)

Explanation:

Placement Group is basically a logical grouping of instances within the single availability zone. They are recommended for that application that are beneficial for low latency network, high latency throughputs or both. To provide the low latency and high packet per second network performance for the placement group, select the instance type that supports enhanced networking.

141.**A** (Use CloudTrail Log File Integrity Validation.)

Explanation:

To detect that the log file is deleted, modified and updated after the CloudTrail delivers it, CloudTrail log file integrity validation is used. This feature is built using industry standards algorithms.

142.   **B** (Rolling Deployments.)

Explanation:

By default, it uses the rolling deployments mechanism when the application is created through the console or EB CLI. Or use all at once deployment when created with different clients (API, SDK or AWS CLI).

143.   **B** (Store your data in Amazon S3, and use lifecycle policies to archive to Amazon Glacier.)

Explanation:

Amazon Glacier is a long term secure and durable storage service that is used for data archiving and long-term back-ups.

Life Cycle Configuration enables you to specify life cycle management rules on the objects in the buckets. The configuration refers to the set of rules, where each rule defines an action on Amazon S3 to apply to the group of objects.

144.   **A** (Deploy.)

Explanation:

AWS OpsWorks stacks triggers deploy events which run each layer deploy recipes when you deploy an application.

145.   **C** (Pending)

Explanation:

Each EC2 instance has a lifecycle, a path that is different from other instances. The instances in Standby state are handled by the auto-scaling group. They are not the active part until you put them back in the service in an application.

146.   **C** (CloudTrail, AWS Config, IAM Credential Reports.)

Explanation:

The AWS CloudTrail is used to get the history of API calls and all the relevant events for your account. The AWS Config enables you to assess, audit and evaluate the configurations of your AWS resources. Ans you can download or generate the credential report which lists all the users in your account and the status of their different credentials.

147.   **B** (Model an AWS EMR job in AWS CloudFormation.)

Explanation:

With AWS CloudFormation, you can update the resources in the existing stack.

148.   **A** (Create a global AWS CloudTrail Trail. Configure a script to aggregate the log data delivered to S3 once per week and deliver this to the CTO.)

Explanation:

AWS CloudTrail is a service that helps you enabling governance, compliance and operational and risk auditing on your account. CloudTrail is used to view, search, archive, download, analyze and respond to the account activity across your AWS infrastructure.

149.   **C** (Create a cross-account IAM role with permission to access the bucket, and grant permission to use the role to the vendor AWS account.)

Explanation:

You can use AWS IAM and AWS STS to setup cross-accounts between the AWS accounts. AWS CloudTrail logs the cross-account activity.

150.   **A** (Choosing the type of environment- Web or worker environment.)

   B (Choosing the platform type- Nide.js, IIS, etc.)

   D (Choosing whether you want a highly available environment or not.)

Explanation:

While creating the Elastic BeanStalk environment, these options appear on the screen. The high availability preset includes a load balancer.

151. **B** (Use CloudWatch to monitor the ELB latency.)

Explanation:

On ELB, high latency is caused by Network Connectivity, ELB configuration, backend web application server issues.

152.   **B** (Memcache.)

Explanation:

AWS specify that OpsWorks Stacks provide built-in support to Memcache.

153.   **B** (Use the Amazon SQS Extended Client Library for Java and Amazon S3 as a storage mechanism for message bodies.)

Explanation:

Amazon SQS is managed with Amazon S3. Because this is useful for carrying and consuming the message of up to 2GB. Use Amazon SQS Extended Client Library with java to manage Amazon SQS with Amazon S3.

154.   **A** (ELB SSL Termination.)

Explanation:

If you are using SSL termination, your server will never get the secure connection. And you cannot know your user is using a secure connection or not.

155.   **C** (Snapshotting an encrypted volume makes an encrypted snapshot; restoring an encrypted snapshot always creates an encrypted volume.)

Explanation:

Snapshots that are taken from encrypted volume are automatically encrypted, and similarly, volumes that are created from encrypted snapshots are also encrypted.

156.   **A** (Create a second ELB, Auto-Scaling Launch Configuration, Auto-Scaling Group using the Launch Configuration. Create AMIs with all codes pre-installed. Assign the new AMI with Auto-scaling Launch Configuration. Use Route53 Weighted Round Robin Records to adjust the proportion of traffic hitting two ELBs.)

Explanation:

You can shift the traffic all at once, or you can do a weighted distribution. In Amazon Route53, you can define the percentage traffic going through the green environment, and then it gradually updates the weight until the green environment carries the full traffic of production. Weighted Distributions provides the capability to perform the canary analysis., where a little percentage of the production traffic introduced to the new environment.

157.   **C** (You did not request a limit increase on concurrent Lambda function executions.)

Explanation:

Every Lambda function is associated with a fixed amount of allocated resources regardless of memory allocation, and each of the function is allocated with a fixed amount of code storage per function.

158.   **B** (Use the Auto-Scaling Rolling Update Policy on CloudFormation template auto-scaling group.)

Explanation:

The auto-scaling group resource supports an update policy attribute. This defines how auto-scaling group updates when an update in CloudFormation occurs. The auto-scaling group is updated by the rolling update, which is performed by specifying the Auto-Scaling Rolling update Policy

159.   **A** (It will rollback all the resources that were created up to the failure point.)

Explanation:

The AWS CloudFormation ensures that all stacks are created or deleted appropriately. Because CloudFormation treats the stack as a single unit. If a resource is not created, the CloudFormation rolls the stack back and delete the resources that were created.

160.   **B** (Re-deploy with a CloudFormation template, define update policies on Auto-Scaling groups in your CloudFormation template.)

C (Use Update Policy attribute with Auto-Scaling Rolling update policy on Cloud Formation to deploy new code.)

Explanation:

The auto-scaling group resource supports an update policy attribute. This defines how auto-scaling group updates when an update in CloudFormation occurs. The auto-scaling group is updated by the rolling update, which is performed by specifying the Auto-Scaling Rolling update Policy. This retains the same auto-scaling group by replacing the old instances with a new one.

161. **B** (DynamoDB table with roughly equal read and write throughput, with ElastiCache, caching.)

Explanation:

With caching, you can miss a roughly equal number of read and write because majority will hit 1% of scores. So for that reason, we use AWS ElastiCache as caching because it is able to cache DynamoDB query rather than a distributed proxy cache for content delivery. Because CloudFront cannot directly cache DynamoDB queries.

162.   **A** (When using AWS SDKs and Amazon EC2 roles, you do not have to explicitly retrieve API keys, because the SDK handles retrieving them from the Amazon EC2 MetaData service.)

Explanation:

When you use IAM roles, then you do not need to manage the applications access because IAM role securely allow the instance to make API calls without any need of credentials.

163.   **A** (Once a CloudWatch alarm is triggered, use SNS to notify the Senior DevOps Engineer.)

C (Set the threshold your application can tolerate in a CloudWatch metric and link a CloudWatch alarm on that threshold.)

Explanation:

For monitoring of application and system, you use CloudWatch log that has logs data and for notification about the alarm is sent via SNS. On the basis of CloudWatch metric threshold is set.

164.   **C** (Use Elastic BeanStalk and re-deploy using Application Versions)

Explanation:

Using Elastic BeanStalk is best for development as it quickly deploys the application in the cloud and your management complexity reduces and in Elastic BeanStalk versions of the application is automatically managed.

165.   **B** (Saved Configurations)

Explanation:

As you want to save the environment state, so it is the configuration. Save the configuration in S3 which is in YAML format, so it can be used for the creation of a new environment or to restore the running environment on the same state.

166.   **A** (Create an AWS CloudFormation template which creates an instance with the AWS::EC2::Instance resource type and an AMI with Docker pre-installed. With UserData, install Git to download the Node.js application and then set it up.)
    B (Create a Docker file to install Node.js. and gets the code from Git. Use the Dockerfile to perform the deployment on a new AWS Elastic BeanStalk application.)

Explanation:

During the launch of the instance, you can define the configuration tasks and script run on an instance in user data. So using CloudFormation template to create an instance with pre-installed Docker AMI is good. You can also Docker container with Elastic BeanStalk. In a container, you define all requirement and use this container with Elastic BeanStalk to deploy an application.

167.   **C** (Add an Amazon S3 bucket policy with a condition statement that requires multi-factor authentication in order to delete objects and enable bucket versioning.)
    D (Create an Amazon Identity and Access Management role with authorization to access the Amazon S3 bucket, and launch all of your application's Amazon EC2 instances with this role.)

Explanation:

By enabling MFA to delete on versioned bucket you can secure the integrity of bucket, and by defining IAM roles to S3 bucket your application securely makes an API request to instances, and you do not need to share your AWS credentials.

168.　**D** (Create a new load balancer with new Amazon EC2 instances, carry out the deployment, and then switch DNS over to the new load balancer using Amazon Route53 after testing.)

Explanation:

For blue/ green deployment you can carry out this deployment, and for that, you first create new ELB with EC2 instances and then use Route53 weighted routing policy to distribute traffic. Once testing is performed, you switch the DNS over the new environment.

169.　**B** (Store your logs in Amazon S3, and use lifecycle policies to archive to Amazon Glacier.)

Explanation:

For storing logs, you can use S3 to store logs that are frequently accessed and then by defining lifecycle policy you can move the files in Glacier because now they are less frequently access over a long time. Glacier is best to choose for long term archival.

170.　**D** (Ship the logs to an Amazon Kinesis Stream and have the consumers analyze the logs in a live manner.)

Explanation:

For rapid data intake and real-time processing of data like logs, market data, etc. you can use Kinesis Streams.

171. **A** (Implement a Route53 weighted routing policy that distributes the traffic between your on-premises application and the AWS application depending on weight.)

Explanation:

By using Weighted routing policy, you can shift a small percentage of the user to the resource and then gradually increase the number of users on AWS. You can use this routing policy for load balancing on a single domain that is linked to multiple resources and for testing new versions.

172. **C** (Update the launch configuration in the AWS CloudFormation template with the new C3 instance type. Add an UpdatePolicy attribute to the Auto Scaling group that specifies an AutoScalingRollingUpdate. Run a stack update with the updated template.)

Explanation:

To change the instance type, you can change the template and also update policy attribute of auto-scaling in which you specify to perform updates on auto-scaling on updating in the stack. This is done by defining Rolling Update Policy for auto-scaling. So it replaces the old instance with new.

173. **A** (Have the CI system launch a new instance, then bootstrap the code and dependencies on that instance, and create an AMI using the CreateImage API call.)

Explanation:

As the number of calls is less so open source like Jenkins for CI based system. It is used as automation server and as simple CI. So using CI system launch the instance and user data define bootstrap code and then create AMI by using CreateImage API.

174. **B** (Update the template and then update the stack with the new template. Only those resources that need to be changed will be changed. All other resources which do not need to be changed will remain as they are.)

Explanation:

In CloudFormation whenever you perform changes, then the stack is updated with a new template and changes perform to only those resource on which changes occur otherwise remaining resources work same as they are in the previous template.

175. **B** (Use an Amazon RDS Multi-AZ deployment.)
     D (Set up an Auto Scaling group for the web server tier along with an Auto Scaling policy that uses the Amazon EC2 CPU utilization CloudWatch metric to scale the instances.)

Explanation:

For high availability and durability of RDS, you can perform Multi-AZ deployment as it synchronously replicates the data to standby instance in other AZ. For scaling of EC2 instance in Auto Scaling, you use CPU utilization metric.

176.   **C** (Pre-build stage: Login into ECR using "aws ecr get-login" and set the repository URI. Post-build stage: Push the image to your ECR repository such as "docker push $REPOSITORY_URI:latest.")

Explanation:

In pre-build stage login to ECR with aws-ecr get-login command and set the repository URL with Git commit ID of the source. Then in build, the Docker image is built with the tag of recent Git commit ID. Now in post-build stage, this image is pushed to ECR with both tags.

177.   **B** (For EC2 instances including Amazon Linux, Ubuntu, and Windows, the ECS agent can be installed. However, for on-premise Redhat server, unfortunately, the ECS agent cannot be installed since Amazon ECS container agent is only supported on Amazon EC2 instances.)

Explanation:

ECS agent is used to connecting your instance to cluster. You can install it on EC2 instance as it only supported by EC2 if you have any on-premises server than ECS agent is not supported.

178.   **A** (Create a new Change Set and use it to identify what changes may happen. Do the necessary backup before executing the Change Set. If everything is good, execute the Change Set and use the CloudFormation console to monitor.)

Explanation:

By using the changeset, you identify what changes happen when the stack is updated. Also, perform some backups before applying changeset. Because it shows how changes in stack impact the resources that are running. Once you view that everything is rightly done then execute the changeset.

179.   **C** (The team should use revision control to manage the CloudFormation template, for example, using GitHub otherwise it is hard to track who and how the changes are made. The changes need code reviews as well to ensure the quality.)

Explanation:

As per given scenario's, you observe that anyone from developer's department can change the template and upload directly, so you do not have revision control to manage the

template. For keeping all the resources changes history, you need to use code review and revision controls. In this way, you can track changes of a different version of templates.

180. **D** (Associate the Amazon RDS database server when the developer creates the app or later by editing the app. When the app is deployed, AWS OpsWorks Stacks creates a file on each of the built-in application server instances containing the connection data. Then a custom recipe can be used to extract the connection information from the deploy attributes and put it in a file that can be read by the application.)

Explanation:

For connecting RDS MySQL DB, you need to associate it with the app while creating or later. Now deploy an app via OpsWorks stacks. Stack create each built-in application instances file in which connection data is present. But you can't access this data it can only be accessible via recipes. Through this data, you can connect to DB. So for access, you need to create a custom recipe that takes the connection information from the deploy attributes and puts it in a file that can be read by the application.

181. **B** (In this case, as CodeStar has used CodeCommit to manage the code repo, you can modify application resource name in the template.yml file in the CodeCommit Repo. This is also the AWS CloudFormation file that models your application's runtime environment.)

Explanation:

Rather than manually changing the resources from infrastructure you can use CloudFormation. Because via this you can modify any application resource in runtime by editing in the template. Like you want to change the name of the resource, so you define this in it.

182. **C** (Use an editor to write a template using JSON, Add a parameter section for the SSH Key such as "MyKeyPair." For new instances, use the keyword of "Ref" to use this parameter. Save the template in S3 and upload it during stack creation.)

Explanation:

For template writing in JSON or YAML format you can use AWS CloudFormation, and in this template, there is parameter section for customizing the template. Via parameter, you enable input value during the creation of stack and by using Ref function the input value is used as the provision of stacks.

183. **D** (Modify the environment's capacity settings to a load balanced environment type with autoscaling. Select all availability zones. Also, add a scaling trigger if average CPU Utilization is over 85% for a 5 minutes period.)

Explanation:

In Elastic Bean Stalk you can choose either load balancing, auto-scaling or single instance type. Depends on your requirements. Like from single instance deployment you can change the environment to load balancing.

184. **A** (Create a new Data Pipeline to transfer the data from DynamoDB table to an S3 bucket. Add a schedule for this pipeline to activate it every day at a suitable time and then open the collected files in S3.)

Explanation:

For automating the movement and processing of any amount of data, you can use AWS Data Pipeline that uses data-driven workflows and built-in dependencies checking. You have multiple options like Run Once, run on activation, Run repeatedly within a data range. Once Data Pipeline is created you can add schedule like run every day or starting and ending time.

185. **A** (Amazon CloudWatch Events can be used to monitor the AWS Cloud resources including CodePipeline. The operation team can create a rule in Amazon CloudWatch Events based on CodePipeline metrics that you define such as "CodePipeline Pipeline Execution State Change." And then use an SNS topic as the target of this Cloudwatch Event rule.)

D (AWS CloudTrail can be used to log AWS CodePipeline API calls and related events made by or on behalf of an AWS account. By CloudTrail, users can determine the request that was made to AWS CodePipeline, the IP address from which the request was made, who made the request, when it was made, and additional details.)

Explanation:

To monitor AWS services, so that ensure everything is running properly then use CloudWatch Events for monitoring of resource and CloudTrail to log API calls and respective events. So for monitoring of CodePipeline: CloudWatch and CloudTrail are best.

186.   **A** (The DevOps engineer should create a trigger in AWS CodeDeploy that publishes an Amazon Simple Notification Service (Amazon SNS) topic for the relevant AWS CodeDeploy deployment event. Then, when that event occurs, all subscribers to the associated topic will receive notifications through the endpoint specified in the topic, such as an SMS message or email message to the development lead.)

Explanation:

To notify the development Lead in time then the most straight forward way is to use SNS. As SNS is the best tool to notify all subscriber about the event occur.

187.   **B** (Nothing as data in AWS CodeCommit repositories is already encrypted in transit and at rest.)

Explanation:

When data is inserted in CodeCommit repository, then it encrypts the data when it receives as it stored in the repository. When the user pulls data from it, CodeCommit decrypts and send so in that encryption of data is done at rest or at transit.

188.   **A** (The "Swap URL" has used Route53 to change the DNS settings. It may bring in some TTL issue as DNS clients may exist at various levels and not all of them obey TTL rules.)

Explanation:

When you use Swap URL then after completing swap operation must verify that the new environment responds by using old environment URL before deleting old environment as DNS changes are propagated. DNS client exists at various level and all of then not carry out TTL rules.

189.   **B** (In CodePipeline, add a Source stage with CodeCommit. Add a Build stage with CodeBuild to build a new Docker container image and push it to ECR. Add a Deploy stage that uses CloudFormation to create a new task definition revision that points to the newly built Docker container image and updates the ECS service to use the new task definition revision.)

Explanation:

In the source stage, you use CodeCommit for accessing the source code repository. Secondly, the Build stage uses CodeBuild to create a new Docker container image based upon the latest source code and pushes it to an ECR repository. The Deploy stage uses CloudFormation to create a new task that points to the newly built Docker container

image and updates the ECS service to use the new task definition revision. After this is done, ECS initiates a deployment by fetching the new Docker container from ECR and restarting the service.

190.   **C** (Use a parameter for the user to input the AMI ID when the stack is created. Make sure that the parameter has the type as AWS::EC2::Image::Id.)

Explanation:

For AMI id Fn::FindInMap and mapping is best but here there is no need to use this. So by using Parameter, you can define specific parameter type in details as it only uses one AMI id.

191. **D** (Create a new CloudTrail and configure an S3 bucket for the trail. By default, CloudFormation service is included, and all CloudFormation API calls will be recorded as CloudTrail events. The events contain lots of useful information that the security team cares about.)

Explanation:

For API tracking we use CloudTrail, and for the trail, we use S3 bucket. By default, CloudTrail has the capability to track all API calls as CloudTrail event.

192.   **A** (The stack should have three 24/7 instances, which are always on and handle the base load. Add 12 time-based instances and modify the number of time-based instances every two hours. Add 2 load-based instances to handle traffic spikes.)

Explanation:

As you want to manage multiple application server instances then use mix-up of all three types;

24/7 instances are manually started and run continuously until they are manually stopped.

Time-based instances are started automatically and stopped on the basis of schedule by OpsWorks stack

Load-based instances are started and stopped on the basis of load metrics.

193.   **A** (IAM users that have been added to an AWS CodeStar project as team members.)

B (Git credentials (user name and password) for the IAM users that the developers use.)

Explanation:

If CodeStar uses CodeCommit to store source code, then the user must be a member of CodeStar project. To use Eclipse as code changes directly user must be IAM user which is added to CodeStar as a member if source code store in CodeCommit then Git credentials is used for IAM user and enough permission to install Eclipse and toolkit of AWS to Eclipse on the computer.

194.   **A** (In CodeStar management console, on the "Team members" page, add the developers as Contributor, add the UI designer and the scrum master as Viewer as both of them need read-only access)

Explanation:

In CodeStar you can add any team member in the project if you have full access policy or owner role in CodeStar. In CodeStar role you can define owner, contributor and viewer role to the user. So for we assign UI and Scrum master a viewer role as they need read-only access and Developer a contributor role. The head developer has Owner Role.

195.   **D** (Use dockerrun.aws.json v2 for the multidocker environment. This file describes the containers to deploy to each container instance.)

Explanation:

For deploy multicontainer environment in Elastic BeanStalk then you need to use dockerrun.aws.json v2. As this command define he to deploy Docker container as EB application.

196.   **A** (Since it is for production, it is suggested to put the RDS database outside of the Elastic BeanStalk environment. This can be done by using your application to connect to it on launch.)

Explanation:

For production environment best choice to connect RDS to EB environment is to create RDS outside the environment. Because if you create an instance within the environment, then it attaches with the lifecycle policy of Applications' environment.

197.   **A** (Launch an Amazon EC2 instance to host the Jenkins server and use an IAM role to grant the instance the required permissions for interacting with AWS CodePipeline.

Then create a new CodePipeline. In the build stage, choose "Add Jenkins" and configure correct "Provider name" and "Server URL.")

Explanation:

When you use Jenkins, CodeBuild as build provider in CodePipeline. So in build stage select Jenkins as build provider. Then enter the provider name as Plugin for Jenkin that you define in CodePipeline. In Provider name, type the name of the action you provided in the AWS CodePipeline. In Server URL, type the URL of the Amazon EC2 instance where Jenkins is installed. In Project name, type the name of the project you created in Jenkins.

198.   **A** (Make sure the correct SNS topic is created because when CodeDeploy Deployment Group is being created, one SNS topic is required to subscribe to the CodeDeploy application, which is a mandatory step)
C (Make sure that you have a service role that trusts AWS CodeDeploy with correct permissions. This should be done before creating the Deployment Group in CodeDeploy. IAM should be involved for that by creating a new role, and the role type is AWS Service.)
D (Prepare an autoscaling group with Min 4 and Max 8 instances. Make sure that the autoscaling group has the correct autoscaling launch configurations attached. You can use the prebaked AMI to install some configuration packages for the instances.)

Explanation:

These are the following steps that need to be created first before creating a deployment group in CodeDeploy.

- Make sure the correct SNS topic is created because when CodeDeploy Deployment Group is being created, one SNS topic is required to subscribe to the CodeDeploy application, which is a mandatory step
- Make sure that you have a service role that trusts AWS CodeDeploy with correct permissions. This should be done before creating the Deployment Group in CodeDeploy. IAM should be involved for that by creating a new role, and the role type is AWS Service.
- Prepare an autoscaling group with Min 4 and Max 8 instances. Make sure that the autoscaling group has the correct autoscaling launch configurations attached. You can use the prebaked AMI to install some configuration packages for the instances.)

199.   **C** (In order to work on existing CodeCommit Repo for other developers, create an IAM group with a suitable CodeCommit policy. Add users to that group. Then all developers are able to git clone the CodeCommit Repo and start working on their own branches.)

   D (Set up new CodeCommit Repo using AWS CLI. Find the repo url which may be an HTTPS or SSH one. Use git push to upload the repo from local to CodeCommit server. After that, inspect if the files show properly in CodeCommit.)

Explanation:

To shift the Git repository to CodeCommit then first create repository in CodeCommit then clone the repository and push in the CodeCommit and view files in CodeCommit. Now give this repository to the other developer by creating IAM group with policy.

200.   **C** (The health check is not accurate. The classic ELB HTTP health check should point to a file that only exists after the new instances are ready to serve.)

Explanation:

In ELB health checks is used to specify whether the instance is able to send traffic to it or not.

201.   **B** (Deploy 3 EC2 instances in one availability zone and 3 in another availability zone and use Amazon Elastic Load Balancer.)

Explanation:

ELB supports in multiple AZ not across the region so for high Availability best option is to place 3 in one AZ and other 3 in other AZ.

202.   **C** (Create an AMI of the EC2 instance and copy the AMI to the desired region)

Explanation:

AMI of instances can be copied into another region or within the region via console, CLI and SDK.

203.   **C** (You hit the soft limit of 5 EIPs per region when creating the development environment.)

Explanation:

There is a limit of EIP's in a region, so when creating a development environment you hit the limit of EIP, that's why the creation of a production environment fails.

204. **B** (Use Route53 with the failover option to failover to a static S3 website bucket or CloudFront distribution.)

Explanation:

By configuring DNS failover in Route53, you can route traffic from one resource that is unhealthy to the healthy resource. If multiple resources perform the same function.

205. **C** (Modify the Auto Scaling Group cooldown timers) and **D** (Modify the Amazon CloudWatch alarm period that triggers your AutoScaling scale down policy.)

Explanation:

In auto scaling group cold down timer is configurable so try to change it does not launch and terminate the instances before the effect of previously task taken. Or by defining the threshold in CloudWatch trigger which is appropriate for scaling down, you can overcome this issue.

206. **B** (Use Lifecycle policies to move the data onto Amazon Glacier after a period of 3 months)

D (Store the log files as they emitted from the application on to Amazon Simple Storage Service)

Explanation:

First store file in S3 as this is most durable storage and by defining lifecycle policies to move it after 3 months into Glacier.

207. **A** (us-west-2a with 6 instances, us-west-2b with 6 instances, us-west-2c with 0 instances)

C (us-west-2a with 3 instances, us-west-2b with 3 instances, us-west-2c with 3 instances)

Explanation:

As they want 6 instances available all the time, so the best option is to deploy 3 instances in each AZ or deploy 6 instances in 2 AZ and one AZ with 0 instances.

208. **D** (Create CloudWatch alarms for StatuscheckFailed_System metrics and select EC2 action-Recover the instance)

Explanation:

By creating CloudWatch alarm action, he creates an alarm which automates the stopping, termination, and recovery of EC2 instances if system status check fails.

209.   **C** (Amazon S3, because it provides unlimited amounts of storage data, scales automatically, is highly available, and durable)

Explanation:

S3 is the most durable storage, scale easily and host a huge amount of data.

210.   **A** (Define the tags on the test and production servers and add a condition to the IAM policy which allows access to specific tags)

Explanation:

Tagging is the best option to define which instance belongs to which department, and by defining IAM policy, you can define control access to these tags.

211. **C** (Consider not using a Multi-AZ **A** RDS deployment for the development database)

Explanation:

For a production environment, Multi-AZ is best, but for development department multi-AZ DB is not a good option. So to reduce cost, you can remove Multi-AZ DB.

212.   **D** (Output)

Explanation:

By defining in output attribute, you can return the value of DNS of ELB by using Fn::GetAtt.

213.   **A** (Write a cronjob that uses the AWS CLI to take a snapshot of production EBS volumes. The data is durable because EBS snapshots are stored on the Amazon S3 standard storage class)

Explanation:

By taking a snapshot of EBS volume and store it in S3, you store the snapshot in durable storage.

214.   **A** (Encrypt the file system on an EBS volume using Linux tools) and **C** (Enable S3 Encryption)

Explanation:

For storing critical data, you can use encryption in EBS volume and encryption in S3. With EBS encryption at rest, you can encrypt data at rest, in transit and snapshot created from the volume.

215.   **D** (Create a parameter in the Cloudformation template and then use the Condition clause in the template to create an S3 bucket if the parameter has a value of development)

Explanation:

In the template, you can use a parameter which inputs the environment type, and on the basis of the environment, it creates the resources. In this way, you reuse the template.

216.   **A** (This is because the underlying EC2 Instances are created with no persistent local storage)

Explanation:

When you use non-persistence local storage then whenever you terminate the EC2 instance the data will be deleted so try to store the data in persistence storage.

217.   **D** (Use an SQS queue to decouple the application components)

Explanation:

As we know SQS is the best service for message querying and reliable communication at any scale among Distributed components and microservices.

218.   **C** (Enable Multi-AZ feature for the AWS RDS database.)

Explanation:

By using Multi-AZ feature, you can make this architecture more self-healing because of Multi-AZ you can enhance availability and durability of DB. In Multi-AZ a primary DB replicate data synchronously to standby DB in another AZ.

219.   **B** (Create a CloudWatch event which will trigger the Lambda function) and **D** (Create a Lambda function which will write the event to CloudWatch logs)

Explanation:

For logs of the instance, you can create a CloudWatch event in which whenever the instance is added or terminate from auto-scaling group it triggers Lambda function then Lambda writes event in CloudWatch Logs.

220. **A** (This is because the underlying EC2 Instances are created with no persistent local storage)

Explanation:

The reason behind this issue is that in the environment the instance is created with non-persistence storage so when instance terminated the data is not saved, and it is lost.

221. **A** (Use Web identity federation to authenticate the users)

Explanation:

By using web identity federation, you can configure the identity provider to access resources in AWS. The identity provider which is supported is FB, Google, and Amazon.

222. **D** (5 minutes)

Explanation:

In OpsWorks stack each instance has an agent that communicates continuously with service for monitoring the health if the agent is not able to communicate with the service for more than 5 minutes then OpsWorks stack declare it as a failed instance.

223. **B** (Ensure the recipe is placed as part of the Setup Lifecycle event as part of the Layer setting.)
      D (Ensure the custom cookbooks option is set in OpsWorks stack.)

s:

In OpsWorks layer there is lifecycle event which has its built-in recipes. When particular lifecycle event occurs that associated recipe runs on that stack. By enabling option custom Cookbooks, you can use custom cookbooks.

224. **C** (Enable CloudTrail logs so that the API calls can be recorded)

Explanation:

Via CloudTrail you can track the API calls on any AWS resource in AWS account. So by enabling CloudTrail in CloudFormation, you can keep track of all API calls made to the CloudFormation.

225. **D** (AutoScalingRollingUpdate)

Explanation:

In the auto scaling group, you have an update policy attribute which performs updates whenever the CludFormation stack is updated. The common approach to performing the update is a rolling update that can be done by defining AutoScalingRollingUpdate policy.

226. **B** (eb create)

Explanation:

To deploy an application quickly and easily you can use Elastic BeanStalk. EB CLI has multiple supported commands:

- eb init – Use eb init to create an Elastic Beanstalk directory in an existing project directory and create a new Elastic BeanStalk application for the project.
- eb branch – EB CLI 3 does not include the command eb branch.
- eb push and git aws.push – EB CLI 3 does not include the commands eb push or git aws.push. Use eb deploy to update your application code.
- eb start – EB CLI 3 does not include the command eb start. Use eb create to create an environment.
- eb update – EB CLI 3 does not include the command eb update. Use the eb config to update an environment.
- eb stop – EB CLI 3 does not include the command eb stop. Use eb terminate to completely terminate an environment and clean up.

Now EB CLI is depreciated and using CLI in which eb create command is used to create a new environment and deploy application version in it. With this command, you define the specific environment name.

227. **C** (Use the Elastic Beanstalk service to provision an IIS platform web environment to host the application.)

D (Create a source bundle for the .Net code and upload it as an application revision.)

Explanation:

By using Elastic BeanStalk to deploy an application you can define your desired platform with the application code. Make the code in Zip or WAR format.

228. **A** (CreationPolicy attribute)

D (AWS::CloudFormation::WaitCondition)

Explanation:

To coordinate the stack resource creation with other configuration actions which are outside the creation of stack and for tracking the status of the configuration process, you can use Creation policy and AWS::CloudFormation::WaitCondition resource.

229.   **A** (Create a Docker container for the custom application and then deploy it to Elastic BeanStalk.)

Explanation:

By using Docker container, you can move your custom applications to AWS. Docker Container is supported in EB. Docker Container is used in such cases where the EB supported platform is not valid for the desired application.

230.   **C** (All at once)

Explanation:

In that deployment technique, there is no downtime, and it deploys code to all existing instances and in case of deployment failed the downtime occurs and for rollback redeploy occur.

231.   **B** (CloudTrail)

Explanation:

Integration of DynamoDB with CLoudTrail you can keep track of all the API request that is made to the table and then these logs are stored in S3 bucket.

232.   **B** (AWS CodeDeploy) and **D** (AWS CodePipeline)

Explanation:

For automatic deployment of the application, you can use AWS CodeDeploy that automates the deployment of AWS instances and On-premises instances. For continuous delivery, you can use CodePipeline so it can model and automate the steps required for software releases.

233.   **D** (appspec.yml)

Explanation:

When you deploy the application via CodeDeploy then in the source file you must add appspec.yml which include what needs to be installed on instances from application files

in S3 or Github and lifecycle event that attach to run on the response of lifecycle event at deployment.

234.   **C** (The stack has an S3 bucket defined which has objects present in it.) and **D** (The stack has an EC2 Security Group which has EC2 Instances attached to it.)

Explanation:

Before deleting the stack, you need to delete some resources like objects in S3, EC2 instances in Auto Scaling group, etc.

235.   **A** (Use the CloudFormation service. Create separate templates for each application revision and deploy them accordingly.)
        B (Use the Elastic Beanstalk service. Use Application versions and upload the revisions of your application. Deploy the revisions accordingly and rollback to prior versions accordingly.)

Explanation:

For the provision of all resource in a cloud environment, you can use CloudFormation. In simple template file you define the resources, and then CloudFormation automatically and securely provision the resources. By using Elastic BeanStalk, you can deploy your application with its versions. Each version is unique, and you can deploy any version at any time quickly.

236.   **A** (In the App for OpsWorks deployment, specify the git url for the recipes which will deploy the applications in the docker environment.)
        C (Use custom cookbooks for your OpsWorks stack and provide the Git repository which has the chef recipes for the Docker containers.)

Explanation:

In OpsWorks you can deploy and manage any application regardless of size and shape. In OpsWorks you can create a layer of Docker which uses Chef recipes for Docker container. The recipes are in the Git repository, and for that, you must use custom cookbooks option. In the app, you define URL for recipes that need to be deployed on the application in a container.

https://aws.Amazon.com/blogs/DevOps/running-docker-on-aws-opsworks/

237.   **C** (buildspec.yml)

Explanation:

For build process in CodeBuild, you need to define buildspec.yml file in the source code that contains the build command and its related setting in YAML format.

238.   **B** (AWS::CloudFormation::Stack)

Explanation:

The nested stack is a concept in which you create a stack in another stack, and for that, you use AWS::CloudFormation::Stack command. Deployment and management of all resources for nested stack can be done from a single stack. You can also use the output of one stack as input to another stack.

239.   **A** (Use an HTTPS front end listener for your ELB) and **C** (Use an SSL front end listener for your ELB)

Explanation:

When you use ELB which uses SSL/TLS protocol for encryption, then this enables encryption at transit between a client that initiates with HTTPS or connection to EC2 instance. If you use HTTPS or SSL for frontend connection, then for that you need to deploy an X.509 certificate (SSL server certificate) on your load balancer. The load balancer decrypts request from clients before sending them to the back-end instances.

240.   **C** (Deploy the application to an Elastic BeanStalk environment. Have a secondary Elastic BeanStalk environment in place with the updated application code. Use the swap URL's feature to switch onto the new environment.)
        D (Deploy the application using OpsWorks stacks. Have a secondary stack for the new application deployment. Use Route53 to switch over to the new stack for the new application update.)

Explanation:

By using Elastic Beanstalk and OpsWorks, you can deploy an application without worrying about management. In both services, you can deploy Blue/Green deployment.

241.   **B** (Use the CFN helper scripts to signal once the resource configuration is complete.)
        D (Use the CreationPolicy to ensure it is associated with the EC2 Instance resource.)

Explanation:

By defining creation policy of resource with additional actions you can proceed the creation of stack. And by using CFN helper, you can define that one the resource configuration complete its provide signal.

242. **C** (The stacks were created without the custom cookbooks option. Just change the stack settings accordingly.)

Explanation:

For the use of Custom cookbooks, you need to enable the option of custom cookbooks at creation time. If it is not enabled, then you cannot define the custom recipes.

243. **A** (Ensure that the CodeDeploy agent is installed on the EC2 Instance)
      D (Ensure an IAM role is attached to the instance so that it can work with the Code Deploy Service.)

Explanation:

For working of EC2 instance with CodeDeploy, you need to install CodeDeploy agent on the instance and ensure that IAM role is attached to the instance to allow work with CodeDeploy.

244. **D** (Create a new CloudTrail trail with one new S3 bucket to store the logs and with the global services option selected. Use IAM roles S3 bucket policies, and Multi-Factor Authentication (MFA) Delete on the S3 bucket that stores your logs.)

Explanation:

When you integrate an IAM with CloudTrail then what are events made on behalf of your account CloudTrail keep logs of this. These logs files then sent to S3 bucket.

245. **B** (Use server-side encryption for S3)
      C (Encrypt all EBS volumes attached to EC2 Instances)
      D (Use SSL/HTTPS when using the Elastic Load Balancer)

Explanation:

In EBS encryption can be done by encryption all data on EBS volume, in S3 encryption at rest or transit is done via SSL/TLS, Client-side encryption, and server-side encryption. ELB uses SSL/TLS protocol for encryption. When you use ELB which uses SSL/TLS protocol for encryption, then this enables encryption at transit between a client that initiates with HTTPS or connection to EC2 instance. If you use HTTPS or SSL for frontend connection, then you need to deploy an X.509 certificate (SSL server certificate)

on your load balancer. The load balancer decrypts request from clients before sending them to the back-end instances.

246.   **C** (Bake an AMI when deploying new versions of code, and use that AMI for the Auto Scaling Launch Configuration.)

Explanation:

As they want to provide instances as quickly as possible, then it's better to choose the creation of AMI rather than defining in User data. In AMI you define the information that is needed for the launching of instances.

247.   **C** (EC2 system manager)

Explanation:

With the use of EC2 system manager, you can automate the collection of software inventory, applying of patches, system image creation, and configuration of OS (Linux and Windows). The system manager is automation which can be used for patches, bake Application on AMI and update agents.

248.   **B** (Send the logs from the instances onto CloudWatch logs.)

   D (Search for the keyword "ERROR" in CloudWatch logs)

Explanation:

In CloudWatch you can use a metric filter to search your desired match term or values in log events. But for that first send the logs to CloudWatch log and search with ERROR keyword.

249.   **D** (All of the above)

Explanation:

The AWS service which you integrate your Jenkin tools are:

EC2, ECS, SNS, ECR, S3, CloudFormation, Elastic BeanStalk, CodeCommit, CodeDeploy, CodePipeline and Device Farm.

250.   **B** (CloudWatch)

Explanation:

To monitor the resources of AWS you use CloudWatch service of AWS. It keeps track of all metrics, monitoring of logs and you can also set the alarm on a certain threshold.

251.   **B** (Create an Auto Scaling launch configuration with the new AMI to use the new launch configuration and to register instances with the new load balancer)

D (Use Amazon RouteS3 weighted Round Robin to vary the proportion of requests sent to the load balancers.)

Explanation:

By using Route53 weighted Round Robin policy, you can define the number of the user to gradually move toward green deployment. For green deployment, you need to create an Auto Scaling launch configuration with the new AMI to use the new launch configuration and to register instances with the new load balancer.

252.   **A** (Terminating:Wait)
        D (Pending:Wait)

Explanation:

When you add lifecycle hooks to autoscaling group then when instance put in Wait state then there are two states: Terminating:Wait or Pending:Wait.

On scale out, it responds to launch an instance and on the scale in it responds to terminate the instance.

253.   **D** (Use the Active Directory connector service on AWS)

Explanation:

In AWS AD connector is a gateway for directory through which you redirect your request to the on-premises directory. It can support up to 5000 users.

254.   **B** (On the web servers, create a scheduled task that executes a script to rotate and transmit the logs to an Amazon S3 bucket.)
        D (Use AWS Data Pipeline to move log data from the Amazon S3 bucket to Amazon Redshift in order to process and run reports)

Explanation:

For durable storage, S3 is the best option and for analyzing the data by use of SQL or existing business intelligence tool in cost effective and simple way is Redshift.

255.   **C** (In the AWS CloudFormation template, set the DeletionPolicy of the AWS::RDS::DBInstance's DeletionPolicy property to "Retain.")

Explanation:

By use of Deletion policy, you can define which resource you want to be preserved on deletion of the stack. Otherwise by default hen stack is deleted all resources are also deleted.

256.   **B** (AWS Elastic BeanStalk)

Explanation:

By use of Elastic BeanStalk, you can deploy and manage application quickly and easily without any worry of infra. EB supported PHP, Python, Go, Java, .NET, Node.js and Ruby

257.   **B** (Re-deploy your application behind a load balancer that uses Auto Scaling groups, create a new identical Auto Scaling group, and associate it to the load balancer. During deployment, set the desired number of instances on the old Auto Scaling group to zero, and when all instances have terminated, delete the old Auto Scaling group.)

Explanation:

For blue/green deployment best option is to create a new identical auto scaling group and attach it to existing ELB put the instances from old auto scaling group into a standby state in case of a rollback. If the rollback occurs detach the load balancer from new auto scaling group.

258.   **C** (Make use of container command)

Explanation:

By use of container command, you can define the execute commands that need to affect your application source. This command runs after setting up of application and web server, but application version is not deployed.

259.   **A** (Use ElastiCache in front of your Amazon RDS DB to cache common queries)
       C (Create Amazon DB Read Replica's. Configure the application layer to query the read replicas for query needs)

Explanation:

To enhance the performance of DB, you make read replica of DB, so the read-intensive workload is reducing by querying multiple read replica and for caching common queries you can use ElastiCache in front to DB.

260.   **C** (AWS Config)

Explanation:

Any information related to the configuration can be done by using AWS Config

261. **C** (Use CloudWatch metrics to check the utilization of the web layer. Use Autoscaling Group to scale the web instances accordingly based on the CloudWatch metrics.)

   D (Utilize the Multi-AZ feature for the Amazon RDS layer)

Explanation:

For high availability and durability of RDS, you can perform Multi-AZ deployment as it synchronously replicates the data to standby instance in other AZ. For scaling of EC2 instance in Auto Scaling, you use CPU utilization metric.

262. **B** (Use Amazon S3 to store the logs and then use Amazon Kinesis to process and analyze the logs in real time)

Explanation:

For real-time processing and analyzing you can use Kinesis Stream, and for storing logs you can use S3 as Glacier is for archival.

263. **A** (Install CloudWatch logs agent on the instance and send all the logs to CloudWatch logs.)

Explanation:

As log data is only viewed in CloudWarch console, so you need to install CloudWatch logs agent on instance so it takes logs from resource to CloudWatch Logs.

264. **B** (In-place)

   C (Blue/Green)

Explanation:

The deployment types that are supported by CodeDeploy are In-place and Blue/Green.

265. **D** (Dockerrun.aws.json)

Explanation:

By use of Dockerrun.aws.json, you can define the way of deploying a group of Docker container with every detail. It's a JSON file.

266.   **B** (Use lifecycle hooks to ensure the processing is complete before the termination occurs)

Explanation:

By defining the lifecycle policy to put the instance in terminating:wait for state and once the processing is complete send single to terminate.

267.   **B** (Ensure the Instances are launched only when the build tests are completed.)
         D (Ensure that all build tests are conducted using Jenkins before deploying the build to newly launched EC2 Instances.)

Explanation:

For cost optimization bets solution is to build a test in Jenkin servers and after completing the build, tests move this to newly created instances.

268.   **A** (Use CloudWatch Events to trigger the snapshots of EBS Volumes)

Explanation:

For automating the creation of EBS snapshot, you can use built-in service of CloudWatch which is CloudWatch event. This service delivers real-time stream of events.

269.   **B** (The ELB would have deregistered the older instances)

Explanation:

When you are using existing ELB then must ensure that this ELB is not used for another purpose as well as it does not contain any instance because when ELB attach to OpsWorks layer, it removes existing instances and uses this ELB only for the handling of layer's instances.

270.   **B** (Create an IAM Role that allows write access to the DynamoDB table)
         D (Add an IAM Role to a running EC2 instance)

Explanation:

By creating a role with the permission EC2 instances want and assign that role to EC2 instances. In this way, you do not need to share keys.

271.   **C** (Use the Elastic Beanstalk service and use Docker containers to host each application environment for the developer community)

Explanation:

The best way to deploy applications that contain multiple dependencies and belongs to multiple Programming languages is Elastic BeanStalk with Docker container. With Docker Container you can deploy your own runtime environment.

272.   **C** (Create a second Elastic BeanStalk environment running the new application version, and swap the environment CNAMEs.)

Explanation:

As they need no downtime and instant rollback, then the best option is to use Blue/Green deployment. With this deployment technique, you create the second environment which is a replica of first and then swap the DNS/CNAMEs of the environment.

273.   **B** (Create a cross-account IAM Role with permission to access the bucket, and grant permission to use the Role to the vendor AWS account.)

Explanation:

For cross-account access you can use IAM role and STS between AWS accounts.

274.   **A** (Use an S3 bucket policy that ensures that MFA Delete is set on the objects in the bucket)
   B (Create an IAM Role and ensure the EC2 Instances uses the IAM Role to access the data in the bucket.)

Explanation:

IAM role is best to assign secure permission to the resource without sharing AWS credentials. And for integrity put MFA delete in bucket policy.

275.   **A** (Bitbucket repositories)
   B (S3 buckets)
   C (GitHub repositories)

Explanation:

In AWS CodeDeploy you can deploy the content that is stored in S3, Github and bitbucket repositories for code deployment.

276.   **D** (In the properties section of the EC2 Instance in the resources section)
Explanation:

In the template resource section of the instance, you can define user data.

```
"MyInstance" : {
  "Type" : "AWS::EC2::Instance",
  "Properties" : {
    "KeyName" : { "Ref" : "KeyName" },
    "SecurityGroups" : [ {
       "Ref" : "logical name of AWS::EC2::SecurityGroup resource"
    } ],
    "UserData" : {
       "Fn::Base64" : {
         "Fn::Join" : [ ":", [
           "PORT=80",
           "TOPIC=", {
              "Ref" : "logical name of an AWS::SNS::Topic resource"
           } ] } }
  }
}
```

277.   **A** (Consider using the Trusted Advisor)

    B (Create budgets in billing section so that budgets are set before hand)

    C (Use the Cost Explorer to see the costs of AWS resources)

Explanation:

To view, the graph on AWS spend data then quick and high level analyzing is done by Cost Explorer. It updates data daily.

By setting a budget in which you define the cost and usage that not exceed your budget amount.

AWS Trusted Advisor works like a customized cloud expert, analyzing your AWS environment and providing best practice recommendations to help you save money, improve system performance and reliability, and close security gaps.

278.   **B** (Post your log data to an Amazon Kinesis data stream, and subscribe your log-processing application, so that is configured to process your logging data.)

Explanation:

For rapid data intake and real-time processing of data like logs, market data, website clickstreams, etc. you can use Kinesis Streams.

279. **B** (Use AWS Cost Allocation Tagging for all resources which support it. Use the Cost Explorer to analyze costs throughout the month.)

Explanation:

By using the tag on resources by making resources more organize. So first allocate cost allocation tags for cost allocation reports for easily keeping track of the cost. These tags can appear of cost allocation report or cost explorer.

280. **A** (Create a new load balancer with new Amazon EC2 instances, carry out the deployment, and then switch DNS over to the new load balancer using Amazon Route53 after testing.)

Explanation:

- Firstly, create a new ELB to show new changes in production.
- For the distribution of traffic to the 2 ELB based on an 80- 20 percent traffic scenario use the Weighted Route Policy for Route53. This is the normal scenario, according to the requirement, the percentage can be changed.
- Finally, if all modifications have been tested, Route53 can be set to 100% for the new ELB.

Option B is incorrect, as the deployment scenario is not blue-green. You are not able to control the users for a new EC2 instance.

Option C is incorrect because this is not a Blue Green Deployment Failure scenario. You need to have 2 environments working side by side in Blue Green deployments.

Option D is wrong because the changes will run side by side with a production stack.

281. **D** (Have the CI system launch a new spot instance bootstrap the code and apps onto the instance and create an AMI out of it.)

Explanation:

You can add Automation as a post-build step to pre-install application releases to Amazon Machine Images (AMI) if you use Jenkins software within a CI / CD pipeline. The Jenkins scheduling function can also be applied to call Automation and create your own OS patching cadence.

282. **E** (Use data pipelines to migrate your DynamoDB table to a new DynamoDB table with a primary key that is evenly distributed across your dataset. Update your web application to request data from the new table.)

Explanation:

The table's provisioned throughput optimal depends on the following factors:

- The primary key selection.
- The workload patterns on individual items.

Each item in a table is uniquely defined by the primary key. The primary key can be simple (partition key) or composite (partition key and sort key).

DynamoDB divides the items of a table into multiple partitions when saving data and mainly distributes the data based on the key partition value. Consequently, you keep the workload evenly across key partition values to achieve the full amount of query throughput provided for a table. Distributing requests across partition key values distributes the requests across partitions.

We can create a new index when we import data from S3 with the DataPipeline into a new dynamodb table.

Following are the steps:

i.   Log in to the console and select DynamoDB

ii.   Select the table you have to copy

iii. Select Export / Import. For copying DynamoDB table to S3 or from S3 to DynamoDB table export / import uses DataPipeline and EMR.

iv.   If you do not have two IAM roles for export / import, you must create them.

v.   Click export table option

vi.   You will need to specify the following:

- S3 bucket to copy the table data and another bucket to store log files for operation. The same bucket can be used

- The percentage of the throughput capacity for the table to be used to read data from the table(to copy to S3) that was provided. The default value is 25%. The increased percentage will accelerate backup

- The IAM roles : The values will default

vii. Choose the option "create data pipeline," and the backup will be scheduled. Depending on the table size, the backup may take time.

viii. After exporting, check logs to verify that no bugs are there.

ix.   Note the hash and range key information of the table

     x.   Delete the table

    xi.   Create a table with the right index. Set the provisioned throughput

    xii.   Using import option, import into a table from S3.

    xiii.   After completion, do check that it is error-free.

283.   **D** (Provide your VP with a link to IAM AWS documentation to address the VP's key rotation concerns.)

Explanation:

Instead of using access keys to access the service this question focuses on IAM roles, AWS will look into the temporary credentials provided by the roles in accessing these services.

284.   **C** (Use an AWS OpsWorks stack to re-deploy your web application and use AWS OpsWorks DeploymentCommand to initiate a rollback during failures.)

Explanation:

AWS DeploymentCommand contains a rollback option in it. Apps can use by the following commands:

deploy: Deploy App.

Ruby on Rails apps has an optional migrate args parameter. To migrate the database, set Args to{ "migrate":["true"]}.

The default setting is {"migrate":["false"]}.

The app will roll back to the previous version with the "rollback" feature.

AWS OpsWorks stores the previous versions, up to five versions, when we update an app.

We can roll an app back in four versions with this command.

285.   **C** (Elastic Load Balancing, Amazon EC2, and Auto Scaling)

Explanation:

The issue was a scalable web tier, not a database tier. Thus, the A,B and D options are eliminated, since a database option is not required.

In elastic and scalable web tier an Elastic Load balancer is connected to 2 EC2 instances connected via Auto Scaling. Scaleable refers to an increase or decrease in the number of EC2, as required using autoscaling process.

286. **C** (Log into the instance and check if the recipe was properly configured.)

Explanation:

Failure to use a recipe will lead to the instance setup failed state rather than online. While the instance of AWS OpsWorks Stacks is not online, it is often useful to log in to resolve the matter in EC2. The EC2 instance is running. You can check whether that an application or personalized cookbook is installed correctly. The AWS OpsWorks Stacks built-in support for SSH and RDP login is available only for the online state instances.

287. **A** (Package the application and dependencies with Docker, and deploy the Docker container with Elastic BeanStalk.)

Explanation:

The deployment of a web application from Docker containers is supported by Elastic BeanStalk. You can set your own runtime environment with Docker containers. You can choose a platform, programming language, and any application dependencies that are not supported by other platforms, such as package managers or tools. Docker containers are autonomous and contain all the configuration information and software needed to run your web application.

288. **C** (Namespaces)

Explanation:

The namespaces of CloudWatch are metric containers. Metrics in various namespaces are isolated so that they are not mistakenly aggregated into the same statistics for metrics from different applications. A namespace string starts with AWS/ for all AWS services that offer Amazon CloudWatch data. You also need to specify a namespace as a container for custom metrics to create your custom metrics.

289. **D** (Install the CloudWatch Logs agent and send Nginx access log data to CloudWatch. Then, filter the log streams for searching the relevant errors.)

Explanation:

For searching and matching terms, phrases or values in your log events you can use metric filters. In your log events, you can increase the value of a CloudWatch metric when a metric filter finds a term, phrase or values. For example, to scan and count the occurrence of the word ERROR in your log events, a metric filter can be created.

290. **B** (60 minutes)

Explanation:

The instance will wait for an hour by default, and Auto Scaling will carry on with the launch or terminate the process (Pending:Proceed or Terminating:Proceed). You can reboot the timeout period by recording a heartbeat if you need more time. You can finish the lifecycle action that continues the launch or termination process if you finish before the time limit ends.

291. **C** (Can include parent directories)

Explanation:

If a new application or application version is to be deployed using the AWS Elastic Beanstalk console, a source package is needed. The following requirements must be met by your source bundle:

- It should be consists of one ZIP or WAR file(multiple WAR files can be included within your ZIP file)
- Not exceed 512 MB
- Not include a parent folder or top-level directory (subdirectories are fine)

292. **A** (Deploy the new application component as an Elastic BeanStalk application, read the data from the social media sites, store it in DynamoDB, and use Apache Hive with Amazon Elastic MapReduce for analytics.)

Explanation:

For all applications requiring a consistent single-digit millisecond latency at every scale, Amazon DynamoDB is a fast and flexible NoSQL database service. It is a cloud database which is fully managed and supports key-value storage and document models. Due to its flexible data model, reliable performance and automated throughput capacity scaling, the system fits mobile, web, gaming, ad technology, IoT and many other applications greatly.

293. **B** (Near zero-downtime release for new changes

   C (Better rollback capabilities)

   D (Good turnaround time for application deployments)

Explanation:

Blue / green deployments offer near-zero downtime and rollback functionality. The basic idea behind blue / green deployment is to shift traffic between the same environments running different applications. The blue environment is the current version of the application for production traffic. In parallel, a different version of your application runs via a green environment. The production traffic will then be transported from blue to green when the green environment is ready and tested.

294. **A** (Use the AWS CloudFormation console to view the status of your stack.)

   D (See the logs in the /var/log directory for Linux instances)

Explanation:

You can view a list of stack events in the AWS CloudFormation stack while your stack is being created, updated, or deleted. Select the failure event from this list and then view the status reason for the event. You can see the cloud- init and cfn logs for Amazon EC2 problems. These logs can be found in the /var / log/ directory on the Amazon EC2 instance. These logs record processes and command outputs during instance set up by AWS CloudFormation. View EC2Configure service and CFN logs for Windows in the%ProgramFiles%\Amazon\EC2ConfigService and C:\cfn\log .

295. **A** (Run command)

Explanation:

You can configure instances by using the Run Command from the Amazon EC2 console without logging in to each instance.

296. **C** (Use the DependsOn attribute to ensure that the database server is created before the web server.)

Explanation:

You may specify with the DependsOn attribute that a particular resource creation follows another. If you want to restrict the creation of any resource that it should create after the specific resource creation, then add that resource in DependOn attribute.

297. **D** (Use a Stack-based policy to protect the production-based resources.)

Explanation:

All update actions are permitted on all resources when a stack is created. Updating all of the resources on the stack can be used by default, the one who has stack update permission. During an update, some resources may need to be interrupted or replaced

completely, leading to new physical identities or entirely new storage. You can avoid unintended updating or removal of stack resources during a stack update via stack policy. A stack policy is a JSON document defining update actions on designated resources.

298. **B** (Create a new pre-baked AMI with the new OS and use the User Data section to deploy the application.)

Explanation:

The ideal way is to continue the same deployment process that was used previously and create a new AMI and use the user data section in order to deploy the application.

299. **D** (CloudWatch Logs Agents)

Explanation:

The CloudWatch Logs agent offers an automated method of sending log data from Amazon EC2 instances to CloudWatch Logs. The agent consist of the following components:

- A plug-in to the AWS CLI that pushes log data to CloudWatch Logs.

- A cron job that ensures that the daemon is always running.

- A script (daemon) that initiates the process to push data to CloudWatch Logs.

300. **D** (Add the appropriate driver packages to ensure the application can work with the database)

Explanation:

For Linux Stacks, you have to add the appropriate driver package to the associated application layer if you want to associate an Amazon RDS service layer with your application, to add it follow the given steps:

i. Click Layers in the navigation pane and open the app server's Recipes tab.

ii. Click Edit and insert OS Packages with the appropriate driver package. For example, if a layer contains instances of Amazon Linux or mysql- client, you should specify mysql if the layer contains instances of Ubuntu.

iii. Save changes and redeploy the app.

301. **B** (Use TCP load balancing on the load balancer. SSL termination on the Amazon EC2 instances. OS-level disk encryption on the Amazon EBS volumes and Amazon S3 with server-side encryption.)

E (Use SSL termination on the load balancer an SSL listener on the Amazon EC2 instances, Amazon EBS encryption on EBS volumes containing PHI and Amazon S3 with server-side encryption.)

Explanation:

HTTPS/SSL Listeners

The following security features can be used to create a load balancer.

SSL Server Certificates

You have to deploy X.509 certificates (SSL server certificates) on your load balancer if you use HTTPS or SSL for your front- end connections. Before sending requests to the backend instance (known as SSL termination), the load balancer decodes requests from clients.

You can use TCP for front and back- end connections and deploy certificates on registered instances processing requests if you do not want a load balancer to handle SSL termination (known as SSL offloading).

Create a classic Load balancer with an HTTPS Listener

A load balancer receives requests from customers and distributes the load balancer requests throughout the EC2 instances registered with the load balancer.

You can create a load balancer that listens on both the HTTP (80) and HTTPS (443) ports. If you specify the HTTPS listener to send requests to port 80 instances, the load balancer ends the requests, and no load balancer communications to the instances are encrypted. If the HTTPS listener sends requests to port 443 instances, the load balancer communication is encrypted to the instances.

Options A & C is not correct because the transit between ELB and EC2 instances is missing in encryption.

Option D is incorrect because the data related to the EC2 instances lack encryption at rest.

302. **E** (Set up a cron job to actively monitor the AWS CloudTrail logs for increased traffic and use Amazon SNS to alert your team.)

Explanation:

NetworkIn Metric: The number of bytes received by each instance on all network interfaces. The metric shows the amount of input traffic of the network on a particular instance. The number of bytes received during the period is the number of bytes reported. This number can be divided by 300 bytes per second if you are using basic monitoring. Divide it by 60, if you have detailed monitoring.

303.　**A** (Use a Docker container that has the third party application server installed on it and that creates the load balancer and an Amazon SQS queue using the application source bundle feature.)

Explanation:

The deployment of a web application from Docker containers is supported by Elastic BeanStalk. You can set your own runtime environment with Docker containers. You can choose a platform, programming language, and any application dependencies that are not supported by other platforms, such as package managers or tools. Docker containers are autonomous and contain all the configuration information and software needed to run your web application.

304.　**D** (Amazon S3 Standard- Infrequent Access)

Explanation:

The Amazon S3 Standard- Infrequent Access(Standard- IA) is a less frequently accessed Amazon S3 storage class, but requires quick access where required.Standard - IA offers the high durability, throughput, and low latency of Amazon S3 Standard, with a low per GB storage price and per GB retrieval fee.

305.　**A** (AWS Lambda Functions)

　　B (Amazon ECS Tasks)

　　C (Amazon EC2 Instances)

Explanation:

You can configure Amazon EC2 instances, AWS Lambda functions, Streams in Amazon Kinesis Streams, Delivery streams in Amazon Kinesis Firehose, Amazon ECS tasks, SSM Run command, SSM automation, Step functions state machine, Pipelines in AWS CodePipeline, Amazon inspector assessment template, Amazon SNS topics, Amazon SQS

queues, Built-in Targets, and the default event bus of another AWS account as target for CloudWatch events.

306.   **B** (AWS CodePipeline)

Explanation:

Continuous delivery is a release practice in which changes in code are automatically built, tested and ready for release to production. The CodePipeline with AWS CloudFormation and AWS allows you to use continuous delivery to automatically build and test changes before promoting your AWS CloudFormation templates onto the stacks. You can make changes to your AWS infrastructure quickly and reliably with this release process.

307.   **D** (Use the CodePipeline Service)

Explanation:

AWS CodePipeline is an ongoing delivery service for modeling, visualizing and automating the steps needed to release the software. The different steps of software release can be quickly designed and configured. AWS CodePipeline automates the steps necessary to continuously release your change of software.

308.   **B** (Use the NoEcho property for the parameter value)

Explanation:

Set the NoEcho property to true for sensitive parameter values(e.g., passwords). In this way, the value of your parameter is displayed as asterisks(****) , whenever anybody describes your stack.

309.   **A** (Create a second Elastic BeanStalk environment running the new application version, and swap the environment CNAMEs.)

Explanation:

Due to the fact that Elastic BeanStalk performs an in-place update to your application versions, your application may not be available to users for a short period of time. This downtime may be avoided by using a blue / green deployment in which the new version is deployed to a separate environment, and the CNAMEs of both environments can be switched on instantly to the new version to redirect the traffic.

310.   **D** ("UserData": {   "Fn::Base64": {})

Explanation:

The intrinsic Fn::Base64 function returns the input string Base64 representation. This function is typically used to transfer encoded data via the UserData property to Amazon EC2 instances

311. **A** (You can use instances running on your own hardware.)

   B (You can start and stop instances manually.)

   D (You can use EC2 Instances that were created outside the boundary of OpsWorks.)

Explanation:

- You can start, stop, or automatically scale the number of instances by AWS OpsWorks Stacks. With any stack you can use automatic time- based scaling; Linux stacks can also use load-based scaling.

- You can also register instances with a Linux stack that have been created outside of AWS OpsWorks Stacks in addition to the use of AWS OpsWorks Stacks in Amazon EC2 instances. This includes EC2 instances and instances on your own hardware. However, they have to run one of the Linux distributions supported, however. You may not be able to register on-premise Windows instances or Amazon EC2.

- A stack can run Linux or Windows instances. A stack may have various Linux versions or distributions on various instances, but Linux and Windows cannot be mixed.

312.   **C** (A Classic Load Balancer can span across AWS OpsWorks Stacks layers.)

Explanation:

To use Elastic Load Balancing with the stack, the Elastic Load Balancing console, CLI, or API must be used first to create one or more load balancers in the same region. The following should be considered:

- Only one load balancer can be attached to a layer.

- Only one layer can be handled by each load balancer.

- The application Load Balancer is not supported by AWS OpsWorks Stacks. You can only use Classic Load Balancer with AWS OpsWorks Stacks.

313. **A** (Create separate logical templates, for example, a separate template for networking, security, application, etc. Then nest the relevant templates.)

Explanation:

When infrastructure grows, common patterns may arise, in which each of your templates declares the same components. You can create dedicated templates and separate common components. In this way, you can mix and match various templates, but use nested stacks to create a single stack. To create other stacks within a stack, one should use nested stacks. AWS::CloudFormation::Stack resource is used in your template to reference other templates to create nested stacks.

314.   **C** (Uninstall)

Explanation:

Lifecycle events available in OpsWorks are Setup, Deploy, Undeploy, Shutdown, and Configure.

315.   **C** (Launch an Amazon Elastic Compute Cloud (EC2) instance in the staging VPC in response to a development request, and use configuration management to set up the application. Run any testing harnesses to verify application functionality and then use Amazon Simple Notification Service (SNS) to notify the development team of the results.)

Explanation:

It would take more time to install Amazon Kinesis and would not be ideal to notify the concerned team as shortly as possible.

Since the test must be performed at the staging VPC, it is best to launch EC2 in the staging VPC.

The best answer to this question would be the management of AWS configuration together with SNS.

AWS Config provides a detailed inventory of current AWS resources and records configuration modifications on a continuous basis such as the tags value in the instance, security group entry / exit rules, and network ACL rules in VPCs.(see the AWS Config website for the list of supported AWS resources). The AWS Config allows customers to determine how a resource was configured at any time, to view resource dependencies and to send notifications when the resource settings change. The AWS Config Rules are a new package that enables customers to assess whether their AWS resources meet the configuration requirements. In order to assess compliance of AWS resources, customers can either use predefined AWS- managed rules or define themselves.

The application should be tested in a staging VPC that is not described in option A., therefore, option C is correct.

316. **C** (Update the stack with the template. If the template fails rollback will return the stack and its resources to exactly the same state.)

D (Use the AWS CloudFormation Validate Template to validate the syntax of the template)

F (When creating the stack, specify an Amazon SNS topic to which your testing system is subscribed. Your testing system runs tests when it receives notification that the stack is created or updated.)

Explanation:

The validate-template command of AWS CloudFormation has been intended to check only your template's syntax. It will not check that the specified property value from you for a resource is valid for that source or not. The number of resources that will exist when the stack is created is also not determined.

You must create the stack to verify the operational validity. AWS CloudFormation stacks are not subject to a sandbox or test area, so the resources created for testing is charged.

Option F is for notifications requirement.

317. **D** (4)

Explanation:

Restores the app version previously installed. For example, the server will serve the app from the second deployment when you have deployed the app three times and run Rollback. The server will serve the app from the first deployment when you run Rollback again. The five latest deployments are stored by AWS OpsWorks Stacks by default, so up to four versions can be restored. When the number of versions stored is exceeded, the command fails and leave the oldest version in place.

318. **D** (Ensure that the Amazon EBS volumes have been pre-warmed by reading all the blocks before the test.)

Explanation:

As the AMI gets all the data from S3 as snapshots, it should be checked always that the volume is prewarmed before the load test is set.

319.   **A** (Use CloudFormation changesets to check for the impact on the changes.)

Explanation:

When you need to update a stack, it helps you to update stacks in confidence if you understand how your changes affect running resources before implementing them. Change sets allow you to preview how proposed stack changes can affect your running sources, e.g., whether your changes will delete or replace critical resources, and AWS CloudFormation will only make the changes to your stack when you decide to run the changeset, allows you to decide whether to follow the proposed changes or find other changes by creating another changeset. The AWS CloudFormation Console, AWS CLI or AWS CloudFormation API allows you to create and manage changesets.

320.   **D** (Post your log data to an Amazon Kinesis data stream, and subscribe your log-processing application, so that is configured to process your logging data.)

Explanation:

Amazon Kinesis makes collecting, processing, and analyzing data in real time easier and enables you to get timely insights and respond quickly to new information. Amazon Kinesis offers key capabilities to process streaming data in a cost-effective manner, and flexibility to choose the tools that best fit your application. With Amazon Kinesis, you can enter into real times data such as application logs, website clickstreams, IoT telemetry data, and more into your databases, data lakes and data warehouses, or build your own real-time applications using this data. Instead of having to wait for all your data to be collected before the processing can start, Amazon Kinesis can process and analyze data as it arrives and responds in real time.

321.   **B** (Create and start new instances to replace your current online instances. Then delete the current instances.)

   C (On Linux-based instances in Chef 11.10 or older stacks, run the Update Dependencies stack command.)

Explanation:

By default, after an instance booting is completed, AWS OpsWorks stacks automatically install the most recent updates during setup. AWS OpsWorks stacks do not automatically install updates after an instance is online, In order to prevent interruptions such as restarting of the application server. Instead, you manage online updates yourself, so that any disturbance can be minimized.

You may use one of the following for update:

- Create and launch new instances to replace your current online instances. Then delete the existing instances.

- Run the command Update Dependencies Stack on Linux based instances in Chef 11.10 or previous stacks, which installs a current set of security patches and updates in the instance you specified.

322.   **C** (Build a custom Amazon Machine Image that includes all components pre-installed, including an agent, configuration artifacts, application frameworks, and code. Create a startup script that executes the agent to configure the system on startup.)

Explanation:

Since new instances must be installed in 3 minutes, all components should be pre-bake in an AMI as a result. When you attempt to use the User Data option, it takes time to install and configure various components based on the time mentioned in the question.

323.   **D** (All at once)

Explanation:

All at once is the fastest deployment method because in this method all the deployment occurs at once on all the instances.

324.   **A** (AWS OpsWorks)

Explanation:

AWS OpsWorks is a configuration management service that helps you by using chef for configurations and operations in all shapes and sizes. You can define the architecture of the application and the specification for each component, including package installation, software configuration, and storage resources. Start with templates for common technologies such as app servers and databases, or create your own to accomplish any scripted tasks. AWS OpsWorks includes automation to scale your application based on time or load and dynamic configuration to orchestrate changes as your environment scales.

325.   **C** (Create a new AWS Elastic BeanStalk application and configure a Go environment to host your application, Using Git check out the latest version of the code, once the local repository for Elastic BeanStalk is configured using "eb create"

command to create an environment and then use "eb deploy" command to deploy the application.)

D (Write a Dockerfile that installs the Go base image and fetches your application using Git, Create a new AWS Elastic BeanStalk application and use this Dockerfile to automate the deployment.)

Explanation:

Option B is incorrect because OpsWorks works with Chef recipes and not with Docker containers.

Option A is incorrect because there is no AWS::EC2::Container resource for CloudFormation.

The deployment of a web application from Docker containers is supported by Elastic BeanStalk. You can set your own runtime environment with Docker containers. You can set your own runtime environment with Docker containers. You can choose your own platform, the language of programming, and any application dependencies that are not supported by other platforms, such as package managers or tools. Docker containers are independent and contain all configuration information and software required to execute your Web application.

326.   **A** (Elastic Container Service)

Explanation:

With Amazon EC2 Container Service (ECS), Docker enabled applications can easily be run and manage across a cluster of EC2 instances. Container packaged applications will deploy and operate locally in the same way as Amazon ECS managed containers. If you are using Amazon ECS, there is no need for your own cluster management infrastructure to be installed, operated and scaled, and enables you to plan your Docker enabled applications across your cluster based on your resources and availability needs.

327.   **B** (AngularJS)

Explanation:

Following are the supported platforms on Elastic BeanStalk

- Go

- Java SE

- Java with Tomcat

- .NET on windows server with IIS

- Node.js

- PHP

- Python

- Ruby

- Packer Builder

- Single container Docker

- Multicontainer Docker

- Preconfigured Docker

328. **B** (Use lifecycle policies in Elastic BeanStalk)

Explanation:

Elastic Beanstalk creates an application version whenever you upload your application's new version with the Elastic Beanstalk console or EB CLI. You will eventually reach the application version limit and not be able to create a new version of that application if you do not delete previously created versions that you are no longer using. The application version lifecycle policy can prevent you from reaching the limit. An Elastic BeanStalk lifecycle policy tells Elastic BeanStalk to remove old versions of an app or remove versions of the application if the total number of versions of the app exceeds the specified number.

329. **D** (cfn-init)

Explanation:

cfn-init: Used to recover and interpret the metadata of resources, install packages, start services and create files.

cfn-signal: A simple wrapper to signal the creation policy or WaitCondition of AWS CloudFormation so that you can sync other resources within a stack to ready for use in the application.

cfn-get-metadata: A wrapper script facilitates either the retrieval of all metadata defined for a resource or path to a particular metadata key or subtree.

cfn-hup: A daemon that checks for metadata updates and performs the custom hooks when detecting changes.

330.   **C** (Use Amazon Data Lifecycle Manager to automate the process.)

Explanation:

Amazon Data Lifecycle Manager (Amazon DLM) is used for EBS volume backup through automation of creation, retention, and deletion of snapshots.

Managing the automation of snapshots helps you in the protection of valuable information by implementing a schedule of regular backup, retaining backups that are required by internal compliance or auditors, storage cost reduction by deleting old backups.

331.**D** (aws cloudformation list-stack-resources)

Explanation:

This command returns all stack resources descriptions. ListStackResources returns resource information for deleted stacks for up to 90 days from deletion. list-stack-resources is a paginated operation . In order to get the whole data set of results, multiple API calls could be issued. By providing -no-paginate argument, you can disable pagination. The -query argument must extract data from the results of the following query expressions: StackResourceSummeries by using the -output text and the -query argument on a paginated response.

332.   **B** (Create a CloudWatch alarm which would then send a trigger to AWS Lambda to increase the Read and Write capacity of the DynamoDB table.)

C (Monitor the ConsumedReadCapacityUnits and ConsumedWriteCapacityUnits metric using CloudWatch.)

Explanation:

ConsumedReadCapacityUnits and ConsumedWriteCapacityUnits over the specified time period can monitor for a DynamoDB table to track the usage of your provisioned throughput.

333.   **A** (Analyze the application logs to identify possible reasons for message processing failure and resolve the cause for failures.)

Explanation:

The best option here is to examine the application logs and fix the failure. In the application, you may have a functionality problem which causes messages to queue up and increase the number of fleet instances within the Autoscaling group.

334.   **A** (Availability zone is not added to Elastic load balancer)

Explanation:

The Elastic Load Balancing creates a load balancer node in the Available Zone when you add an Availability Zone to your load balancer. Load balancer nodes accept customer traffic and forward requests in one or more Availability Zones to healthy registered instances.

335.   **D** (Create a new CloudTrail trail with one new S3 bucket to store the logs and with the global services option selected. Use IAM roles S3 bucket policies, and Multi-Factor Authentication (MFA) Delete on the S3 bucket that stores your logs.)

Explanation:

AWS CloudTrail service is integrated with AWS Identity and Access Management (IAM). It is a service that logs AWS events from or on behalf of your AWS account. CloudTrail logs AWS authenticated API calls as well as AWS sign-in events and collects information of this event in the files that are supplied to Amazon S3 buckets. You must make sure all services are included. Therefore, option C is partly correct.

Options A and B is incorrect because it just adds overhead for having 3 S3 buckets and SNS notifications.

336.   **A** (Stream the log data into Amazon Elasticsearch for any search analysis required.)
    B (Stream the log data to Amazon Kinesis for further processing)
    D (Send the log data to AWS Lambda for custom processing)

Explanation:

For fast and continuous data intake and aggregation, Amazon Kinesis can be used. The data used include IT infrastructure log data, application logs, social media, feeds for market data, and clickstream data.

Amazon Lambda is a web service that can be used to compute logs published by CloudWatch logs without servers

To deploy, operate, and scale Elasticsearch for log analytics, full-text search, application monitoring, and many more in the simplest way, and Amazon Elasticsearch Service can be used.

337. **C** (Use DynamoDB streams to monitor the changes in the DynamoDB table.)

Explanation:

A stream of DynamoDB is an ordered flow of information on item changes in a DynamoDB table in Amazon. DynamoDB captures information on every change to data items in the table when you enable a stream on a tab.

DynamoDB Streams writes a stream record with a primary key attribute(s) of the items that have been modified when the application creates or updates or deletes items in the table. Data modification information for a single item in a DynamoDB table is included in the A stream record. The stream can be configured to capture additional information in Stream records, like the images of modified items "before" or "after."

338. **C** (Use Web identity federation and register your application with a third-party identity provider such as Google, Amazon, or Facebook.)

   D (Create an IAM role which has specific access to the DynamoDB table.)

Explanation:

You don't have to create a customized login code or manage your own user identities with a web identity federation. Instead, application users can use well- known identity provider IdP for sign in, such as Amazon Login, Facebook, Google or other OIDC compatible IdPs, and then exchange the received authentication token for AWS temporary security credentials, that map in an IAM role for the resources access in your AWS account. Using an IdP helps you maintain your AWS account secure because your application needs not to integrate and distribute long- term security credentials.

339. **A** (Define an AWS CloudFormation template to place your infrastructure into version control and use the same template to deploy the Docker container into Elastic BeanStalk for staging and production.)

Explanation:

The deployment of a web application from Docker containers is supported by Elastic BeanStalk. You can set your own runtime environment with Docker containers. You can choose a platform, programming language, and any application dependencies that are not supported by other platforms, such as package managers or tools. Docker containers are

autonomous and contain all the configuration information and software needed to run your web application.

If you create your infrastructure by using Docker with Elastic BeanStalk, it handles capacity supply details, load-balancing, scaling and application health monitoring automatically.

340.   **B** (Use roles that allow a web identity federated user to assume a role that allows access to the RedShift table by providing temporary credentials.)

Explanation:

The ideal approach for accessing any AWS service is to use roles. That's the first choice. Options A and C are therefore incorrect. You must also use the web identity federation for any web application. Option B is, therefore, the correct option.

You will request for AWS services, which must be signed with an AWS access key while writing such an app. However, It is recommended to develop a web application that its long term AWS credentials should not be installed or distributed with apps even in an encrypted store that a user downloads. Instead, build your app to require the AWS temporary security credentials dynamically web identity federation is required. The temporary credentials map to an AWS role only allows executing the tasks required by the mobile app.

341.   **D** (Create an AMI from an instance, and set up an Auto Scaling group with an instance type that has enhanced networking enabled and is Amazon EBS-optimized.)

Explanation:

An Amazon Machine Image (AMI) gives the necessary information for launching an instance that is a virtual cloud-based server. When you launch an instance, you specify an AMI, and you can start as many instances as you need from an AMI. You can also launch instances from as many AMIs as you want.

342.   **A** (Create a new launch configuration with the updated AMI and associate it with the AutoScaling group. Increase the size of the group to six and when instances become healthy revert to three.)

Explanation:

A single launch configuration is associated to an Auto Scaling Group, and after creation, you cannot change the launch configuration. You can use an existing launch configuration as the foundation for a new launch configuration, then upgrade the Auto Scaling group to use a new launch configuration. After changing the launch setup for an

autoscaling group, any new instances are launched with the new configuration options without affecting the existing instances. Then to check the launching of new instances, change autoscaling group size to 6 and once the instances are initiated, turn it back to 3.

343. **B** (Create a new launch configuration with the new instance type and update your Autoscaling Group.)

Explanation:

A Launch configuration is a template used by an Auto Scaling Group for EC2 startups. You specify information for instances like the Amazon Machine Image (AMI) ID, the instance type, a key pair, one or more security groups, and a block mapping device when creating the launch configuration. You specified the same information to launch the instance if you had previously launched the EC2 instance. You must specify a launch configuration when creating an auto-scaling group. You can specify your launch configuration with multiple Auto Scaling groups. However, you can set only one launch configuration at a time for an Auto Scaling group, and after you have created this, you cannot modify the launch settings.

Therefore to change the launch configuration of an autoscaling group, you should create a launch configuration and then update your Auto Scaling group with the new launch configuration.

344. **A** (Build)
 B (Production)
 C (SourceControl)

Explanation:

Basic stages of CI/CD Pipeline are as follows:
  i.   Build
  ii. SourceControl
  iii. Staging
  iv. Production

345. **D** (Use Elastic Load Balancing to distribute traffic to a set of web servers, configure the load balancer to perform TCP load balancing, use an AWS CloudHSM to perform the SSL transactions, and write your web server logs to a private Amazon S3 bucket using Amazon S3 server-side encryption.)

Explanation:

By using a dedicated Hardware Security Module (HSM) appliances within the AWS cloud, The AWS CloudHSM service helps you meet corporate, contractual and regulatory compliance needed for data security. CloudHSM can control the encryption keys and cryptographic operations performed by the HSM.

Option A is wrong with the CloudHSM option because of the ephemeral volume which this is temporary storage.

346.   **C** (AutoScalingRollingUpdate)

Explanation:

The AWS::AutoScaling::AutoScalingGroup resource supports an UpdatePolicy attribute which defines how an Auto Scaling group resource is updated when an update to the CloudFormation stack occurs. A common approach is executed rolling update for updating an Auto Scaling Group by defining the AutoScalingRollingUpdate policy. This keeps the same Auto Scaling Group and, according to the indicated parameters, replaces old instances with new ones

347.   **B** (Use the CreationPolicy to ensure it is associated with the EC2 Instance resource.)

   C (Use the CFN helper scripts to signal once the resource configuration is complete.)

Explanation:

You might specify additional measures to set up the instance, like installing software packages or Bootstrap applications, for provisioning an Amazon EC2 instance in an AWS CloudFormation stack. Normally, after creating the instance successfully, CloudFormation proceeds with stack creation. However, you can use a Creation Policy so that only after your configuration actions are done, CloudFormation continue with stack creation. You will, therefore, know that your apps are ready to go when the stack is successful.

348.   **A** (Create a CloudWatch alarm to send a notification to the Auto Scaling group when the aggregated CPU utilization is less than 30% and configure the Auto Scaling policy to remove one instance.)

Explanation:

You should define two policies, one for scale in (terminating instances) and one for scale out (launching instances) for monitoring each event. For example, when the network bandwidth reaches a certain level you want to scale out for that purpose you have to

create a policy specifying that Auto Scaling should start a certain number of instances to help with your traffic. But, if the network bandwidth level goes down when the network bandwidth level goes back down you have to define scale in policy.

349.   **C** (Deploy 3 EC2 instances in one availability zone and 3 in another availability zone and use Amazon Elastic Load Balancer)

Explanation:

Option B is incorrect because question requirement was high availability so in option A, down of AZ will cause failure of the entire application.

ELB cannot be accessed across multiple regions, therefore options A and D are wrong.

In elastic and scalable web tier an Elastic Load balancer is connected to 2 EC2 instances connected via Auto Scaling. Scaleable refers to an increase or decrease in the number of EC2, as required using autoscaling process.

350.   **B** (Create a load balancer. Create an Auto Scaling launch configuration with the new AMI to use the new launch configuration and to register instances with the new load balancer. Use Amazon Route53 weighted Round Robin to vary the proportion of requests sent to the load balancers.)

Explanation:

Because you want to control the use of the new application, the best way is to use the weighted method of Route53. Weighted routing can assign a single domain (example.com) or subdomain name (acme.example.com) to multiple resources and choose the amount of traffic that is routed to each resource. This can be helpful for a range of purposes such as load balancing and testing of new software versions.

351.   **B** (Update the launch configuration specified in the AWS CloudFormation template with the new C3 instance type. Also, add an UpdatePolicy attribute to your Auto Scaling group that specifies an AutoScalingRollingUpdate. Run a stack update with the new template)

Explanation:

The AWS::AutoScaling::AutoScalingGroup resource supports an UpdatePolicy attribute which defines how an Auto Scaling group resource is updated when an update to the CloudFormation stack occurs. A common approach is executed rolling update for updating an Auto Scaling Group by defining the AutoScalingRollingUpdate policy. This

keeps the same Auto Scaling Group and, according to the indicated parameters, replaces old instances with new ones

352. **D** (By default ELB access logs are disabled.)

Explanation:

Access logging is by default disabled. It is an Elastic Load Balancing feature. Once the load balancer logs are enabled, Elastic Load Balancing captures the logs and keeps them in a specified Amazon S3 bucket. The access logging can be disabled at any time.

353. **C** (In the AWS OpsWorks stack settings, enable Berkshelf. Create a new cookbook with a Berksfile that specifies the other two cookbooks. Configure the stack to use this new cookbook.)

Explanation:

You need a way to install and manage dependencies to use an external cookbook in an instance. A cookbook that supports a dependency manager named Berkshelf is the preferred approach. In addition to work with the test kitchens and Vagrants, Berkshelf is working on Amazon EC2 instances such as AWS OpsWorks Stacks instances.

354. **B** (Blue/Green)

Explanation:

Blue-green deployment requires the least time to rollback.

355. **C** (Using a custom CloudWatch metric insert the elapsed time since the instance launch to the time the instance responds to an Elastic Load Balancing health check, and periodically adjust the Pause Time and the CoolDown property on the AutoScaling group to be over the value of the metric.)

Explanation:

The question focuses on adding traffic-related instances with an Auto Scaling Group.

To control how rolling updates are performed when changes are made to the launch configuration of the auto scaling group, you can add a UpdatePolicy attribute to your Auto Scaling Group. It's mainly used in combination with AutoScalingGroup resource CloudFormation Templates.

In AutoScalingGroup 's UpdatePolicy attribute, PauseTime is used.

If you don't have the correct settings configured, a rolling update on an auto-scaling group can lead to unexpected behaviors.

PauseTime refers to the amount of time that AWS CloudFormation takes to start Software applications after making a change to a set of instances. For example, to scale up the instances in an Autoscaling group, you might need to specify PauseTime.

356.   **C** (5 minutes)

   D (60 minutes)

Explanation:

Elastic Load Balancing publishes a log file at the specified interval for each load balancer node. When you activate your load balancer Access Log, you can enter a publishing interval of either 5 minutes or 60 minutes. Elastic Load Balancing releases logs by default at a time interval of sixty minutes.

357.   **D** (AWS CloudFormation)

Explanation:

AWS CloudFormation provides developers and system managers with an easy way to create, manage a set of related AWS resources, supply, and update in an orderly and predictable manner.

To run your application, you can use samples templates from AWS CloudFormation, or create your own templates to describe AWS resources as well as any corresponding dependencies or runtime parameter. The order for AWS services or the subtleties to make these dependencies work, you do not have to figure. This is what CloudFormation cares for you. After the use of AWS resources, the version controls on your AWS infrastructure can be modified and updated in a controlled and predictable way, just as you are doing with the software.

AWS CloudFormation Designer allows you to visualize your templates as diagrams and edit them using a drag-and-drop interface.

358.   **A** (Store data in Amazon S3 and use lifecycle management to move data from S3 to Glacier after 2 months.)

Explanation:

The configuration is a set of rules to define the action on Amazon S3 bucket for a group of objects. Lifecycle configuration enables you to manage S3 lifecycle. Following actions can be defined for Amazon S3:

Transition actions: Transition actions describe the transition of one storage class to another storage class, for example, you want to change your S3 storage to Glacier after 30 days.

Expiration actions: This action defines the expiration timeline of objects. S3 deletes the expired objects automatically.

359.   **D** (Dockerrun.aws.json)

Explanation:

Elastic BeanStalk specific json file, i.e., Dockerrun.aws.json describes the deployment of a set of Docker container as an Elastic BeanStalk application. This command can be used to deploy a multi-container Docker environment.

Dockerrun.aws.json describes the containers to deploy to each container instances in the environment. It also describes the data volume to create on the host instance for the containers to mount.

360.   **A** (Configuring IAM role)

  B (Setting up federation proxy or identity provider)

  E (Using AWS STS service to generate temporary tokens)

Explanation:

Firstly the access request is sent to the identity provider which directs the request to the corporate identity store which authenticates the user and sends the request to STS which issues the temporary token to the user, and then the user can log in to the console and get access of the desired bucket.

361.   **B** (Task Runner)

  D (Pipeline Definition)

Explanation:

AWS pipeline components work together to manage your data.

- **Pipeline Definition**

    It identifies the business logic of your data management.

- **Pipeline schedules and run tasks**

To perform the required activities which include uploading of pipeline definition and then pipeline activation. It enables you to edit your running pipeline and its activation. You can deactivate pipeline, update your data source and then again activate your pipeline. Pipeline can be deleted when your work is finished.

- **Task Runner**

    Task runner polls the task to perform. You can use default or custom task runner application as per requirement. It is installed and run automatically.

362.   **A** (Deploy ElasticCache in-memory cache running in each availability zone)

    C (Add an RDS MySQL read replica in each availability zone)

Explanation:

Enhanced performance and durability for database instances are provided by Amazon RDS read replicas. For read-heavy database workloads, this replication feature makes it easy to scale out beyond a capacity constraint of single DB instance.

Amazon ElastiCache is used to deploy, run and scale an in-memory data store or cache in the cloud. It provides the high-performance web application because it allows you to fetch information from fast, managed, in-memory data stores.

363.   **C** (Ensure CloudTrail is enabled. Create a user account for the IT Auditor and attach the AWSCloudTrailReadOnlyAccess Policy to the user.

Explanation:

AWS CloudTrail is used to record user actions by the history of AWS API calls from your account. API calls are made through the management console, SDK or command line. These API calls include the identity of the caller, request parameters, the name of the API, time of the API and responses get back by AWS service.

Purpose of CloudTrail is to enable security analysis, track changes to your account and provide compliance auditing.

364.   **B** (Define a deletion policy of type Retain for the Amazon RDS resource to assure that the RDS database is not deleted with the AWS CloudFormation stack.)

    C (Define a deletion policy of type Snapshot for the Amazon RDS resource to assure that RDS database can be restored after the AWS CloudFormation stack is deleted.)

Explanation:

If the user wants to control any resource, then DeletionPolicy should be attached to it. DeletetionPolicy attributes allow the user to preserve or in some cases backup a resource when its stack is deleted. AWS CloudFormation deletes a resource by default if no DeletionPolicy attribute is attached to it.

If the user specifies the Retain for any source, this will prevent the resource deletion if its stack is deleted.

365.   **A** (Create an IAM cross-account role in the development account that allows the user from production account to access the S3 bucket in the Development account.)

Explanation:

For setting up a cross-account access between AWS accounts, user should use AWS IAM roles and AWS STS service. AWS CloudTrail logs cross-account activities when user attach an IAM role in another AWS account for cross-account access.

366.   **B** (Create a scheduled policy to scale up on Monday and scale down on Friday)

Explanation:

Scheduling based scaling allows you to scale according to the change in a load of application. i.e., if the traffic level is high, then it will scale up, and when it's low, it will scale down.

367.   **C** (list-stacks)

Explanation:

This command returns the stack information of all the stacks whose status is matched with StackStatusFilter. If the command doesn't find any stack filter, it will return the information of all stacks. Information of deleted stacks is kept in record for 90 days.

368.   **D** (Availability zone is not added to Elastic Load Balancer)

Explanation:

Elastic Load Balancer creates a load balancer note in the AZ. When traffic arrives from the client side, the load balancer node directs that traffic to the suitable instances in one or more Availability zone.

369.   **B** (Cool down period)

Explanation:

The cooldown period feature enables the user to check not to launch or terminate any additional instances before the previous scaling action takes place. Auto-scaling waits for the completion of the cool-down period before resuming the auto scaling activities. By default not to wait for the cooldown period is enabled when you manually scale your Auto Scaling group.

370.   **D** (AppSpec file)

Explanation:

AppSpec file is an application specification file, which is particular to AWS CodeDeploy. It is a YAML formatted file used to specify custom permissions for deployed files, specify scripts to be run on each instance at various stages of the deployment process and map the source files in your application revision to their destinations on the instance.

371.   **A** (Use your on-premises SAML 2 O-compliant identity provider (IDP) to grant the members federated access to the AWS Management Console via the AWS single-sign-on (SSO) endpoint.)

Explanation:

You can use a role to set up your SAML 2.0 IDP and AWS so that your federated users can access the AWS management console. The role empowers the user to perform tasks in the console.

372.   **A** (Use the DependsOn attribute)

Explanation:

For troubleshooting the dependency error, you must add the DependsOn attributes to the resources that depend on any other resource in a template. You may declare dependencies exceptionally for creation and deletion process correctly in AWS CloudFormation.

373.   **C** (Store your data in Amazon S3, and use lifecycle policies to archive to Amazon Glacier.)

Explanation:

The configuration is a set of rules to define the action on Amazon S3 bucket for a group of objects. Lifecycle configuration enables you to manage S3 lifecycle. Following actions can be defined for Amazon S3:

Transition actions: Transition actions describe the transition of one storage class to another storage class, for example, you want to change your S3 storage to Glacier after 30 days.

Expiration actions: This action defines the expiration timeline of objects. S3 deletes the expired objects automatically.

374.   **A** (The user can use the WaitCondition resource to hold the creation of the other dependent resources.)

Explanation:

You can use the wait condition to coordinate stack resource creation with external configuration actions and to stack creation to track the configuration process status.

375.   **D** (Kubernetes)

Explanation:

- Following are the supported platforms on Elastic BeanStalk

- Go

- Java SE

- Java with Tomcat

- .NET on windows server with IIS

- Node.js

- PHP

- Python

- Ruby

- Packer Builder

- Single container Docker

- Multicontainer Docker

- Preconfigured Docker

376.   **B** (RDS uses DNS to switch over to standby replica for a seamless transition.)

Explanation:

Amazon RDS Multi-AZ deployments enhance the availability and durability of database(DB) instances and make them a natural fit for workloads in the production database. Amazon RDS creates a primary DB instance automatically when you provide a Multi-AZ DB instance and synchronously replicates the data to a standby instance in a different Availability Zone(AZ). Each AZ runs on its own independent physically distinct infrastructure and is designed to be highly reliable. In the event of an infrastructure failure(e.g., hardware failure, storage failure or network disruption), Amazon RDS automatically failover to the standby mode so that you can resume database operations once the failover has been completed.

And according to the AWS documentation, when the primary one fails, the cname is changed to the standby DB.

Q: What happens and how long does it take during the multi- AZ failure?

Failover is automatically handled by Amazon RDS so that you can resume database operations without any administrative intervention as soon as possible. If you fail to do so, Amazon RDS simply flips the canonical name record (CNAME) to the standby for your DB instance, which is promoted to become the new primary.

On this basis, RDS Multi-AZ uses DNS to create the CNAME and therefore **B** is the right choice.

377.   **B** (Use CloudWatch monitoring to check the size of the queue and then scale out using Autoscaling to ensure that it can handle the right number of jobs.)

Explanation:

SQS can be used to manage communication between the web and the roles of the worker. The number of messages in the SQS queue can be used to determine the number of instances the AutoScaling group should have.

378.   **D** (Delete the Autoscaling launch configuration after the instances are terminated)

Explanation:

Option A is incorrect because Elastic IP consumes costs if it is not deleted. Option B is incorrect because EBS volumes have a costing aspect and therefore the removal of the

volumes saves on costs. Option C is incorrect because of ELB costs. Only Autoscaling groups are free of charge. You are only charged for the underlying resources.

379. **C** (Use CloudWatch Events to trigger the snapshots of EBS volumes.)

Explanation:

The best thing to do is to use CloudWatch's built-in service as CloudWatch events to automate the creation of EBS snapshots. With Option A, you should only run the power shell script on Windows machines and keep the script itself. And you have the overhead to just run this script with a separate instance.

When you go to CloudWatch events, you can use the Target as EC2 CreateSnapshot API call.

CloudWatch Events provides an almost real-time stream of system events describing changes in Amazon Web Services (AWS) resources. You can match and route events to one or more target functions or streams by using simple rules that you can set up quickly.

380. **A** (Use the Active Directory connector service on AWS)

Explanation:

AD Connector is a directory gateway that allows you to redirect directory requests to your Microsoft Active Directory on- site without caching any cloud information. AD Connector is available in two sizes, small and large. A small AD connector for smaller companies with up to 500 users is designed. A large AD connector can support larger enterprises with up to 5,000 users.

381. **B** (Create an IAM role for cross-account access allows the SaaS provider's account to assume the role and assign it a policy that allows only the actions required by the SaaS application.)

Explanation:

Many SaaS platforms provide access to AWS resources via created AWS cross-account access. You will see the ability to add a cross-account role if you go to Roles in your identity management.

382. **B** (Deploy)
    C (Shutdown)
    D (Setup)

Explanation:

Lifecycle events available in OpsWorks are Setup, Deploy, Undeploy, Shutdown, and Configure.

383.   **D** (Have one single dashboard to report metrics to CloudWatch from different regions)

Explanation:

AWS resources can be monitored through a single CloudWatch dashboard in several regions. For example, you can create a dashboard that displays the use of CPUs for an EC2 instance in the us- west-2 region with your billing metrics in the us- east-1 region.

384.   **A** (Make an S3 notification configuration which publishes to AWS Lambda of the manifest bucket. Make the Lambda CloudFormation stack which contains the logic to construct an Autoscaling worker tier EC2 G2 instances with the artificial neural network code on each instance. Handle the CloudFormation Stacks creation success or failure using another Lambda function. Create an SQS queue of the images in the manifest. Tear the stack down when the queue is empty.)

Explanation:

The S3 Events are the best way to be informed when the images are sent to the bucket. You do not need to provide infrastructure here in advance, and since the S3 source provides event management, this should be used.

Amazon S3 can publish events (e.g., when an object is created in a bucket) to AWS Lambda and use your Lambda function as a parameter by passing the event data. This integration allows you to write Amazon S3 events Lambda functions. In Amazon S3, you add bucket notification settings that identify the type of event you want Amazon S3 to publish and the Lambda function you want to invoke.

Further information as to why the second function of Lambda is required:

You can use AWS Lambda to create a CloudFormation stack. CloudFormation stack creation is an asynchronous call, so we don't have to wait for until the whole stack moves to FAILED / SUCCEEDED state.

385.   **D** (Configure a Dead Letter Queue)
Explanation:

Elastic BeanStalk worker environment supports Amazon SQS queue service dead letter queues. In dead letter queue, other queues can send messages that for some reasons could not be processed. Messages that are unsuccessful in processing are targeted from source queue to the dead-letter queue. you can gather these type of messages in dead-letter queue to find the reason of their failure.

386. **D** (Docker)

Explanation:

Below are the Elastic BeanStalk components:

1) Application: A logical collection of Elastic BeanStalk components, including environments, versions and environmental configurations, is an Elastic BeanStalk application. An application is conceptually similar to a folder in Elastic BeanStalk

2) Application version: An application version of Elastic BeanStalk refers to a specific, labeled iteration for a web application of the deployable code.

3) Environment: An environment is a version used on AWS resources. Each environment only operates one single application version at a time, although in many environments you can run the same or other versions simultaneously.

4) Environment Configuration: A set of environment parameters and settings that define the behavior of an environment and associated resources are identified by Environment Configuration.

5) Configuration Template: It is a starting point for the creation of unique configuration template.

387. **B** (AWS Config)

Explanation:

AWS Config allows you to do the following:

- Judge the configuration of your AWS resources for the desired settings.

- Recover one or more resources configuration that exist in your account.

- Recover one or more resource historical configurations.

- Get a notification when creating, modifying, or deleting a resource.

- View resource relationships. For example, all resources that use a specific security group could be found.

388.   **D** (You can only use intrinsic functions in a specific part of a template. You can use intrinsic functions in resource properties, metadata attributes, and update policy attributes.)

Explanation:

AWS CloudFormation offers multiple built-in functions for the management of your stacks. To assign values to properties that are not available until runtime, use the intrinsic functions in your templates.

Only in certain parts of a template can intrinsic functions be used. Currently, intrinsic functions can be used to update policy attributes, outputs, Metadata and resource properties. You can also use intrinsic functions to build stack resources on condition.

389.   **B** (In a stack you can use a mix of both Linux and Windows operating systems)

Explanation:

According to AWS documentation, following are the features of OpsWorks stack:

- A stack may run Linux or Windows instances. (A stack may have various Linux versions or distributions, but you can't mix Linux and Windows instances.)

- Custom AMIs (Amazon Machine Images) are available but must be based on one AMI that is supported by AWS OpsWorks Stacks.

- You can manually start and stop instances or automatically scale the number of instances with AWS OpsWorks Stacks. (Automatic time-based scaling with any stack is possible; Linux stacks can also use load-based scaling.)

- AWS OpsWorks Stacks is used to create Amazon EC2 instances, instances created outside the AWS OpsWorks Stacks can be also registered with a Linux stack.

390.   **B** (Having the web and worker roles running on separate EC2 instances)

   C (Using SQS to establish communication between the web and worker roles)

Explanation:

You can use SQS and separate environments for web and worker processes. Communication between the web and worker roles is managed by SQS queue.

391.   C (aws ec2 run-instances)

Explanation:

This command uses AMI to launch the mentioned number of instances for which user have permission. The user can specify the number of options, or it could be left default. Following are the rules:

- [EC2-VPC] AWS select a default subnet for the user from user default VPC if the user does not enter the subnet Id. The user needs to specify a subnet ID in the request when user does not have a default VPC.

- IPv6 addresses do not support all instance types.

- [EC2-Classic] An Availability zone is selected for the user if it is not specified.

- [EC2-VPC] Every instance has a primary private IPv4 network address. AWS choose one from the IPv4 range of user subnet if user does not specify this address.

- Some types of instances have to be started in a VPC. If user has no default VPC or do not specify a subnet id, the request fails.

- If a security group ID is not specified, AWS uses a standard security group.

- If any of the AMI is provided with a product code is not subscribed by the user, the request fails.

392.   A (Resources)

Explanation:

The resources are the only compulsory field, Mention the stack resources and their properties such as an Amazon Simple Storage Service bucket or Amazon Elastic Compute Cloud Instance.

393.   D (Use a T2 burstable performance instance)

Explanation:

AWS recommends using T2 instance type for that instance which don't utilize more CPU. T2 are Burstable Performance Instances that provide a baseline level of CPU performance that is capable of above the baseline.

T2 Unlimited instances can maintain high CPU efficiency as long as it is necessary for the workload. T2 Unlimited instances offer ample functionality without any further charges for most general workloads. If an instance needs to run for an extended period with higher CPU usage, it can do so for a flat extra charge of 5 cents per CPU hour.

CPU credits govern basic performance and capacity to burst. T2 instances continuously receive CPU credit at a specified instance- size rate, accumulate CPU credits when idle and use CPU credits when active. T2 instances are an excellent choice for a wide range of general purpose workloads including micro-services, interactive low- latency applications, build and stage environment, small and medium databases, virtual desktops, code repositories, and product prototypes.

394.   **B** (Rolling based on instances)

Explanation:

- Elastic BeanStalk will wait for instances in batch pass health checks before proceeding to a next batch using health-based rolling updates.

- The amount of time Elastic BeanStalk is waiting for after launching a number of instances can be set up for time- based rolling updates before moving on to the next batch. This pause time allows you to bootstrap and begin serving requests.

- Immutable updates in the environment are an alternative to rolling updates, which ensure efficient and safe application of configuration modifications requires to replace of instances. In the case of the failure of an immutable update of the environment, only an auto-scaling group is necessary for the rollback process. On the other hand, an unsuccessful rolling update requires a further update to roll back changes.

395.   **D** (All of the above)

Explanation:

In a configurable weekly maintenance window with Managed Platform Updates, you can set up your environment to apply minor and patch version updates automatically. Elastic BeanStalk applies managed updates without downtime or reduced capacity and immediately cancels the update if your application fails health checks of running instance when the new version executes your application.

396.   **A** (Enable SSL termination on the ELB)

Explanation:

You were supposed to tell the wrong implementation.

Option A is the right thing to do. The traffic will be encrypted all to the way to the back-end if you disable the SSL termination on the ELB. SSL termination enables encrypted traffic between client to ELB, while unencrypted traffic from the ELB to the backend (suspected EC2 or ECS / Task).

Option C is wrong because the S3 SSE encryption helps the rest of the data in S3 to be encrypted.

You must use layer 4 in order to have traffic encrypted throughout if SSL is not terminated on the ELB.

Option D "Enabling sticky sessions on your load balancer" cannot be used because Layer 4 (TCP endpoint) does not support sticky sessions.

397.   **B** (AWS CloudFormation)

Explanation:

The automatic choice is CloudFormation when you want to automate the deployment. Below is the cloud information from AWS.

AWS CloudFormation provides developers and system managers with an easy way to create, manage a set of related AWS resources, supply, and update in an orderly and predictable manner.

To run your application, you can use samples templates from AWS CloudFormation, or create your own templates to describe AWS resources as well as any corresponding dependencies or runtime parameter. The order for AWS services or the subtleties to make these dependencies work, you do not have to figure. This is what CloudFormation cares for you. After the use of AWS resources, the version controls on your AWS infrastructure can be modified and updated in a controlled and predictable way, just as you are doing with software

In your Elastic BeanStalk environment, AWS Elastic Beanstalk supports the running of Amazon Relational Database Service (Amazon RDS) instances. This works great for environment development and testing. However, it is not ideal for a production environment as it links the database instances lifecycle to the lifecycle of the environment of your application.

398. **A** (Create a new stack that contains a new layer with the Python code. To cut over the new stack the company should consider using Blue/Green deployment)

Explanation:

Blue/green deployment is the technique for application release by shifting of traffic from different application versions in two identical environments. Blue / green deployments can reduce common risks associated with software deployments, such as downtime and rollback.

399. **B** (Single instance)

  D (Load balancing, Autoscaling)

Explanation:

You can create a load balancing, autoscaling or a single- instance environment with Elastic BeanStalk. The environment type is dependent on the deployed application. You will be able to see the environmental type when you go to the configuration for your environment.

400. **A** (Use the User data section and use a custom script which will be used to download the necessary LAMP stack packages.)

  B (Create a CloudFormation template and use the cloud-init directives to download and install the LAMP stack packages.)

Explanation:

You can always ensure that the latest version of the LAMP stack is downloaded and given to development teams using user data and cloud- init directive. The AMI's version will always be the same, and you must create an AMI each time you change the version of the LAMP stack.

You can transfer your user data to the Instance when you launch an instance in Amazon EC2, which can be used to carry out common automated configuration tasks and even run scripts after the instance is started. The two types of user data that can be passed to EC2 instance are shell scripts and cloud-init directives. You can also transfer that data into a launch wizard either as a file (which can be used to launch instances using the command line tools), as simple text or as a base64-encoded text (for API calls).

401. **A** (Use the Trusted advisor to see the underutilized resources)

C (Create CloudWatch alarms to monitor underutilized resources and either shut down or terminate resources which are not required.)

Explanation:

CloudWatch alarms can be used to see if resources threshold level for a long time period that it is below or not. If so, you can decide either to stop or terminate the resources.

With Trusted Advisor you will obtain all kinds of checks that can be used to optimize or reduce the costs of your AWS resources.

402.   **B** (Use the complete-lifecycle-action call to complete the lifecycle action. Run this command from Command Line Interface.)

Explanation:

Use the complete- lifecycle- action command to allow the Auto Scaling Group to continue to launch or terminate the instance after completing your custom action before the time period expires. You can use the following command to specify the lifecycle action token:

Aws autoscaling complete-lifecycle-action –lifecycle-action-result

403.   **C** (Create a cross-account IAM role with permission to access the bucket, and grant permission to use the role to the vendor AWS account.)

Explanation:

You can set cross-account access between AWS accounts by using AWS Identity and Access Management(IAM) Roles and the AWS Security Token Service(STS). AWS CloudTrail logs cross- country activity if you assume an IAM role in another AWS account for access to services and resources in that account.

404.   **A** (All data moving between the volume and instance)
   B (All snapshots created from the volume)
   C (Data at rest inside the volume)

Explanation:

You don't need to build, maintain and secure your own key management infrastructure in Amazon EBS encryption for EBS volumes. If you create and attach an encrypted EBS volume to a supported instance type, the following kind of data is encrypted:

   • Data at rest

- All snapshots created from the volume

- All volume created from those snapshots

- All data moving between the volume and instances

405. **D** (Use the Deletion policy of the CloudFormation template to ensure a snapshot is created of the relational database.)

Explanation:

When the resource stack is deleted, you can save or(in some cases) backup a resource with the DeletionPolicy attribute. For each resource you would like to control, you have to specify a DeletionPolicy attribute. AWS CloudFormation can remove the resource by default if a resource has no DeletionPolicy attribute. Please note that this ability also covers the update operations which result in the removal of resources.

406. **C** (Use the mappings sections in the CloudFormation template, so that based on the relevant region, the relevant resource can be spinned up)

Explanation:

The key to a set of named values is matched by the optional Mappings section. For instance, you could create a mapping with a key using the region's name and with the values to be specified for each region for setting values based on a region. You would use the intrinsic function Fn::FindInMap to recover values from a map.

407. **A** (Create another parallel environment in Elastic BeanStalk. Use the swap URL feature.)

Explanation:

As the requirement is the least downtime, it's ideal for creating a blue-green deployment environment and use the Swap URL function to swap new deployment environments and then swap back in case of deployment failure.

When you update your application versions, Elastic BeanStalk implements in-place update which may make your application unavailable for a short period of time.

This downtime can be prevented by a blue-green deployment where the new version is deployed in a different environment. CNAMEs of both environments can be swapped, and the traffic can be redirected to a new version instantly.

408. **B** (Configure)

C (Execute Recipes)

D (Update Custom Cookbooks)

Explanation:

Command types available for OpsWorks are as follows:

- Update Custom Cookbooks: This command does not run any recipes. The current version of the instances cookbook is updated from the repository.
- Execute Recipes: Specified set of recipes are executed on instances
- Configure: Runs the instances configure recipes
- Setup: Runs the instances setup recipes

409. **D** (Create an IAM role for cross-account access allows the SaaS provider's account to assume the role and assign it a policy that allows only the actions required by the SaaS application.)

Explanation:

Many SaaS platforms provide access to AWS resources via created AWS cross-account access. You will see the ability to add a cross-account role if you go to Roles in your identity management.

410. **D** (Use AWS Config to create a rule to check EC2 instance type)

Explanation:

If you want to check that EC2 instances are following a specified instance type, you can create a rule in AWS config.

411. **B** (Create a launch configuration with Spot Instances. Ensure the user section data details the installation of the custom software. Create an Autoscaling group with the launch configuration.)

Explanation:

The application can sustain the failures and solution should be cost effective therefore spot instances are best for this purpose. The launch configuration can be used to request spot instances.

412. **B** (Configure the lifecycle hook to record heartbeats. If the hour is up, restart the timeout period.)

C (If the software installation and the configuration is complete, then send the signal to complete the launch of the instance.)

Explanation:

The instance will wait for an hour by default, and Auto Scaling will carry on with the launch or terminate the process (Pending:Proceed or Terminating:Proceed). You can reboot the timeout period by recording a heartbeat if you need more time. You can finish the lifecycle action that continues the launch or termination process if you finish before the time limit ends.

413. **B** (Create an IAM user who will have read-only access to your AWS VPC infrastructure and provide the auditor with those credentials.)

Explanation:

Option B fits well in this case because it is only providing the required permissions as high-level permissions should be avoided.

414. **A** (Use the CloudWatch billing alarm to notify you when you reach the threshold value)

Explanation:

CloudWatch enables you to monitor your AWS costs. You can create billing alerts with CloudWatch when your usage exceeds your defined thresholds. When creating the billing alert, you specify these threshold amounts. An email notification is sent by AWS in the result of excessive usage.

415. **A** (Create one AWS OpsWorks stack create two AWS OpsWorks layers create one custom recipe.)

Explanation:

Only one OpsWorks stack with multiple layers is available, one for Node.js and one for the standard app.

The configuration of your entire application is defined by an AWS OpsWorks Stack: load balancers, server software, database, etc. You control each part of the stack by building layers that define the software packages and other configuration details such as Elastic IPs and security groups. You can also deploy your software on layers by identifying the

repository and using Chef Recipes optionally to automate everything Chef can do, such as creating directories and users, setting up databases, etc. You can use the built-in automation of OpsWorks Stacks to scale your application and recover from instance failures automatically. You can check and control who can view and manage the resources your application uses, including ssh access to the instances your application uses.

416. **A** (The application authenticates against LDAP and retrieves the name of an IAM role associated with the user. The application then calls the IAM Security Token Service to assume that IAM role. The application can use the temporary credentials to access any AWS resources.)

B (Develop an identity broker that authenticates against LDAP and then calls IAM Security Token Service to get IAM federated user credentials. The application calls the identity broker to get IAM federated user credentials with access to the appropriate AWS service.)

Explanation:

If you need an in-premise environment to work with a cloud environment, you usually have two artifacts for authentication.

An Identity Store: This is the on-site store like Active Directory, where all the user and groups information is stored.

An Identity Broker: It acts as an intermediate agent between the cloud environment and the on-premise location. This facility is provided by a system called Active Directory Federation Services in Windows.

The outside user is first authenticated by Identity broker using active directories. Then the temporary security token is issued to access console or user access APIs

417. **D** (Use MFA on all users and accounts, especially on the root account)
Explanation:

The user can add an additional protective layer on top of username and password using MFA. When MFA is enabled, the user is prompted for a username and password (first factor, what user know) and an authentication code of their AWS MFA system (second factor, what user have) to be registered on an AWS website.

418. **D** (All of the above)
Explanation:

The disadvantages of the self-hosted version control system include expensive Per-developer licensing fees, hardware maintenance, support staffing. The amount and types of the files to be stored are limited. It has a limited number of branches, the amount of version history, and the other related metadata that can be stored.

419.   **A** (Use the Amazon SQS Extended Client Library for Java and Amazon S3 as a storage mechanism for message bodies.)

Explanation:

Amazon SQS messages can be managed using Amazon S3. This is particularly good for the storage and consumption of messages up to 2 GB size. You can use the Amazon SQS Extended Client Library for Java to manage Amazon SQS messages using Amazon S3. This library can be specifically used to fetch or delete the corresponding message object from S3 bucket, to when the messages are stored to S3 bucket, and to send a message which refers to a single S3 bucket message object.

420.   **C** (Create a billing alarm which can alert you when the costs are going beyond a certain threshold.)

Explanation:

CloudWatch enables you to monitor your AWS costs. You can create billing alerts with CloudWatch when your usage exceeds your defined thresholds. When creating the billing alert, you specify these threshold amounts. An email notification is sent by AWS in the result of excessive usage. You can also enable the notifications for the updates of AWS resources price.

421.   **C** (Create a MySQL RDS environment with Multi-AZ feature enabled)

    D (Create Multiple EC2 instances in the separate AZ. Host MySQL and enable replication via scripts between instances.)

Explanation:

If you want high availability and fault tolerant environment, the instances must be located in multiple availability zones. Therefore, if you host your own MySQL, ensure that you have instances spread over several AZs

By using Multi-AZ deployments, Amazon RDS delivers high availability and failover support for DB instances. Amazon's failover technology is used by Multi-AZ deployments for PostgreSQL, MySQL, Oracle, and MariaDB DB instances.

422.   **A** (Make a copy of the Launch Configuration. Change the instance type in the new launch configuration. Attach that to the Autoscaling group. Change the maximum and desired size of the Autoscaling group to 4. Once the new instances are launched, change the desired and max size back to 2.)

Explanation:

Firstly you should copy the launch configuration and then add the new instance with the required instance type. After that modify the Autoscaling group to add the created instance. Then to launch the new instance type, change the desired number of Autoscaling group to 4. After the new instance is launched, change the desired number to 2 which will enable the Autoscaling group to delete the instances with the old configuration.

Here we assume that the existing instances are distributed equally over multiple AZ 's since the autoscaling process will first use AZRebalance to delete instances.

Option B is invalid because the current Launch configuration cannot be amended. Option C is invalid because your application won't be available if you delete the existing launch configuration. A smooth deployment process needs to be ensured. Option D is invalid since after attaching the new launch configuration, you should change the desired size to 4.

423.   **B** (Create multiple CloudFormation templates for each set of logical resources, one for networking, and the other for LAMP stack creation.)

Explanation:

Creating multiple CloudFormation templates is one of the examples of nested stacks. When infrastructure grows, common patterns may arise, in which each of your templates declares the same components. You can create dedicated templates and separate common components. In this way, you can mix and match various templates, but use nested stacks to create a single stack. To create other stacks within a stack, one should use nested stacks. AWS::CloudFormation::Stack resource is used in your template to reference other templates to create nested stacks.

424.   **A** (Conditions)

Explanation:

In the optional Conditions section, there are statements that define when a resource is created or when a property is defined. For example, you can perform a comparison

between two values. You can create resources based on the result of this condition. Multiple conditions should be separated with commas.

425.　**C** (Use CloudTrail to log all events to one S3 bucket. Make this S3 bucket only accessible by your security officer with a bucket policy that restricts access to his user only and also adds MFA to the policy for a further level of security.)

Explanation:

CloudTrail is used to enable security analysis, track changes to your account and provide compliance auditing. You can log and monitor and retain events relating to API calls throughout your AWS infrastructure continuously with CloudTrail. A history of your account AWS API calls, including API calls via the AWS Management Console, AWS SDKs, command line tools, and other AWS services, is provided by the CloudTrail. This history helps security analysis, tracking, and troubleshooting of resources.

426.　**B** (Change the Max capacity to 2)

　　C (Suspend the launch process of the Autoscaling group)

Explanation:

By either reducing the maximum capacity to 2 or suspending the launch process of the autoscaling group, you can temporarily suspend the creation of new instances so that the 2 current running instances match the maximum limit.

The scaling process of Amazon EC2 instance support Launch and Adds a new EC2 instance to the group, with increased capacity.

Launch suspension will interrupt other processes. For example, you are unable to return from a standby state in service, because the group cannot scale if the launch process is suspended.

427.　**D** (Create an IAM role with the proper permission policy to communicate with the DynamoDB table. Use web identity federation, which assumes the IAM role using AssumeRoleWithWebIdentity, when the user signs in, granting temporary security credentials using STS.)

Explanation:

To access any AWS service, using role is the prior way to approach any application whereas web identity federation is used for any web application. It is recommended to develop a web application that its long term AWS credentials should not be installed or

distributed with apps even in an encrypted store that a user downloads. Instead, build your app to require the AWS temporary security credentials dynamically web identity federation is required. The temporary credentials map to an AWS role only allows executing the tasks required by the mobile app.

428. **B** (Use SQS to assist and let the application pull messages and then perform the relevant operation in DynamoDB.)

Explanation:

SQS is the best option for scalability. DynamoDB is usually scalable, messages in SQS can help in the management of the above- mentioned situation due to the cost-effective solution condition. Amazon Simple Queue Service (SQS), a fully managed service for the communication of message queues between distributed microservices and software components at any scale. It is the best practical design for the modern application.

SQS makes decoupling and coordinating the components of a cloud application simple and cost-effective. You can send, store and receive messages from software components at any volume via SQS without losing messages or demanding the availability of other services at any time.

429. **B** (Using "Rolling Updates" deployment method)

Explanation:

A new set of servers, which can replace the existing set of servers, may be mentioned in rolling deployment. This substitution will occur in a phased out manner. As no swap URL is required, Blue Green deployments cannot be used.

430. **B** (Model the stack in three CloudFormation templates: Data layer, compute layer, and networking layer. Write stack deployment and integration testing automation following Blue-Green methodologies.)

Explanation:

You will use Blue-green deployment and nested CloudFormation stack for deployment.

When infrastructure grows, common patterns may arise, in which each of your templates declares the same components. You can create dedicated templates and separate common components. In this way, you can mix and match various templates, but use nested stacks to create a single stack. To create other stacks within a stack, one should use nested stacks. AWS::CloudFormation::Stack resource is used in your template to reference other templates to create nested stacks.

431.   **B** (Blue-Green Deployments)

Explanation:

When you update your application versions, Elastic BeanStalk implements in-place update which may make your application unavailable for a short period of time. This downtime can be prevented by a blue-green deployment where the new version is deployed in a different environment. CNAMEs of both environments can be swapped, and the traffic can be redirected to a new version instantly.

Deployments in blue / green require your environment to run independently of your production database if your application uses one. If you have an Amazon RDS DB instance attached to your environment, the data will not be transferred to your second environment and will be lost if the original environment is terminated.

432.   **A** (Send the log data to AWS Lambda for custom processing or to load into other systems)
        C (Stream the log data to Amazon Kinesis)
        D (Stream the log data into Amazon Elasticsearch in near real-time with CloudWatch logs subscriptions.)

Explanation:

The CloudWatch Logs are used to monitor, store, and access your log files from EC2 instance, CloudTrail and other sources. The associated log data from CloudWatch Logs can then be retrieved.

433.   **A** (Create Docker containers for the custom application components)
        D (Use Elastic BeanStalk to deploy the docker containers)

Explanation:

Elastic Beanstalk supports the use of web applications from Docker containers. You can set your own runtime environment with Docker containers. You can choose your own platform, the language of programming, and any application dependencies that are not supported by other platforms, such as package managers or tools. Docker containers are independent and contain all configuration information and software required to run your Web application.

434. **C** (Creates an SNS topic and adds a subscription ARN endpoint for the SQS resource created under the logical name SQSQueue)

Explanation:

The Fn::GetAtt intrinsic function gives a value from the resource of an attribute in the template, so the options are suggesting adding parameters, allowing endpoints and invoking relevant calls.

435. **A** (Setup Auto-scaled workers triggered by queue depth that use spot instances to process messages in SQS. Once data is processed, change the storage class of the S3 objects to Glacier.)

Explanation:

RabbitMQ was used internally that's why SQS should be used. Therefore option B is invalid.

The best option for reducing costs is Glacier, as everything was stored on tape at the on-site location. Option C is therefore out.

No need to modify the objects in S3, hence option A is more suitable.

436. **C** (Use AMI's which already have the software installed.)

Explanation:

As you use the AMI which already has the required software installed therefore it will the fastest. You can configure the public AMI as a custom AMI with your own defined configuration. The instance launched from that AMI will contain all the modifications you have made.

437. **D** (User data)

Explanation:

In the Advanced Details section, User can enter custom scripts in the User Data section to create an instance in "Configure Instance Details" step.

About Our Products

Other products from IPSpecialist LTD regarding AWS technology are:

 AWS Certified Cloud Practitioner v2 Technology Workbook

 AWS Certified Solution Architect - Associate Technology Workbook

 AWS SysOps Administrator Associate v3 Technology Workbook

 AWS Certified Developer Associate Technology Workbook

 AWS Certified Solution Architect - Professional Technology Workbook

Upcoming products from IPSpecialist LTD regarding AWS technology are:

 AWS Certified Security - Specialty Technology Workbook

 AWS Certified Advance Networking – Specialty Technology Workbook

 AWS Certified Big Data – Specialty Technology Workbook

Note from the Author:

Reviews are gold to authors! If you have enjoyed this book and it helped you along certification, would you consider rating it and reviewing it?

Link to Product Page:

www.ingramcontent.com/pod-product-compliance
Lightning Source LLC
Chambersburg PA
CBHW060527060326
40690CB00017B/3413